State Law, Dispute Processing, and Legal Pluralism

This book presents an ethnography of dispute processing by non-state forums and actors in rural India. As such it sheds light on a much neglected and contested topic. Arising in the context of recent legal and political debates that question the legitimacy of non-state actors engaged in dispute processing, the book explores the nature, form, and functioning of such forums and actors in two locations in rural India. Focusing on a fishermen's community belonging to the caste of Hindu Machimār Koḷīs in coastal Maharashtra and an agrarian community in Uttarakhand with members from the Pandit, Thakur, Bhotiā, and Harijan caste groups, this study shows the manner in which non-state forums and actors engage with state law and its regulatory systems.

Dr Kalindi Kokal is a post-doctoral fellow in the Centre for Policy Studies at the Indian Institute of Technology (IIT) in Mumbai, India. She completed her doctorate in law from the Martin Luther University in Halle, Germany, with a fellowship from the Department of Law and Anthropology at the Max Planck Institute for Social Anthropology, Germany. Kokal's interest in exploring law as a social process stems from her earlier experience as a practising lawyer in the Bombay High Court. Her current work broadly focuses on themes related to law and society in India in particular and in South Asia more generally.

Law and Anthropology

Series Editor: Marie-Claire Foblets, Max Planck Institute for Social Anthropology, Germany

The series is intended as a forum for the publication of outstanding scholarly contributions that strive systematically to involve legal practitioners in the research, thinking, and theorizing about the search for justice and the accommodation of diversity in contemporary pluralistic societies. It focuses on applied legal anthropology, giving equal weight both to an anthropologically informed understanding of diversity of normative orders (often existing side-by-side within a single state system) and to the practical, pragmatic experience and concerns of legal practitioners (judges, lawyers, legal services representatives, etc.) who, in their daily practice, confront the phenomenon of 'internormativity' – situations where different normative logics come into contact (and often conflict) with one another – and the resulting need for state legal systems to accommodate this diversity.

https://www.routledge.com/Law-and-Anthropology/book-series/LAWANTH

State Law, Dispute Processing, and Legal Pluralism

Unspoken Dialogues from Rural India

Kalindi Kokal

Routledge
Taylor & Francis Group
LONDON AND NEW YORK

First published 2020 by Routledge

2 Park Square, Milton Park, Abingdon, Oxon, OX14 4RN
605 Third Avenue, New York, NY 10017

Routledge is an imprint of the Taylor & Francis Group, an informa business

First issued in paperback 2020

British Library Cataloguing in Publication Data
A catalogue record for this book is available from the British Library

Library of Congress Cataloging-in-Publication Data
A catalog record has been requested for this book

ISBN: 978-1-138-62521-1 (hbk)
ISBN: 978-0-367-72682-9 (pbk)

Typeset in Galliard
by Taylor & Francis Books

I dedicate this book, my first, to *Ajee*, my grandmother, who taught me that it is one's willingness to learn that makes life a richer and fuller experience.

Contents

Figures

Preface

The journey of this book began long before my doctoral programme started. It was in 2010 that I began working on the project "Accessing economic and social rights in India's lower courts" with my friends and colleagues, Jayanth Krishnan and Shirish Kavadi.[1] At the time, I had been practising civil law in the Bombay High Court for a few years, and participating in a research project was a new experience for me. It felt different, not being behind the dais to represent a party, but instead watching these arguments from a back seat in those crowded courtrooms. Lengthy, casual conversations with judges, intense debates with local lawyers, and mindful interactions with litigants were insightful experiences, but also jolted me into the reality of how much of dispute processing in India occurs beyond the walls of the courts and police stations. At the time I had no opportunity to delve into this further, but the keenness and enthusiasm to understand how disputes find their way to state forums remained with me for several years thereafter. An interdisciplinary doctoral programme set the ball rolling.

When I started this study, debates about the existence of non-state forums of dispute processing were at their peak. Petitions in the Supreme Court of India and media coverage of incidents indicating the arbitrary use of power by political and caste factions in the villages curated the flow of popular discourses about justice. Having spent several months over the course of eight years volunteering in different parts of rural India, I found the complexities underlying seemingly straightforward arguments, based on a presumed binary between the state and non-state, both perplexing and inspiring. Even casual conversations with people living in villages revealed how aware and sensitive they were to national- and state-level politics. People had opinions about the slack implementation of laws, of corruption hampering bureaucratic institutions, and of the consequences of affirmative action policies. Engagement in government jobs and mass enrolment in the Aadhar scheme,[2] only added to the indicators pointing to the inevitable

1 This project resulted in the publication Krishnan et. al (2014).

2 Aadhar was an initiative launched by in the Indian Government in 2009. It proposed assigning a unique identification number to every citizen of India. Data related to the people's age, residence, and biometrics were collected across the country. Aadhar enrolment went from being voluntary to compulsory and is now, with a recent judgment of the Supreme Court (Aadhaar Judgment.pdf 2018), once again voluntary and

engagement between the spheres of the state and the non-state. The sphere of law, I was certain, could not have been a stranger to this reality.

What began as a tryst with experiences in state institutions turned into a project focusing on the life of non-state dispute processing, and the role of state law and state forums within it. What made non-state forums so appealing? What did a ***pancāyat*** look like? People still also approached police stations for certain types of disputes. Were people ignorant of state law? How did literacy, development, caste, gender, and religion impact perceptions about dispute processing? What about engagement with state law? Was decision-making an arbitrary or a democratic process? What was the role of disputes in social life? This book works with these and other ideas to develop an understanding about the present condition of non-state actors in dispute processing in India and the legal frameworks within which they conduct actions of dispute processing.

In Uttarakhand, I had been associated with a not-for-profit organisation for the previous eleven years. Ease of understanding Kumaoni, the mother tongue of the majority of residents in the Kumaon region of Uttarakhand, coupled with my familiarity with the *ritī-riwāz* (local rituals and practices) in the region made this location ideal for fieldwork. Little did I know then that relocating to the region would come with its own set of challenges and discoveries. Living in a remote village with a highly caste-conscious community familiarised me with so many of my own prejudices, ideological perspectives, and levels of endurance. I returned more sensitive to the complexity of everyday life and the choices people make within it.

At the other end of the country, I went to Gonjhé in Maharashtra at the insistence of Kaivalya, an old friend of mine from law school. There I met Ravindra Pavshe, an ambitious notable, who would eventually become my host father. After a presentation before the entire team of notables from Gonjhé, I received permission to conduct research in the village. By the time I reached Gonjhé, I had travelled through six other villages along coastal Maharashtra to select an appropriate field site. Gonjhé was the first place I had been where everyone I spoke to caught on to the gist of my project and responded enthusiastically to it, offering many suggestions and insights regarding how I should proceed. One statement from a young notable has stuck with me: "We are all judges here, so don't be concerned about (not) finding data."

This research project, more than anything else, has been a memorable life journey. I have learned that the social barriers of caste, class, education, and norms of hospitality may be superficial, but are nevertheless very real. Navigating them is an endeavour that requires great skill, and while I may never have crossed or broken any of these barriers, even the relationships I built around and between

required only to serve certain purposes. Despite the fact that the assignment of a unique identification code met with a great deal opposition from many sections of society, the vigorous enrolment drives led by the government have resulted in an enrolment of about 1.21 billion people in the country (nearly 90 per cent of India's population) (Press Trust of India 2018).

them provided me with experiences and insights that added value to what this book offers and also to my experience of the world.

I learned how much our educational endeavours influence us even at the subconscious level. This interdisciplinary project challenged some very fundamental ideas that had evolved over five years of law school, crucial years of legal practice, and postgraduate education in the same field. Learning to ask questions differently meant letting go of the presumptions doctrinal legal education had instilled in me. No, not everyone knows state law, even though "ignorance of the law" cannot be an excuse for breaking the law. Justice was not only found in courtrooms, but also in temples, and mosques, and household backyards. I was reintroduced to elements from legal history, a subject that I remember was popularly abhorred in law school, and the nuances between *niti* (rules), *nyāy* (justice), and *nirnay* (decision). People could at once be loyal to and therefore governed by different thought regimes, moral norms, and legal orders. But most of all, this also taught me to recast power in the agency of people themselves. Law school was clearly not a neutral ground. We were taught to survive in courts, police stations, and state institutions. Part of this also included learning how to capitalise on this knowledge and people's ignorance of it. An overwhelming emphasis on these survival skills had clouded my worldview. This project acted as a reality check, and I remain thankful to all my friends in the villages of Uttarakhand and Maharashtra who opened my eyes to this.

This book, to the extent that I have succeeded with its interdisciplinary style and research methodology, is an attempt to represent this journey of experiences and learning. While the findings remain an important academic pursuit, the methodology is detailed and reiterated at every stage to make this book insightful for those who seek to understand how to study law. The discipline of law is as much empowering – and therefore enticing – as it is limiting. But a nuanced approach to studying and understanding law can enhance a method of thinking about its presence in everyday life, which I think is especially important given the several variants of power relationships we have in our societies today. As for justice, the idea of which led to the pursuit of this research project in the first place, it is probably always to be found somewhere in between the solid lines of laws, power, and social relationships, thus making its pursuit ever more desirable, exacting, and amaranthine.

Acknowledgements

This book though conceived several years ago, would not have seen the light of the day without the generous support of the village communities in the Dharamgarh valley and Gonjhé. I learned, not only from our lengthy conversations over dwindling charcoal embers, but also from the questions that were posed, the responsibilities I was given, the routines of everyday life, and the celebrations and silences that were punctuated by cups of *gur*-chai. Anonymity in this publication was preferred by the majority of my friends from these locations and so, even as I thank them, I continue to retain confidentiality in terms of location and identity by using pseudonyms – later followed throughout this book. I am especially grateful to Ravindra and Hema Pavshe for allowing me a place in their home and making me feel like family. To Mohansingh and his wife Mohini – *chāchā* and *chāchi* – you were my angels in Khasi. Thank you not only for entrusting me with the responsibility of the room you let out to me, but also for trusting in my capacity to make this project work, and realise from it a sustainable and thorough analysis. To Latika, thank you for welcoming me with loud and cheerful calls each time I walked up to our home from the school, where I taught.

The fieldwork in Gonjhé was initiated with the help of friends, Kaivalya and Dhanashree Dandekar, and their son Kanaad. They made my pauses from fieldwork comfortable and productive. Their local knowledge and experience of several years in the region lent tremendous insight into building the methodology and context-setting sections in this book. In Uttarakhand, the people of Dharamgarh valley were more willing to welcome me because of Avani, a non-profit organisation that has been working in the region for more than fifteen years. The team at Avani, especially Rashmi Bharati, Rajnish Jain, and Rajendra Joshi, placed their faith in me and allowed me to use Avani as my platform to build relationships in the community. To Janak and Kavita Bhauriyal, Dhana and Amar Rathod, thank you for pushing me to keep going in all the times when I battled with loneliness, frustration, illness, and hunger for home-cooked food. You remain my motivation to continue exploring this region. Words cannot do justice to describe all that I gained from our long exchanges of ideas and experiences. I remain grateful to you for sharing your spaces with me.

This book draws on my doctoral research, which was generously supported by the Max Planck Institute (MPI) for Social Anthropology in Halle, Germany. The team of librarians procured books and articles from different nooks and crannies of this world. The Law and Anthropology Department at the MPI is where this project gained direction. I presented several drafts of many sections in this book amidst a diverse audience of anthropologists, lawyers, religious studies scholars, and historians. Seminars that felt intimidating at times and intense almost always helped me churn out thoroughness in conducting fieldwork and mapping an analysis. It also made me aware of my abilities and limitations, significant now as I think back to pre-fieldwork preparation. Bertram Turner, Brian Donahoe, Katrin Seidel, Martin Ramstedt, and Dominik Müller were friends and mentors who made learning exuberant. For Jonathan Bernaerts, Catherine Larouche, Mareike Riedel, Markus Klank, and Harika Dauth, it was tremendously comforting to know that we were sharing the experiences of charting this journey together. I will always remain thankful for the many cups of coffee and tea that were had in the cafeterias and corridors of the Institute, where concepts, theories, and dilemmas were willingly discussed. All the laughter over anecdotes from the field made this journey enjoyable and lighter.

I also benefited greatly from two doctoral workshops organised by Kyriaki Topidi with the support of the University of Lucerne and the Swiss Institute of Comparative Law, where rigorous brainstorming over questions of legal pluralism and human rights added value to my reflections on the empirical data. I thank Kyriaki also for giving me the opportunity to develop some ideas from this project as chapter contributions in edited volumes following these workshops.

One of the most memorable experiences of this research project was learning to work in an interdisciplinary field. The result, this book, has benefited greatly from all the moments when this journey, at the time, felt exhausting and challenging. So many other lawyer friends across and outside of India encouraged me along the way to push the boundaries, and social science friends helped build the bridges! A heartfelt "Thank you!" to them all.

While this book was being written up, I spent a semester teaching at the Indian Institute of Science, Education, and Research (IISER) in Pune, India. The course allowed several exchanges on law and society relations that have helped me develop many parts of the introduction to this book. It was especially useful to exchange notes with an audience that was not from within the social science fraternity. Umesh K.P., Reema Jalal, Zakhiya P.C., and Himanshu Lagachu, thank you for keeping me actively engaged with your labyrinthine questions.

This book would not have been possible without a dream, an inspiration, and constant motivations. My mentors Prof. Werner Menski and Prof. Marie-Claire Foblets set an example of academic rigour and discipline that laid the foundation for this project. Thank you for believing in me. The works of Erin Moore, Marc Galanter, Gopika Solanki, and Mengia Hong Tschaler must be mentioned because they never moved from my deskside library.

And lastly, but most importantly, my parents, my sister, my in-laws, and Sumit: your prayers, and unbridled companionship, and support allowed me to live this project productively and substantially.

Glossary

bandar	port
beizzati	dishonour, insulting (also to social reputation)
bhāngaḍ	dispute
Bhāvkī, Manḍaḷ, Samāj	types of *Pancāyat* in Gonjhé village.
bhūt	ghost, spirit of a deceased person
birāderi	exogamous segment of caste in India
dev, devtā	male deity
devī	female deity
dharma	notion of righteousness in Hindu philosophy
gomutra	urine of a cow
Grām Pradhān	elected head of a village
Gram Prahari	an informant of the police in the village
izzat	honour, social reputation
kāydā, kānūn	law and order
nyāy	justice
pancāyat	village or caste council
panch	presiding member of *Pancāyat*
puchiāri	a type of priest magician, similar to a *shaman*.
puḍhārī	notable
pūjā	ritual of worship
pundit	priest
sarkār	government or state
shiyāné pl. (*shiyānās*, *shiyānis*)	village wisemen in Uttarakhand (male, female)
tālukā, tehsil	sub-district revenue division

Map 1 Map of fieldwork locations.
Based on map by Jutta Turner.
Note: This is an approximate representation.

1 Setting the context

Miradevi is a mother of four children. Her husband is extremely violent and besides physical aggression, he also subjects her to a great amount of mental stress and torture. "He undresses publicly and speaks openly about our conjugal relations at his workplace and even in the market. There are no traces of shame left in him and he has also caused me a lot of beizzati *(disrepute or dishonour)," narrated Miradevi. She approached a state forum – the police station – for the first time after ten years of her marriage. It was at the insistence of her neighbours, who saw that she had been beaten violently by her husband. When several police complaints did not improve her husband's ways, Miradevi heeded the advice of the police and filed a suit in the local* tehsil *court under Section 125 of the Criminal Procedure Code of 1973.*[1] *She received an order directing her husband to pay a monthly maintenance of Rs. 4,000 (approx. $58) to her and the children. Since this amount was not enough to cover the expenses for food, clothing, and schooling, Miradevi and her children continue to live with her husband. However, confronting the situation through police action and court processes has made Miradevi stronger. She knows now that she has the support of the state authorities. Her act of seeking help with the state machinery also caught the attention of her husband's employer, who now informs Miradevi about the transfer of her husband's monthly salary to his account. Today, Miradevi boldly keeps a close watch on how her husband spends his salary. She even accompanies him to the bank when he goes to encash it. She takes a share of his salary to pay the bills and the children's school fees. "Otherwise, he would just spend all the money on alcohol, like he did earlier," she says. A certified copy of the court order is kept safe by Miradevi at her parents' home. She knows she will enforce it if the situation gets out of hand. At the time of the interview, it had been three years since the court case. By invoking the support of state authorities in a domestic dispute, Miradevi has defied social norms of privacy that often tend to reinforce patriarchal notions of power. But she did so in a situation of distress and believes that she has grown stronger as a result.*[2]

Govindi Devi's son, Lalit, is mentally ill. Sometimes he becomes violent in a fit of madness. Lalit's wife, Suman, left her marital home a year after their marriage.

1 A *tehsil* is an administrative division within a district in a state. *Tehsils* are also known as *tālukā* and *tāluk* in different parts of India.

2 This case study is followed up in Chapter 5.

Govindi Devi is concerned about her son who cannot manage on his own. "He needs someone to take care of him," she said. Govindi Devi feels that the most practical solution would be for Suman to inform Lalit in writing that she does not wish to live with him and that she has decided to leave him. "She keeps asking us to give her in writing that Lalit does not want to reside any more with her. But we will do nothing like this. She is welcome here. She should look after her husband and she has a right over all the property here. But if she does not want to look after my son, she should just say so and give it to us in writing so that all of us can move ahead," said Govindi Devi. Govindi Devi has been cautioned by the wise men in her village to ensure that Lalit does not give Suman any written document that reveals "an intention to separate." Govindi Devi has said that since the "(state) law is for women" (aurat ka kanoon hai*), any such piece of writing by Lalit to Suman could lead him into a tricky situation involving courts and police stations.*[3]

That relationships with and between corporate entities, be it in the public or private sector, are influenced by state law by the mere fact of their existence does not come as a surprise. The above two snippets of fieldwork, however, are meant to reveal the various forms dispute processing assumes as a result of the engagement of non-state forums and actors with state law and its systems.

The above two experiences are within the sphere of the family, which, as a social unit has, for a long time, been fairly independent of the state law and its systems in India (Derrett 1968, 1978b). First, the personal law system (Subramanian 2014) in India causes a majority of family matters to be governed by religious law and customary practices.[4] And second, an intricate web of caste, *birāderi* (see Chapter 2, page 52) and community reciprocities keep the regulation of family affairs limited largely to kinship circles, extending at the most to the village. The latter remains true in many parts of rural India, including in the two locations of fieldwork on which the evidence presented in this book is based, where caste and *birāderi* networks still play an important role within the general social structure. However, as the two vignettes at the beginning (and other case studies that follow in the next chapters) reveal, even the processing of family disputes witnesses an intensive engagement with state law and its systems, the presence and penetration of which is today undisputable.[5] As, the title suggests, this book explores the

3 This case study is followed up in Chapter 4.

4 Every individual in India has a right to be governed by his/her personal law in matters of marriage and divorce, infants and minors, adoptions, wills, intestacy, and succession. Personal laws reflect a multicultural rule of law giving religious/cultural minorities an opportunity to be governed by their own customs, norms, and religious laws (Solanki 2011; Sezgin 2013).

5 I use the concept of dispute processing over dispute resolution or dispute settlement because disputes in my observation did not really ever get "settled" entirely. This book adopts the term "dispute processing" in line with Felstiner's (1974, 63) argument that "a significant amount of dispute processing is not intended to settle disputes, that a greater amount does not do so and that it is often difficult to know whether a dispute which has been processed has been settled" and Sen's (2009, 392) comment that "Complete resolution is neither a requirement of a person's own rationality, nor is it a condition of reasonable social choice, including a reason-based theory of justice."

unspoken dialogues between non-state actors, state laws, and the regulatory systems that reveal the nature and form of this engagement. By focusing on the blurred boundaries between state and non-state law, this book establishes that no aspect of Indian society, irrespective of its nature, location, or size, remains entirely autonomous at any point of the state law and its systems. The family, popularly referred to as the basic unit of this society, is only one example.

Experiences like those above indicate the nature of the impact that state law and its systems may have, even on dispute processing that occurs outside state institutions, such as state courts and police stations in India today. Whether in terms of counter-balancing the power disparity with her husband by improving her bargaining power with a court decree, as in the case of Miradevi, or in the form of a transformation in customary practices that occurs in response to legislative interventions regulating social relationships, as highlighted in Govindi Devi's response, the impact of state law and its processes becomes evident in the diverse forms of adoption and resistance through which state law gets translated. The experiences of individuals and communities steering across different "layers of legality" (see page 65 below), characterised by a dynamic of competing values within such layers, establish that the non-state and state spheres of dispute processing are "mutually constitutive" (Merry 1992, 358). This challenges the popular rhetoric of campaigns seeking the elimination of non-state forums of dispute processing on the grounds that such forums work in "parallel" to their state-based counterparts.

Fitzpatrick (2001, 212–215) argues that the fundamental political principles, in this era of neoliberalism where the market is supreme, are democracy, human rights, and the rule of law. The creation of such a state is replete with efforts to capture and control dispute processing, to extinguish local forms, and to develop uniformity. As India is experiencing this phenomenon too, an evident consequence, therefore, is the ongoing debate in India about whether the task of processing disputes and grievances that involve questions of individual freedoms and rights should be left entirely to the devices of the state. This study finds its conceptual roots in this very debate. Drawing on the framework of legal pluralism,[6] a still contested heuristic tool, and proceeding with the methods of participant observation and semi-structured interviews, I present an ethnography of how disputes are handled in rural Indian societies and the nature of engagement with state law that such processing involves. Legal pluralism is "that state of affairs, for any social field, in which behaviour pursuant to more than one legal order occurs" (Griffiths 1986, 2). The present study develops the research question through exploring the agency of various actors embedded within a complex interplay of power, information, networks, and values involved in such processing. Two sections of lower-caste communities located in the rural areas of Maharashtra and Uttarakhand

6 For a detailed understanding and discussion about "legal pluralism," see Sally Falk Moore (1973), John Griffiths (1986), Sally Engle Merry (1988), Masaji Chiba (1989), Werner Menski (2006b), and Brian Tamanaha (2008).

respectively,[7] aid the understanding of the research question, enhancing the contribution of this study with specific reference to the communities perceived to be on the margins of development and social justice.

The book emphasises that, in the sphere of dispute processing, the nature of engagement of non-state forums and actors with state law and its systems can be understood only through examining the extent to which, and the manner in which, the values underlying a community's sense of order and the values of state law compete or coincide with one another during the processing of disputes. How communities generally and individuals within these communities specifically balance these dynamics is equally crucial to such an understanding.[8] Through an ethnographic study of dispute processing in the village communities of Gonjhé and the Dharamgarh valley the present study builds on Masaji Chiba's (1986, 378–391) theory of "identity postulates of indigenous law" (see page 72 for further details), to show how the nature of the engagement between the values of *dharma* and *izzat* underscoring community laws (in both the communities) and the values of state law determined the extent to which state law influenced dispute processing within these village communities and the manner in which it came to be "translated" (Merry 2009).[9]

This chapter first contextualises the research study and its focus. It then introduces the methodology used, followed by a description of the frameworks of thought and terminology that guided the present study. In the next sections, I provide an overview and analysis of the debates surrounding the relationship of state law and non-state actors as perceived by the Indian judiciary and socio-legal activists. These sections also present an outline of the current literature on non-state dispute processing in India generally. Towards the conclusion of this chapter is a brief description of the chapters that follow.

1.1 Law in action: Using ethnography to understand state law

In order to tackle the question of whether, to what extent and in which manner non-state forums and actors in dispute processing engaged with state law and its systems, it did not take me very long to realise that merely having a knowledge of state law, its objectives, and how it works to implement these was insufficient.

7 Maharashtra and Uttarakhand are states in India. Maharashtra is located on the western part of the Indian peninsula, whereas Uttarakhand is located in the northern part of India that borders with Nepal and Tibet. The first site involved research with a fishing community; and in the second location the research focused on a rural agrarian community.

8 A fair share of literature in anthropology (Ramsbotham, Woodhouse, and Miall 2011) discusses the usage of terminology pertaining to "dispute" and "conflict." This book understands "disputes" as a type of conflict (see Nader 1978, 15, for disputes as a stage of conflict); conflict being the "widest set of circumstances in which parties perceive that they have mutually incompatible goals" (Ramsbotham, Woodhouse, and Miall 2011, 9). See also Epstein (1974, ch. 1) and Koch (1974, 26) on similar descriptions of "disputes."

9 For the concepts of *dharma* and *izzat* see Chapter 3, page 67.

State law certainly does not exist in a vacuum, but rather in a society in order to be meaningful. However, societies – and in the context of this study, non-state forums and actors – are not just passive recipients of state law, but are constantly modifying the impact and influence of state law by engaging with it (Sally Falk Moore 1973).

The discipline of anthropology with its emphasis on ethnography "helps us overcome the resistance of law to more nuanced analysis on the ground, among real people. It allows us to begin to explore how law features in different ways for individuals from different ethnic and socioeconomic backgrounds" (Darian-Smith 2012, 555). I approached therefore the concept of "impact of state law" not from within the ambit of legal discourses, but rather as an empirical question. This enabled me to gain a broader, more holistic, contextualised, and realistic picture of the "impact of state law" in terms of how state law actually worked and was received within society.

Approaching the research question with a combination of understandings drawn from both law and anthropology was a fairly challenging task. The amalgam of disciplines necessitated twelve months of ethnographic fieldwork, which was carried out partly in a fishermen's community in western Maharashtra and partly in an agrarian community in Uttarakhand.[10] My own learning about law had to be partly unlearned to reduce the "sense of shock" provided by the "tension between the nature of reality as presented by the ideology of legal centralism and the actual state of the empirical world" (Griffiths 1986, 4). My experience of law school followed by legal practice in the state courts seemed to have provided an exaggerated picture of how frequently state courts are accessed by people. While indeed courtrooms in Indian courts are constantly overflowing with litigants and the sheaves of papers on a judge's desk never seem to end (see Krishnan 2014, 275–279, for a more detailed insight on this point); from the other end of the telescope, this proportion of people seem to be a disparate minority in comparison to those numbers that process their disputes in the compounds of a state court or simply beyond its boundaries. As rightly articulated by Galanter (1981, 31, 34):

> Courts and (other official agencies) comprise only one hemisphere of the world of regulating and disputing. To understand them we must learn how they interact with the other normative orderings that pervade social life. To fulfil our commitment to enlarge justice requires that we embark on research that will illuminate the complex relationship between official forums and indigenous law.

Ethnographic fieldwork using methods like participant observation and semi-structured interviews allowed me to observe how these communities engaged with state law in the context of their cultural and religious backgrounds, caste, and kinship reciprocities together with the dynamics of gender, power, and

10 The descriptions of fieldwork and what it entailed are given in more detail in Chapter 2.

class.[11] The anthropological perspective on state law was particularly crucial in order to be able to comprehend "(strong) legal pluralism as a fact" (Griffiths 1986, 4) and disputing as a social process (Miller and Sarat 1980). In line with the interdisciplinary approach adopted, this study follows Sally Falk Moore's understanding of "law" and Griffiths' explanation of it.[12] Moore argues that the state is not the only source of "legal" rules and that law is the self-regulation of a "semi-autonomous field" (Sally Falk Moore 1978, 57–58).[13] Pursuing Moore's definition of "law," Griffiths (1986, 38) explains:

> The idea that only the law of the state is law "properly so called" is a feature of the ideology of legal centralism and has for empirical purposes nothing to be said for it. Distinctions can, where appropriate, be made between more or less differentiated forms of law.

Accordingly, this study differentiates between "state law" and other types of law. It explores a situation of legal pluralism, a concept that was devised essentially to counter the idea that all law was created by the state (von Rossum and Taekema 2013). As part of the process of challenging the hierarchy accorded to state law within legal centralist approaches (R. Michaels 2015), which, as this study will establish, does not exist within the various dispute processing mechanisms adopted by the communities studied, the usage of terminology in this study therefore does *not* limit the term "law" (and legality) to state law alone (see also Woodman 2001 in the context of "customary law").[14]

11 I remain sensitive at all times to Laura Nader's (2002) observation that ethnography is a craft and that ethnographic fieldwork goes beyond just participant observation and the conducting of interviews. To that extent of course this ethnography of disputing processes remains limited, in that it is carried out not by a researcher trained in anthropology, but one who is a student of law.

12 I remain aware, however, that Griffiths (2006) subsequently changed his views in this context.

13 While I follow Sally Falk Moore's understanding of law as well as her framework of "semi-autonomous social fields" described later in this chapter (see page 20), which explains how the non-state and state interact in the sphere of dispute processing, it was not Moore alone who argued that state law was not the only source of everything "legal." Along with Moore, scholars like Leopold Pospisil (1978), Eugen Ehrlich (2002 [1936]), and M. G. Smith (1974) have argued similarly.

14 But see Pirie (2013, chap. 2) who raises concerns about extending the term "law" to all types of normative orders. She proposes that it is important to "talk about law in the way in which people talk about it" (2013, 45), so as to be able to tease out the distinctions in their perceptions, if any. In this context, it becomes important to note that here the use of the term "law" in the way stated above also resonates with the manner in which both village communities that were observed perceived laws. They referred to both – the norms comprising their respective community's sense of order and state law – as "law" (*kāydā* in Maharashtra and *kānūn* in Uttarakhand) making the distinction only in terms of community laws and state law.

1.2 State–non-state, formal–informal, official–unofficial: Choice of terminology

Discourses within anthropology have long debated the dichotomy between that which constitutes the "state" and the "non-state" (Hertogh 2007; Kötter et al. 2015; Helfand 2015). It has also been argued that the use of "state" and "non-state" inherently implies a hierarchy of state over non-state. I remain sensitive to this critique and adopt the use of "state" and "non-state" with reference to types of law and forums only as analytical categories.

Non-state forums of dispute processing have been variously referred to as informal systems of justice, informal systems of dispute settlement, and unofficial systems, in different pieces of literature, often being used interchangeably.[15] In this section I will clarify my choice of "non-state" over these other terms. In the larger scheme of studies on dispute processing, the concept of "non-state forums and actors" has included private mediation centres, legal aid clinics, lawyer's offices, as well as non-governmental organisations. In this book, however, the terms non-state forums and non-state actors are a reference only to *community*-based forums and individuals active in the actual processes of dispute processing.[16] In Galanter's words, "It includes any forum that is part of (and embedded within) the social setting within which the dispute arose" (1981, 2). In the context of the study, this solely refers to such forums and individuals engaged in dispute processing that are organised, managed, and maintained by and rooted within a community, which may be village-, religion-, or caste-based, to handle disputes that cannot be resolved by everyday processes.[17] Ordinarily, the state is not a direct stakeholder, whether in terms of providing financial support or through the appointment of any of its members, in such non-state forums. Conversely, the use of the terms "state forums" and "state actors" refers to any forum or actor whose position is established by the state. State actors and the employees of a state forum may be appointed either by the state independently or in consultation with it. I make a difference between state forums and actors and state-supported forums and actors, the latter being actors who are not state-appointed but find the legitimacy for their existence in either state law or state measures or recommendations, and are expected to function in consonance with state law.[18]

15 See Baxi (1976), Galanter (1981), Felstiner, Abel, and Sarat (1981), and Cohn (1965) on how state and non-state institutions and law are referred to in different ways.

16 While I remain conscious of the debates surrounding the terms "forum" and "institution," for the sake of brevity, in this book the terms may be used interchangeably.

17 Here the term "everyday processes" (Galanter 1981, 3) refers to all adjustments in a relationship, "resignation," "lumping it," "avoidance," "exit," or "self-help" by a party. Also the term non-state institutions includes any community-managed body organised specifically for the purpose of dispute processing, or one whose functions are socially recognised to be so. Therefore, a council of elders or influential kin, a *pancāyat*, or a single or group of notables at any level in the village, would ordinarily fit within the scope of non-state institutions in this context.

18 The Dispute Free Village Scheme and Police Patil in Maharashtra and the *Grām Pradhān* and the *Gram Prahari* in Uttarakhand comprise this category of state-supported actors. For more details please see Chapter 3, page 69.

I choose to avoid the terminology of "formal" and "informal" to refer to forums and actors as I perceive these terms to have greater relevance in terms of understanding methods and procedures. Just like a state forum can have or may include informal procedures (Galanter and Krishnan 2003; Nagaraj 2010a),[19] non-state forums, as I found, may have an extremely formal set-up and method of working.[20] To refer to non-state forums as informal forums therefore would be quite confusing as well as, in certain instances, misleading, sometimes drawing clear-cut boundaries, where they do not exist.[21]

Similarly, in the context of the empirical evidence I gathered, the vocabulary of "official" and "unofficial" seemed extremely limiting and unclear, especially in regard to describing (and distinguishing) between non-state and state forums. The use of the terms "official" and "unofficial" particularly with reference to different types of laws and forums, I realised, partly depended on how the author using these terms positioned himself/herself in a narrative. Legal centralists, viewing law in a top-down manner or with an inside-out view when positioning themselves within a state forum, are likely to term state law and its systems as "official" and non-state forums, processes, and laws as "unofficial." However, such a positivistic perception of "official," which is by definition law and other systems officially authorised by the state as the standard legal system of the people, excludes some other systems of law valid in practice for the lives of people (Chiba 1989, 135–136). Being located within a community I realised quickly that there was an internally diverse understanding of the "official" and "unofficial."

With regard to discourses about disputes, my own experience in conducting fieldwork was an eye-opener. I remained both an insider and outsider in both the communities where fieldwork was conducted (see Chapter 2, page 31). As Naples (2003, 49) argues, the identities of "insider" and "outsider" are not static, rather they are "ever-shifting and permeable social locations." Likewise, my position as "insider" or "outsider" was decided by the community according to the context and also depended a great deal on my relationships with the different people in these communities (Narayan 1993). This positionality also determined the type of data I could collect. Often, I received information about certain ongoing disputes in the village, which, according to the village community at large, only an "insider" should have known. Since at the given point in time, my informants considered me an "insider" vis-à-vis themselves, this information was passed on to me, albeit "unofficially." With the exception of my informants (for whom I remained an "insider" in the majority of circumstances), in the broader context of the village I was still an "outsider" in certain contexts, and it was perceived to be

19 The absence of insistence on rules of evidence, representation by lawyers, and payment of court fees is perceived by many scholars as an informalisation of judicial intervention.

20 The *Samāj* – village forums – in Gonjhé village met on the 10th of every month, maintained a register of the proceedings, entertained applications inviting intervention in disputes, and even sent notices to parties. (see Chapter 2, page 43 and Chapter 4, page 101)

21 A similar understanding of formal and informal is reflected in Cohn's (1959, 83) description of *Chamar panchayats* in eastern Uttar Pradesh, India.

"inappropriate" to tell an outsider about the intimate details of certain village disputes. Therefore, a constant reminder from close friends and informants in the village during the collection of these "unofficial" narratives was that this information was "off the record" and that it was "unofficially provided." The "official" narrative about the dispute of course was what was discussed openly in the *Samāj* or in any of the other non-state forums in the village.

Whether a forum or strategy was considered "official" or "unofficial" really depended on the perception of the people using such a forum or practising such strategy. Within the Koḷī community in Gonjhé, one of my fieldwork sites, the *Samāj* – the village *pancāyat* – was considered the "official" forum in the village.[22] The *Samāj* was distinguished from the *Grām Pancāyat*, the latter being known as the *sarkāri* (government) body. Similarly, in the villages in the Dharamgarh valley in Uttarakhand, the second location for my fieldwork, the partition of family property in the presence of *shiyāné* individuals (see Chapter 2, page 52 for a description of *shiyāné*) was the "official" method of property partition. This method, however, involved no paperwork or written documentation. According to Chiba (1989 139) such laws:

> generally function in consonance with, or at least without seriously affecting, the state law concerned. But they may function, in exception, in nonconformity or in conflict with the state law depending on the relative autonomy of their authorities.

On the whole, I gathered that the "official" nature of a particular forum or practice depended on the extent of its acceptance.[23] The more accepted and publicly

22 There are various definitions and descriptions of *pancāyats* in the literature that deals with them (Bose 1960, 2; Berreman 1963, 280–281; Cohn 1965). In this book, I use a combination of these descriptions to describe the overall nature of *pancāyats*, which do however differ vastly in their actual working from village to village. The word *pancāyat* literally means a council of five people. However, present-day *pancāyats* may consist of more persons. *Pancāyats* are ad hoc rather than permanently constituted bodies, marked by processes of adjudication, arbitration, and mediation. Their membership usually comprises a combination of people with a representation from at least one if not all of the following groups: The elderly, politically active, religiously prominent, and professionals such as doctors or teachers. Their membership may vary with circumstance.

I use the word *pancāyat* to refer specifically to the non-state forum in the village; it would be the *Samāj* or *Mandaḷ* in the case of Gonjhé and *birāderi* meetings in the villages in Dharamgarh valley. This should not be confused with the Gram Panchayat, which will be referred to as "Gram Panchayat" itself, a state body of local self-government constituted under the U.P. Panchayat Raj Act 1947 (Uttaranchal Amendment) Act, 2002, in Uttarakhand and Bombay Village Panchayats Act, 1958, in Maharashtra. See Chapter 4, 4.4.1, for a detailed description of the *pancāyats* observed.

23 Chiba attributed this feature to what he termed "unofficial laws" and mentioned in the initial description of unofficial law that "which is not officially sanctioned by official law but is in practice sanctioned by the general consensus of a certain people" (Chiba 1989, 136). I however, I argue that what Chiba called "unofficial laws," would actually be "official" in the perception of the communities.

acknowledged a practice or forum was within a community, the greater the likelihood of it being considered "official." In the light of these complexities, where notions of "official" and "unofficial" varied so widely depending on time, positions, and contexts, a blanket reference to state forums and laws as "official" and non-state forums and laws as "unofficial," as is quite often the case, would have in fact amounted to partial-sightedness.

1.3 The Indian judiciary's relationship with non-state actors of dispute processing

Relevant to the study of non-state forums of dispute processing is the context of their position vis-à-vis the state. Since the Indian state enables the people of India to be governed by a variety of laws – state laws, religious laws, customs – in different aspects of their life, by implication, space is made for a variety of actors and forums to regulate the affairs of people.

The issue of non-state forums of dispute processing acting *in parallel* to state and state-supported forums of dispute processing and being "extrajudicial," "illegal," and "regressive" has become a persistent argument put forward by scholars, activists, and organisations engaged in the effort to concentrate all powers of "dispute settlement" and the regulation of individual rights in the hands of the state. On the international landscape, the delivery of justice by non-state institutions has escalated to a controversial issue during recent years as a result of widespread debates crosscutting the management of cultural and religious diversity, citizenship, migration, and human rights. As Grillo (2015, 2) notes, there is hardly any country in the West – or elsewhere, including India – where this is not an issue, as may be observed from newspapers, television, and the internet, in election manifestos, parliamentary debates, and ministerial statements, and in policy initiatives at local, national, and international levels. Canada, it seems, took the lead in 2003–2004 when debates surrounding a proposal by the Islamic Institute of Civil Justice to set up Dar-ul-Qadas (a "Muslim Arbitration Board") ended with the much-cited declaration by Ontario Premier Dalton McGuinty, where he stated that "There will be no Shariah law in Ontario. There will be no religious arbitration in Ontario. There will be one law for all Ontarians" (Korteweg 2006; Razack 2007; Boyd 2013). In the United Kingdom, Baroness Caroline Cox, a member of the House of Lords, has attempted to introduce, on three occasions at least, a Private Member's Bill proposing the criminalisation of any act by a person where s/he "falsely purports to exercise any of the powers or duties of a court or to make legally binding rulings." This Bill, if passed, would be detrimental to community-run dispute settlement forums such as Shari'a Councils in the UK (Grillo 2015, ch. 7).

The relationship of the Indian state with non-state forums of dispute processing and the actors involved therein has never been clearly defined, more so probably because it has never been questioned until recently. Commentaries in the media (Shedge 2014; IBN Lokmat 2015) and public campaigns (Correspondent 2015; Waghmode 2015) concerning the legitimacy of non-state forums and actors in the scheme of dispute processing have arisen in the context of four cases before the

Indian Supreme Court in the last ten years.[24] As Redding (2014, 951) correctly notes, these pieces of litigation are "evidence of the continuing global reach and penetration of liberal legality in the twenty-first century, including liberal norms pertaining to the rule of law."[25]

1.3.1 The course of litigation: Trends and developments

In April 2011, in a judgment upholding the decision of the Madras High Court for a case under the Scheduled Castes and Scheduled Tribes (Prevention of Atrocities Act), 1989, a Division Bench of the Supreme Court made a comment on *khāp pancāyats* labelling them as "kangaroo courts … which are wholly illegal."[26] The issue in the special leave petition in response to which this judgment came did not, in itself, pertain to *khāp pancāyat* or any other non-state forums, but was rather concerned with whether calling someone "*pallan*" amounted to an offence under the Scheduled Castes and Scheduled Tribes (Prevention of Atrocities Act), 1989. Justice M. Katju, a judge popular for his fairly controversial views, however, also seems to have thought it appropriate to make a comment on "honour killings" and "*khap panchayats*" in the same judgment (*Arumugam Servai v State of Tamil Nadu 2011*, (2011), vol. 6, para. C). While the judgment as a whole received very little attention in the media, references to Justice Katju's statements were made in news articles on *khāp pancāyats* and "kangaroo courts," which became the subject of a campaign for human rights activists and a sensational topic for the media in the next few years (Dasgupta 2014; R. Sharma 2014; R. Iyengar 2015).

In January 2014, the Supreme Court through a *suo motu* writ petition took cognisance of an incident of gang rape of a 20-year-old woman from a village in the Birbhum district of the state of West Bengal. This offence occurred on the orders of a "community panchayat as punishment for having relationship with a man from a different community" (Re: Indian woman says gang-raped on orders of Village Court, published in *Business & Financial News* dated 23.01.2014, 2014, Order dated March 28). The Court proceeded to investigate and decide the question of rape as an offence under the Indian Penal Code, 1860. In the judgment, the Court made a comment on the benefits of inter-caste marriages and briefly referred to *Arumugam Servai v State of Tamil Nadu* in the context of honour killings and the

24 See footnote 43 on the role of the mass media.

25 Redding (2014) makes his observation with respect to the case of *Vishwa Lochan Madan v Union of India*, but owing to the similarity in the nature of the court cases described in this section, Redding's observation can be easily extended to describe them all.

26 *Khāp pancāyats* are "modern-day avatars of traditional social assemblies in rural north-western India that were primarily engaged in resolving disputes and ensuring adherence to custom" (A. Kumar 2012, 59). Kumar (2012, 59–60) notes that *khāp pancāyat* form a very old institution, with some scholars tracing their origins to even tribal times. Sources of information on *khāps* before the advent of feudalism and even during it are few and far between. They have been observed to exists "by around the 14th and 15th centuries" as "an informal but well-established social institution in the Jat-dominated areas that fall in present-day Haryana, western Uttar Pradesh and parts of Rajasthan."

"community *panchayats*" that were highlighted in the circumstances of these cases. In the media, however, the theme – rape as a gruesome diktat of community-based non-state forums – became prominent (R. Sharma 2014; Press Trust of India 2014).

An important judgment on July 7, 2014, by the Supreme Court of India seemed to have possibly put to rest questions of the legitimacy of non-state forums and actors by establishing that Dar-ul-Qazas were an "informal justice delivery system with an objective of bringing about amicable settlement between the parties" and that the grievance of the petitioner being "that Dar-ul-Qazas and Nizam-e-Qaza are running a parallel judicial system" was clearly "misconceived" (*Vishwa Lochan Madan v Union of India & Ors 2014*, vol. (2014) 7, paras 13, 15; also see Redding 2013). This judgment disposed of a public interest litigation (PIL) filed by activist lawyer Vishwa Lochan Madan in 2005 that raised as an issue the eligibility of Dar-ul-Qazas to engage in dispute processing. Dar-ul-Qazas are "non-state Muslim courts" (Redding 2014, 959) popular within certain sections of the Muslim community in India. The judgment of the Supreme Court further went on to clarify that while Dar-ul-Qazas were not part of the "corpus juris of the State," their existence could not be deemed as "illegal." The Court continues to consider them as "informal justice delivery system(s) with an objective of bringing about amicable settlement between the parties" (*Vishwa Lochan Madan v Union of India & Ors 2014*, vol. (2014) 7, para. 15). In the early days after this judgment was passed, a rush of headlines commending the Supreme Court for banning "sharia courts" and "*dar-ul-qazas*" filled the newspapers (Nairita 2014; IANS 2014; Ghosh 2014). However, in the weeks that followed a steady flow of opinion pieces by careful readers of the judgment corrected this misrepresentation (Polanki 2014; Dhawan 2014; Gurjar 2014; see also Kokal 2014).[27]

But as we see from the nature of events that followed, the media (FP Politics 2014; *The Hindu* 2014), campaigners and socio-legal activists refused to take the hint. In August 2015, Amnesty International circulated a petition campaigning for an order of protection to be granted to "two Dalit sisters who had been told they had been ordered to be raped and paraded naked by a khap panchayat" (Bashi 2017). While Amnesty International, in most of the interviews to the media, stated that the focus of their campaign was to demand protection from the state for these two sisters, it was

27 A similar trend seems to have been followed with regard to an order of the Madras High Court on dispute processing activities within a mosque in Tamil Nadu. The order is an interim one in a public interest litigation filed by Abdur Rahman who initially sought the services of a certain "Makka Masjid Shariat Council" to be reunited with his wife and upon being made to sign an order of *talaq* instead, rushed to the High Court with this PIL (Express News Service 2016b). Whereas the Court observed, on the basis of the documents brought before it, that certain activities with the "colour of a judicial forum" had taken place in a mosque and along with criticising places of worship being used for "purposes other than prayers and more specifically to create extra judicial forums" directed the authorities to stop "these activities" (*Abdur Rahman v The Secretary to Government 2017*, Order dated January 19). The newspapers reported the Madras High Court having passed an order banning Sharia courts altogether (Subramani 2016; Ahmed 2016).

once again *khāp pancāyats* and "unelected village councils," and their existence as "parallel systems," that became the target of the several news reports and opinion pieces that flooded the media during this period (R. Iyengar 2015). The said case, a writ petition (criminal), was filed in the Supreme Court by Meenakshi Kumari, one of the sisters who felt threatened for her life on account of a village council allegedly having passed an order of rape as punishment against her, for the fact that her brother had eloped with a girl from the higher caste of "Jats" in their village. The case was regularly heard till November 30, 2015, and thereafter once on April 19, 2016 (*Meenakshi Kumari v State of Uttar Pradesh and Ors 2015*, Order dated August 17, 2015; September 14, 2015; September 15, 2015; September 16, 2015; November 30, 2015; April 19, 2016). During this period, the petitioner, her parents and her siblings were examined in camera by the Court and an order for the protection of the "person and liberty of the petitioner and her family members" was passed by the Supreme Court (*Meenakshi Kumari v State of Uttar Pradesh and Ors 2015*, Order dated September 15). The Court made no comments on the nature of "unelected village councils" during this period and continued to pass procedural orders to implead other respondents in order to facilitate cross-examination and other procedures. The details of how this case proceeded in the Supreme Court are unavailable as most of the procedure was conducted in camera. After being heard intermittently in 2016 and 2017, Meenakshi Kumari's petition was dealt with more swiftly in 2018. During this period the criminal cases against the petitioner's brother were also heard jointly with this writ. Cross-examination revealed that the petitioner's brother was not guilty of the offences he had been accused of. In April 2018 the Supreme Court directed the state to compensate the petitioner and her brother for the agony they had gone through as a result of the (wrongful) cases being foisted on them. Meenakshi Kumari's case has however not been closed by the Court. Again, here, the Court has dealt with the petition in order to pronounce only on such orders that are of consequence to the individual parties in the case. On the subject of *pancāyats*, the Court remained silent.

The beginning of 2018 also witnessed a final judgment in the case of *Shakti Vahini v Union of India & Ors*, a public interest litigation filed by an NGO – Shakti Vahini – in 2010 and heard for the first time in March 2012. This case was particularly important to the future of non-state actors because the issues raised in it directly sought the abolition of non-state forums engaging in dispute processing activities and particularly those of the nature of *khāp pancāyats*. Seeking the protection of young couples who married inter-caste or within the same *gotra* from the wrath of the *khāp pancāyat*, the final disposal of this petition came on March 27, 2018. Amidst the furore over *khāp pancāyat* decisions alleged to be generally in violation of human rights[28] and individual freedoms that took over the media through the voices of different NGOs and socio-legal activists in this period, the Supreme Court, through an

28 The tone of demands with regard to human rights in this as well as in other petitions and that of several human rights activists indicates that human rights are understood as a concept that develops from a "modernist understanding of the self and its capacity to act autonomously as well as an emphasis on equality and the security of the body" (Merry 2009, 268). In this book the use of the term "human rights" is intended to echo this same understanding.

interim order in this case on January 4, 2013, invited certain prominent *khāp pancāyats* to represent their views in the case, if they so wished (*Shakti Vahini v Union of India & Ors 2013*, Order dated January 4; Kokal 2013). A leading newspaper, *The Times of India*, quoted the Division Bench presiding over the case saying:

> We are getting the views on khap panchayats from those who are adverse to them. We may share the views but we must hear from them about their views on this issue. We may at the end of the day reject their views as unconstitutional. But it will be more satisfying in a judicial proceeding if the khaps were heard more so because all the parties before the court are hostile to them.
>
> (Mahapatra 2013)

This is a clear reference to the general principle that all parties to a litigation ought to be heard (*audi alteram pertem*). Since July 2013 till the date of final hearing, none of the orders in the case said anything about *khāp pancāyat*. In the final decision in this case, the Court wholly concerned itself with issues of class and caste-based power struggles, honour crimes and the freedom of individual choice and autonomy. Grounding its decision in the estrangement of human rights and human dignity caused by honour-related violence, the Supreme Court held "protection of human rights is *élan vital* of our Constitution" (Supreme Court of India 2018, vol. 7, para. 52) and that any *pancāyat* of any nomenclature creating a dent in the exercise of such rights would not be acceptable (Supreme Court of India 2018, vol. 7, para. 41). The primary intent of this judgment seemed to be the necessity to legislate on individual choice particularly with regard to its exercise in the case of such rights that are guaranteed as fundamental freedoms under the Indian Constitution. Given the nature of the petition, the Court specifically referred to *khāp pancāyats* as groups of persons who have assembled at any time with the:

> view or intention of condemning any marriage, not prohibited by law, on the basis that such a marriage has dishonoured the caste or community tradition or brought disrepute to all or any of the persons forming part of the assembly or the family or the people of the locality concerned.
>
> (Supreme Court of India 2018, vol. 7, para. 28)

This definition was adopted by the Court from "The Prohibition of Interference with the Freedom of Matrimonial Alliances Bill," which was drafted by the Law Commission of India following the directions of the Court during the proceedings of this case. The Bill creates a "threshold bar" on any congregation that objects to individuals of marriageable age entering into a union of their choice if the only ground for such an objection is the honour and social reputation of the community s/he belongs to. This judgment at many points reiterates individual choice and autonomy as an integral part of human dignity within the framework of liberty that the Indian Constitution seeks to protect. Interference in the fructification of an individual's right to make an autonomous choice is thus perceived as a violation of one's fundamental rights secured under the Constitution. Even though this PIL raised questions crucial to the determination of the role of non-state forums in dispute processing activities, the Court limited itself to speaking about the activities of "assemblies" and "*panchayats*" that intervene in an individual's right to express one's choice about who to marry. Simultaneously, in para 49 of its judgment, the Supreme Court clarified that "an assembly or Panchayat committed to engage in any constructive work that does not offend the fundamental rights of an individual will not stand on the same footing of Khap Panchayat." Here the Court seems to have taken the very same stance it took with respect to the functioning of Dar-ul-Qazas in the judgment that came in 2014 discussed earlier. Without commenting on their legitimacy in state law, the Supreme Court discreetly lets them function, but with an obligation to act responsibly and in line with the Constitution.

While a discussion or commentary from the Supreme Court lending the clarity that is being sought through these various strategic litigations on the issue of what is to be the "legal" status of non-state forums and actors engaged in dispute processing has remained more or less absent, the litigation-based campaigns at the national level have accelerated the efforts of several smaller movements that are working towards delegitimising such forums and actors. In Maharashtra, for instance, where one of the locations for fieldwork for this study was located, a state-based NGO, Maharashtra Andhashraddha Nirmoolan Samiti (ANIS), campaigned for a law against "jaat panchayats." Popularly perceived as a variant of their north Indian counterparts, the *khāp pancāyats*, *jāt pancāyats* can be broadly described as caste-based non-state bodies that engage in dispute processing, among other activities, (Kulkarni 2015). Seen as a positive step in this direction, human rights activists rejoiced, when, in April 2016, the Maharashtra state legislature, in an attempt to regulate the working of these caste *pancāyats*, unanimously passed a bill making social boycott "by any person or any extra-judicial group" in Maharashtra a criminal offence (Express News Service 2016a; B. Sharma 2016; Kumar Prasanna 2016). Social boycott is used as a tool for castigation within non-state mechanisms of dispute processing.

The campaigns against non-state forums and actors, though vigorous in their approach, continue to act "with shallower and narrower 'knowledge' about their new found "outlaw" targets" (Redding 2014, 947) having hardly any to zero information on the working of non-state forums and actors and the manner in which they are used. Difficulty in gaining access to those people engaging "with" or "as" such forums and actors is part of the problem (see Chapter 2, page 28) of acquiring information. But a legal centralist approach rooted in a "rule of law" ideology that seeks to confer state actors with all activities of dispute processing is a graver part of the problem, because this means losing sight of the socio-legal complexities that surround the very act of dispute processing. The legal fraternity in India, which comprises mainly judges and lawyers, but also those advocating the law, seeking or enforcing the intervention of state law in the regulation of social life, seems almost hypnotised by the gravity of state law and its systems. Targeted activism influenced and propelled by the global phenomenon of emphasising positivism and state centric behaviour remains undeterred, strengthened today by human rights arguments.

It is important to highlight the fact that what most of these campaigns aspire to would be for the Indian state a completely unrealistic agenda. People in rural India, as the evidence in this book confirms, use a variety of non-state patterns and strategies to cope with issues ranging from protection of their forests, to maintenance, to domestic violence. Most non-state forums, as we shall see in the following chapters, rely on the legitimacy they gain from their communities – caste-, religion-, and village-based. State actors, be they the police or judges, are very much aware of the existence of such non-state forums. Since the presence of non-state actors is extremely commonplace in dispute processing, particularly in rural India, state actors from the lower rungs of the justice system – many of whom hail from rural regions of the state – readily admit to having witnessed, if not been part of a meeting by such non-state forums.[29]

In fact, this author takes the position that the existence of non-state forums in the sphere of dispute processing has not even been a point of contention for the Indian judiciary as a whole. There are two factors that are indicative of this. One, the judiciary has tried in the past, and continues even now, to draw on the methods of dispute processing characteristic of non-state forums. This is evident from the introduction of initiatives such as Lok Adālats, Gram Nyāyālayas and Dispute Free Village Committees (*Tanṭā Mukta Gāv Samitī*) that emphasise negotiation, conciliation, and mediation, and aim to restore balance rather than meeting the ends of adversarial justice.[30] And, two, the judiciary's response, gathered from the Supreme Court of India's judgments, in the cases described above, about the legitimacy of Dar-ul-Qazas and Khāp Panchayats, among other non-state forums, has been more in the direction of categorising them as forums of "mediation," which "aid the working of the state judiciary," rather than emphasising the obnoxious "parallel" existence they are alleged to hold. While the pattern of judgments indicates that the state legal order has a low threshold for the infringement of human rights, broadly defined to include individual choice and autonomy in *Shakti Vahini v Union of India & Ors*, the Court also understands that "duly secured individual autonomy, exercised on informed understanding of the values integral to one's well-being is deeply connected to a free social order"(Supreme Court of India 2018, vol. 7, para. 26). Such an articulation reveals a sensitivity to the careful exercise of agency that so often crucially determines the nature and form of dispute processing activities.

29 Interviews at police stations and police outpost stations in Gonjhé and Gorāi in Maharashtra and different parts of Pitthoragarh and Bageshwar districts in Uttarakhand.

30 "Lok Adālats" literally translates as "people's courts"; they are promoted by the state judiciary as "having a different source and character than the courts of the state" (Galanter and Krishnan 2004, 790). Gram Nyāyālayas are village courts set up under the Gram Nyayalayas Act, 2008 and are the lowest court of subordinate judiciary in a state (Guruswamy and Singh 2010). The Dispute Free Village Committees are bodies comprised of local residents of the village and a representative of the police to processes petty civil and criminal disputes at the village level (see Maharashtra State Police 2007).

Countering these movements and anchoring their efforts in a human rights agenda (with a particular focus on women in many instances) to weaken non-state systems of governance, this book argues that a massive state like India needs recourse to, and thus also official recognition of, various forms of non-state methods for managing disputes. This is simply a matter of effective management of large-scale dispute processing in a nation of now 1.3 billion people.

1.4 Non-state forums: *The* forgotten story

The state judiciary per se, as we see from the above section, has had a fairly nonchalant attitude to the existence and working of non-state forums and actors in the sphere of dispute processing. The moments when it has woken up to engage actively with any aspect the activity of non-state forums in dispute processing have primarily been at the provocation of the media and broader academic literature on this subject, which, in line with present-day trends, have adopted an evaluative approach to the study of such forums.[31] The literature, academic and otherwise, therefore has a crucial role to play in developing the general public's and, specifically, the state judiciary's understanding about the nature and working of non-state forums and actors in dispute processing.

The study of non-state forums in India has not been very consistent. It marked the literature on law and society between the 1950s and up to the late 1980s. In a postcolonial country, developments in the legal system, particularly with reference to caste and religious personal law, received a lot of attention. Ethnographic studies focusing on the impact that British-styled state courts had on traditional systems of dispute processing, the interaction between the two systems, development of the legal profession and legal culture, and the manner in which state law aimed at "transforming the society radically to build a powerful and unified nation" (Galanter 1968, 83) was perceived and responded to by locals were the main themes of the law and society research on India in these years (Cohn 1959; Gough 1960; Beals 1962; Ishwaran 1964; L. I. Rudolph and Rudolph 1965; Derrett 1968; Galanter 1968; Kidder 1973, 1974a; Baxi 1976; Srinivas 2009c).[32]

31 See page 11 above for the case where the Supreme Court of India ordered enquiry into the gang-rape of a 20-year-old woman in Birbhum District of West Bengal. The ordered enquiry was a *suo motu* action on part of the Supreme Court, following the intensive coverage the incident received in the leading newspapers and news channels of India (Re: Indian woman says gang-raped on orders of Village Court published in Business & Financial News dated 23.01.2014 2014). Similarly, in the case of the two sisters of Dalit background who were allegedly ordered by a *khāp pancāyat* in Uttar Pradesh to be raped and publicly humiliated after their brother eloped with a married woman of a higher caste (see page 13 above), it was the media coverage and campaign by Amnesty International that pushed the Supreme Court of India to take note of the incidence.

32 This list of authors is certainly not exhaustive, but they remained some of the most prominent commentators on the development of the legal profession and legal culture in India until the mid-90s. Between the 1950s and 1970s law and society studies on India were at their peak with several extremely in-depth ethnographic studies about dispute processing in the non-state arena being conducted. Thereafter, this research

Some of the most exhaustive descriptions about the workings of the non-state forums and actors in dispute processing are found in these studies, with many of their findings remaining relevant to date, as is confirmed by evidence in the present study.

Research on non-state forums of dispute processing in India went into a lull for several years after that, until the early 2000s, when an interest in and commentary on the functioning of non-state actors was renewed. Geographically, the states of Rajasthan (E. Moore 1985, 1990, 1993, Sbriccoli 2013), Gujarat (Vatuk 2013; S. Iyengar 2007; Baxi 1976), and Uttar Pradesh (Cohn 1965, 1959; Freed 1995) continued to find reference in the literature, indicating a preference for certain locations when it came to conducting ethnographic studies about non-state forums such as *pancāyats*.[33] However, some studies in the later years were also conducted in Jharkhand (Shariff 2013), Karnataka (Srinivas 2009b, 2009d; Pur and Anirudh Krishna 2009; Hayden 1999), Andhra Pradesh (Nagaraj 2010b), Maharashtra (Hayden 1999), Madhya Pradesh (Holden 2008), and Tamilnadu (Headley 2015), pointing to the fact that the existence of non-state forums of dispute processing is common to many parts of India.[34] The more recent studies have reflected a trend of following-up on different aspects of a community previously studied and known to have a *pancāyat* or forums akin to these for dispute processing. Whilst all of the above studies have focused more on the rural areas in India, that such institutions exist even in cities and urban centres is clearly confirmed as well (Solanki 2011; Mukherji 2014; Ansari 2014).

The literature from the early 2000s, as I observe, commented on non-state forums of dispute processing from three different yet interconnected dimensions. Possibly propelled by increasing initiatives across the world on evaluating and improving the situation of women in multicultural societies (Nussbaum 2001; Shachar 2001; Korteweg 2006; Gill 2009; Merry 2012; Parashar 2013), the studies on non-state forums in India, in one manner, became part of a larger focus on exploring and understanding the position of women and the dynamics of gender in the processes of non-state forums (S. Iyengar 2007; Kotiswaran 2008; Nagaraj 2010b; Vatuk 2013). Second, at this point, the study of NGO-supported forums also saw a beginning (Bhatla and Rajan 2003; Magar 2003; Shariff 2008; Tschalaer 2009), which then took notice of non-state forums in a comparative scenario. And then, adding a third dimension, a commentary on non-state forums also found space in literature evaluating judicially supported initiatives, such as Nyaya Panchayats (Kushawaha and Singhvi 1977; Galanter 1989; Bandyopadhyay 2005), Lok Adālat (Whitson 1992; Galanter and Krishnan 2003; A. Singh and Zahid 2009; Zainulbhai 2011), and Gram Nyayalayas (Guruswamy and Singh 2010; Nagaraj 2010a), introduced as part of reforms in the state judiciary.

area experienced a dip until the 2000s after which there has been a surge of literature once again focussing on Indian law and society, in which non-state dispute processing remains no more the primary focus but finds space, nevertheless.

33 See 22 above for a description of *pancāyat*-s.

34 Cohn (1965) provides on exhaustive overview of the research carried out on caste panchayats up to 1965.

In addition to the differences in type of study, the research on non-state institutions in India adopted two methodological approaches: A "bottom-up" and a "top-down" approach.[35] As a result of the difference in the very manner in which these studies were conducted, the evidence in respect of the relationship of litigants with state and non-state forums and the engagement between the two types of forums themselves is very diverse.

Bottom-up research began more at the ground level from within a community and observed the continued use of non-state forums, often referred to as "traditional forums" in these studies, and the reluctance to approach state courts. The studies within this stream of perspective describe the nature of the specific community studied and the working of its particular non-state forum of dispute processing. They also observe the dynamics of power between actors within such forums and with those that surround it (Cohn 1959; Khare 1972; E. Moore 1985; Hayden 1999; Srinivas 2009d; Shariff 2013). Additionally, they all contain a brief reference of comparison between the particular traditional forum and the working of the most proximate state actors. All these studies describe the preferred use of non-state forums over state courts and make an attempt, which in a way remains limited, towards understanding the possible rationale underlying this preference.

The other strand of research that would be understood as more "top-down" in comparison observes how litigation in state courts has become an integral part of Indian people's dispute processing strategy. These studies, parts of which are also known as "courtroom ethnographies," use a state forum as a beginning point. Some of these studies already began in earlier years (see Galanter 1968, 1972; Khare 1972; Kidder 1973; Baxi 1982) but gained a renewed focus with additional rigour more recently (Whitson 1992; Solanki 2011; Galanter and Krishnan 2003, 2004; Berti and Tarabout 2012). Galanter and Krishnan particularly observed that, instead of adapting the existing courts, the present trend of judicial practice persistently diverts certain types of matters to "alternative dispute resolution forums," which are, however, state-supported.

Closer inspection of the above bulk of literature that follows a "top-down" approach reveals an emphasis on a dichotomy between the concept of "rights" and the processes of "reconciliation" – for instance, Baxi (1976, 1982), Galanter and Krishnan (2003, 2004), and Whitson (1992), in their examination of judicial initiatives towards reducing the case load on state courts; and Vatuk (2013, 83–84), Lemons (2010, 71–72), and Iyengar (2007), in the observation of NGO-supported dispute processing forums, such as all-women *pancāyats*, criticise the conciliatory manner of dispute processing emphasised in such "alternate dispute resolution mechanisms," which in many instances are initiated or supported by the

35 I use the terms "bottom-up" and "top-down" in the sense in which it is frequently understood within the discipline of law, with state actors being located at the top and communities and individuals as subjects of law being located at the bottom. While I do not subscribe to the hierarchical positioning inherent in this terminology, I use these terms for heuristic purposes and the continued familiarity with their usage in legal circles.

state, for its endeavoured similarity with the processes of non-state forums. Here, the authors seem to place the dialogue of rights in opposition to the concept of reconciliation, which, as they rightly point out, is a striking feature of all non-state mechanisms of dispute processing (Hayden 1984).

Thus, the absence of ethnographies of non-state forums in themselves,[36] coupled with literature emphasising the compromise of individual rights in the context of reconciliatory procedures (which mark all non-state forums as well as some judicial initiatives in the present day), highlights the horizon of dispute studies in India today. This has in part been contributory to the widespread belief – which is fast gaining popularity – that non-state forums have only a sporadic existence activated purely to reinforce the arbitrary use of power (*The Hindu* 2014; John 2013; Pandey 2014; Ingole 2015).

1.5 State and non-state: Parallel mechanisms of dispute processing?

Galanter (1981, 24–25) observed that the relation of state law to non-state mechanisms of ordering "is not invariably a matter of mutual exclusion (whether the former ousts the latter), nor one of hierarchic control (where the latter is confirmed to or aligned with the former)." Solanki (2011, 60–65) showed through detailed empirical evidence how state and non-state forms, far from having independent and "parallel" spheres of existence, are intensively engaged with one another through processes of "centralisation" and "decentralisation of law."

Sally Falk Moore as early as the 1970s described and theorised the semi-autonomous social field, which would:

> generate rules and customs and systems internally, but that … is also vulnerable to rules and decisions and other forces emanating from the larger world by which it is surrounded. The semi-autonomous social field has rule-making capacities, and the means to induce compliance; but it is simultaneously set in

36 Baxi (1976) makes a similar observation at the beginning of his paper on the Lok Adālat in Rangpur, Gujarat. The studies by E. Moore (1985), Hayden (1999), Solanki (2011), and Holden (2008), which followed in the next few years, have provided the most exhaustive insights in this sphere. However, as a timeline would reveal, research is in this direction (and in the likes of that of Gluckman 1972; Comaroff and Roberts 1981; Nader 1990; Gulliver 1997, to name a few) about non-state forums in India never really picked up, remaining scattered and uncommon. Speaking about caste *pancāyats* specifically, which are also one focus of this book, Headley (2015) states that caste *pancāyats* were eased from public debate on account of two significant changes following Indian independence. First, "the casteless society rhetoric was enshrined in the Constitution," and, second, "the fantasy of the village self-rule was given a democratic avatar in 1957 … through the constitution of an elected local body." This together with certain changes in the trends in anthropological research on South Asia "relegated the study of caste panchayats in the dustbin of social anthropology" (Headley 2015, 231).

> a larger matrix which can, and does, affect and invade, sometimes at the invitation of persons inside it, sometimes at its own instance.
>
> (Sally Falk Moore 1973, 720)

Different types of dispute processing forums and actors – as semi-autonomous social fields – also engage with one another as part of a larger and complex legal order.[37] This inextricable filiation between the non-state and state forums and actors has an inevitable impact of dispute processing that makes it difficult for the Indian state to do away with any type of non-state forums not only as a whole, but also as a part. And therefore, as Sally Engle Merry (2012, 68) points out about the contemporary world, which "holds a rich diversity of coexisting, overlapping, contradictory and complementary systems of law at the local, national, and international levels," resulting in the formation of different layers of law, any efforts to understand legal pluralism and questions of access to justice must encompass a study of "the relationship among the [such] constituent layers." In consonance with Galanter (1981, 1989), Cohn (1965), Ishwaran (1964), and Baxi's research (Baxi, 1982), within the two communities in which I conducted my fieldwork the use of state courts even today continues to be largely avoided. However, through an observation of the manner in which disputes are processed in the non-state arena, I found that state law can be located and is very much operational within the fold of non-state mechanisms of dispute processing, but more at the level of values or value principles, rather than in the form of direct absorption of state law rules.

Literature from political science (Chatterjee 1986; Nandy 1989; Saberwal 1996; Chatterjee 1997; Kaviraj 1997; Khilnani 1999; Bardhan 2001) suggests that the Indian state is a "weak as well as a strong state" (S. H. Rudolph and Rudolph 1987). It is "strong" because it is imbued with a considerable degree of autonomy by "virtue of the compromise of power between dominant classes," but at the same time it remains weak because of being "tightly constrained in what it is capable of doing" (Hansen 2001, 7), primarily as a result of systemic issues at the bureaucratic level (see also Bardhan 1999). Fuller and Benei (2001, 10–11) highlight that, even empirically, the boundary between the state and society is in reality "unclear, blurred, porous or mobile" and that ordinary people "widely recognise that this is so."

Evidence from fieldwork revealed that such porous boundaries between the state and non-state spheres resulted in an exercise of agency (see Chapter 5, pages 133–154) in the processing of disputes that led people to use the "system" as best they could. Such use, however, also included strategies that finally ended up resisting the state (see Chapter 4, page 80). Women in the mountainous regions of Uttarakhand, for instance, made decisions and found solutions to questions concerning their

37 Galligan (2007, ch. 6) explains a similar phenomenon using the concept of "social spheres." However, I prefer to use the concept of "semi-autonomous social fields" to explain the interaction of non-state forums with state law, as I find it more flexible than the idea of "social spheres," which appears more bounded in some way.

livelihood and maintenance in complex negotiating spaces created by an elaborate interplay between state and state-supported forums, community-based processing mechanisms, social practices, and, as Kotiswaran (2008) also observed in her field site, the red-light district of Sonagachi in West Bengal, "formal legal rules, informal social norms and market structures" (2008, 581). Individuals did not remain merely passive recipients of the law but active agents in negotiating the circumstances in which their lives are situated (Hapke 2001, 229; Sachs 1996). The case studies in Chapters 4 and 5 of this book show how this became particularly evident in the context of statutes, case law, and measures to regulate intra-family relations. Promulgation of such legislation is part of the Indian state's effort to protect women from destitution and domestic violence. In the shadow of these laws and the protection measures they offer, individual women and communities as a whole brought into play a series of mechanisms to confront disputing situations that threatened a woman's physical self or socially assured maintenance. More often, however, such mechanisms fed on traditional concepts of decency, status in society, *izzat*, honour, and so on, and had less to do with modern notions of human rights. Evolving customs and social practices, forum shopping, informal networks, and a diverse range of family arrangements enabled women to strike bargains on the blurred fringes of the state and non-state fields of action.[38]

The efforts to strike a balance between the competing values of state law and those of the community through individual experiences of the exercise of agency and the community's response thereto revealed a subtle but definite impact of state legislation, which, however, rolled out in the context of sociocultural and economic factors. For instance, the concept of *izzat*, particularly with its connection to matrimonial relations, was found to be slowly evolving. Even in the geographically remote rural locations of Uttarakhand, matrimonial breakdown in the context of excessive domestic violence, or the enormous consumption of alcohol by the husband, had begun to be accepted and sensitively understood, even among higher caste communities,[39] although the explanation for the increasing

38 I borrow Purkayastha and Subramaniam's (2004) description to explain this term. "Informal networks have no formal membership requirements and may be dependent on bonds of empathy, obligation or sometimes even a conscious need to present a united front against 'others' … Informal networks involve the community in the processes of decision making through the creation of social spaces for sharing experiences that are particularly empowering for participants" (2004, 2, 8)

As in the analysis of legal realists, the two particularly important categories of rules affecting bargaining strength are "the rules governing the conduct of the parties during bargaining" and "rules that structure the alternatives to remaining in the bargaining situation" (Kotiswaran 2008, 584). This also held true for individuals from both village communities in Gonjhé and the Dharamgarh Valley, as the next chapters will reveal.

39 Notes from fieldwork in Pitthoragarh District, Uttarakhand. More and more girls within the Thakur community in Uttarakhand returned to their natal homes because of their husband's inordinate drinking habits. Mothers of such girls recollected that while this could not have been a justification for separation from the husband when they themselves were younger, in present times this was understandable. The changing market structure has made several families in the hilly regions of Uttarakhand dependent more on private employment as against agriculture for a major portion of their

acceptance of such a practice remained cushioned in the "inability of the man to meet his primary duty of maintaining his wife and family." While these communities remained far away from urban centres physically, notions of individual rights, norms of what is "acceptable and not" in the modern-day world, and changing levels of tolerance were slowly filtering into these communities, which were also witnessing increasing education levels, the introduction of television in many homes, and growth in out-migration.[40]

Traces of the impact of ancient scriptures and ways of life and their reformulation through processes of colonisation were still found in the way these communities chose to organise and regulate themselves, although the tremendous impressions of international developments in both social and political life, new technology, and changing market structures had begun to play a prominent role as well.[41] My analysis of how individuals structured their dispute processing mechanisms that begins in the context of these latter elements, may perhaps seem – albeit unintentionally – to undermine the tremendous bearing of historical developments. The empirical evidence in this study about how factors such as caste, religion, customs, information, and the multiple impacts of state law combine as a consequence of the strategic exercise of agency, highlighting the necessity of long-established debates concerning rights versus reconciliation, personal law versus secular law, and codified law versus custom, and the significance of religion and caste identities in the Indian context (Solanki 2011; Sezgin 2013; Mallampalli 2010; Nagaraj 2010b; Subramanian 2014) to be revisited with a fresh perspective.

The present study contributes to the literature, furthering the understanding of legal pluralism and dispute processing. It attempts to generate, for the legal community in India, a foundation for comprehending whether and how situations of legal pluralism enhance or limit what the Indian state terms "access to justice."[42] I

livelihood. Alcohol consumption was perceived to interfere negatively with the productivity of a man, often with him spending far more hours sitting idle in the village instead of going to look for a job.

40 See for instance a newspaper report about a minister in Madhya Pradesh handing out wooden bats to women as a wedding gift in order for them to be "used if their husbands turned alcoholic, harassed them or did not mend their ways" (Asian News International 2017).

41 Shobha Hamal Gurung (2004), in her study on the women weavers of Nepal, provides a wonderful illustration of how "women's roles and status are constantly changing in the midst of global and macro-economic changes, and within the intricacies of caste, class, ethnicity, marital status, and paid work, along with a complex set of social relations" (Gurung 2004, 90).

42 "Access to justice" is literally understood as "access to state forums." The Indian state, and particularly the judiciary, are engaged in several interventions to improve "access to justice." All these interventions focus on improving and easing people's access to state institutions such as the police, state courts, quasi-judicial bodies and special tribunals. The efforts to enhance "access to justice" also include expanding the awareness among people about "state law" and "human rights" at ground level, through programmes carried out by the national, state, and local Legal Service Authorities. For more information see: http://nalsa.gov.in/index.html; http://www.nja.nic.in/about-us.html#vision-statement.

am unable to conclude with a concrete response in respect of this question, since the understanding and agenda of the Indian state with regard to the concept of "access to justice" is fairly positivist, and therefore quite limiting. Rather than asking whether legal pluralism strengthens or hinders "access to justice," this study proceeds on the footing that legal pluralism is actually a social fact, and, thus, has sought to analyse whether and how non-state actors adapted, interpreted, and appropriated the state law to process disputes and maintain order. The study anticipates that these empirical findings will help us in understanding the manner in which different "legal cultures" (Geertz 2000; Merry 2012, 70) coexist, influence, and engage with one another.

In the background of existing literature, the aim of this study is dual. First, to revive and strengthen within legal and political science debates in India about the multiplicity of legal orders and their consequent hierarchy, a subject of classical legal anthropology – the study of indigenous systems of dispute processing and legal consciousness within small-scale societies (see also Darian-Smith 2012; Nader 1978). And, second, to complement the recent literature that comments on dispute processing in the non-state arena (Solanki 2011; Sezgin 2013; Subramanian 2014; Krishnan et al. 2014), with a perspective that views the engagement between the non-state and state arenas through an observation of the movement of disputes (see Chapter 3, page 65), using a point within the non-state area as a beginning. To this extent, the study follows the strand of research on the antecedents of disputes developing with the use of ethnographic methods in legal anthropology. Concentrating on specific communities, this research examines the emergence and processing of a range of disputes (Miller and Sarat 1980, 531). For anthropologists this study will remain another illustration of the manner in which individuals and rural communities navigate between different legal orders on the basis of perceptions about law and justice that are embedded in their socio- and religio-cultural contexts.

At another level, the empirical evidence presented in this book attempts to respond to the almost ferocious ongoing debates on the ground – within the media, in courtrooms, and in activist circles – about the legitimacy of non-state forums.[43] These are discussions and opinions surrounding whether non-state forums – caste-, religion- or village-based – ought to exist and, if so, to what extent their "diktats" may be tolerated. Such questions, and the discussions that follow, arise as a combined consequence of the perceived dichotomy between "rights" and "reconciliation" and the absence of any research on non-state forums per se. Dispute processing in village communities with intricate kinship networks and a plethora of customs and traditions engages a series of strategies that draw on a combination of state and non-state mechanisms. As the awareness about the influence of state law, international developments, and individual rights increases, non-state forums, as "community based

43 As Gupta (1995, 385) highlights in the context of the state, this study argues that in the context of non-state forums of dispute processing, the media in the form of newspapers and television-based news reports contribute to the development of a discourse about these actors and play a critical role in how these forums have come to be imagined.

groups unencumbered by the imperatives of a large and bureaucratic organisation, often rework ideas and themes from the dominant culture in ways which bring forth hidden and potentially subversive dimensions" (Purkayastha and Subramaniam 2004, 8). By examining how disputes move between the non-state and state spheres, this study enquires into the present state of non-state actors engaged in dispute processing in India, ascertaining particularly how state law and its regulatory systems are perceived and the nature of their engagement with non-state forums at one level and with individuals within communities at another level. In doing so, this study in part explores whether and in what manner notions of individual freedom and rights are translated as a result of this engagement. While the present study has not problematized the added element of "religion" in relation to the Indian state, it is evident that the key findings of this study speak to the modalities of interaction between a body of state law, imagined as largely "secular," and related processes and values, on the one hand, and specific "religious" notions involved in non-state dispute processing on the other. The connecting element established as useful and employed here is the notion of "postulational values" (Chiba 1984) (see also Chapter 3, page 66–67), which are connected to all these processes.

The empirical evidence maps the different forms of non-state actors that exist across the two locations, how they function, and the actual extent of their influence on the community or group of individuals they seek to govern. Simultaneously, it also shows how members of these communities, as individual agents, strategise the processing of their disputes in order to fulfil their own goals without disturbing the values they share with their community as a consequence of being part of its circle of solidarity. Dynamics of kinship networks and power relations, which remain vividly highlighted as a part of the empirical narratives, remind us that disputes being part of a greater social continuum are difficult to be addressed unless they are analysed in the light of their context.

In Chapter 2, I discuss the methodology used during the collection of data and then introduce the geographical locations and communities this study focuses on. This book is divided into three main parts that comprise the first part with the introduction and methodology; the second part with Chapters 3, 4 and 5; and the last section with the conclusion. In Chapter 3, I explain the manner in which disputes move between the different layers of legality that exist within these village communities. Chapter 4 describes the varied types of non-state forums and mechanisms that are available to individuals for dispute processing and the manner in which they are impacted on (or not) by state law, its systems, and the regimes for its implementation. Chapter 5 presents three case studies comprising the experiences of two individuals for each, in order to highlight how dispute processing at the level of the self is equally important to understanding the nature of engagement between the non-state and state sphere of dispute processing. The book concludes in Chapter 6 with a note on how the impact of state law and state forums in the non-state arena is only one side of the spectrum of engagement between state and non-state law, and that further research on different aspects of this engagement remains necessary and urgent in the light of the continuous flow of "judicial reforms" being carried out by the Indian state.

2 Early learnings

People, places and perspectives

As outlined in the introduction to this book, the present study stands at the interface of two disciplines: law and anthropology. What we have could be described as an ethnography of non-state dispute processing mechanisms in two rural communities in India. The study locates the role and function of state law within non-state dispute processing in order to understand the nature of engagement by non-state dispute processing forums and actors with state law and its systems.

Implicit to ethnography, fieldwork for the present book combined participant observation, by living within these two communities and semi-structured interviews that arose as part of the daily interactions, and conversations within these communities. Working on the borders of two disciplines can be a challenging task, especially if the goals of these disciplines (as in the case of law and anthropology) are very different. In my own experience while conducting fieldwork, I realised the impact law school had on the way I approached situations and narratives in the field. At the same time, fieldwork compelled me to reflect on my training as part of my core discipline.

This chapter on methodology is divided into three parts. The first part describes how fieldwork was conducted, how the locations and communities focused on in the present study were selected, and the factors that determined the choice of questions, and modes of interactions within these communities. This section also focuses on contextualising the position of the author in relation to the process of data collection. Through an explanation of the circumstances and experiences of data collection, this part will attempt to clarify why a certain type of data came to be gathered and why certain questions may have remained unanswered till the end. The second part of this chapter provides a background of the geographical locations and communities selected for the study. It introduces the reader to the social structures of the communities observed and provides an overview of certain aspects of their ways of life which, as the empirical evidence in the next chapters will reveal, had an intimate connection with the processing of disputes in these communities. The third part of this chapter draws on the features of both these communities that make them comparable in the broader context of the main research question.

2.1 The community

Students of anthropology, but not so much those of law, are already familiar with the fact that a vast landscape needs to be traversed between what one expects from the field and what one actually gets. Initially, this research project aimed at mapping the various dispute processing mechanisms within a tribal community. As part of preliminary fieldwork, therefore, I explored geographical locations that were largely known to be inhabited by tribal communities. However, I soon realised that it became increasingly challenging to "classify" a community as "tribal" because of the gap that lay between the common understanding and legal understanding of the very word "tribal".

In India, the central government, in consultation with the state governments, categorises certain communities within the lists of Scheduled Caste, Scheduled Tribes, Nomadic Tribes and Other Backward Classes.[1] There is little uniformity within the lists of the different states, and it may be that the same community falls within a different list in different states. Moreover, furthering the complexity, these fixed understandings in the Indian Constitution take on very fluid personalities in reality.[2] People in any location in India today experience an information

1 For a brief description of Scheduled Castes, Scheduled Tribes and Other Backward Classes, see Obeng (2014, 21–23) and M.N. Srinivas (1997). Article 341 and 342 of the Constitution provides that the President may, with respect to any state or union territory, specify the castes, races or tribes or parts of or groups within castes, races or tribes which shall for the purposes of the Constitution be deemed to be Scheduled Castes and Scheduled Tribes in relation to that State or Union Territory (Lokur Committee 1965). Clause (10) of Article 338 of the Indian Constitution specifies that Backward Classes are included within the expression Scheduled Castes. Clause (10) of Article 338 reads as follows: "(10) In this article references to the Scheduled Castes and Scheduled Tribes shall be construed as including references to such other backward classes as the President may, on receipt of the report of a Commission appointed under clause (1) of Article 340 by order specify and also to the Anglo-Indian community." Also see Chapter 4, page 74, for the Koḷī community in Gonjhé's response to this confusing situation created by the state government in their case.

2 I will elaborate on this with the example of the Koḷī community in village Gonjhé in Maharashtra (one of my field sites). Until I began to live within this community I believed, on the basis of prima facie information provided by the locals as well as in the sociological literature, that this was a tribal community, also recognised accordingly as "Scheduled Tribe" under the Indian Constitution. But presently the "Scheduled Tribe" status of the Koḷī community, settled primarily along the coastal region of Maharashtra, is hotly debated. While the community members regard themselves as "Mahadeo Koḷī", a community recognised as a Scheduled Tribe under the Central Government list of Scheduled Tribes in India, government reports and recent caste certificates issued to members of this community address them as "Hindu Machimār Koḷī", a community that falls within the list of Other Backward Classes (OBC) (Government of India). Without going into this issue in detail, it would be sufficient to say that for the present project, I go with the social affirmation of the Koḷī community as a lower caste community with the present-day Constitutional status of "OBC". The status of Scheduled Tribes and Other Backward Classes in India has come to be a highly politicised phenomenon with tribal, caste and religious groups claiming either, or even both, identities – more for the socio-economic benefits and privileges attached to these statuses than on the basis of historical identities. The situation with the Koḷī community is no different in my opinion. See also Ranade (2008, 2) who observed in

overload because of migration, education, the internet and other forms of media. What is witnessed is the tremendous hybridisation of customs and lifestyles, making it difficult to standardise a particular form of behaviour – whether in relation to dispute processing or otherwise – to a particular community defined on the lines of caste, tribe or religion. As Chandra Mallampalli (2010, 1050) has pointed out, proof-of-custom revealed that people were not passive recipients of the legal identities imposed upon them by the colonial judiciary. Likewise, tribal and other communities continue to "interrogate" state-imposed fixed identities as they "produce evidence about alternative cultural practices."

Consequently, as a result of the different understandings of such labels and the long-standing debates in India about the authenticity, on one hand, and politics of the identities such labels give rise to, on the other, I decided to give up the quest to select a community on the basis of its "tribal" or "caste" status. In this respect, the arguments in this book would have been lacking if I had made the choice of a community on the basis of their caste or tribal identity without addressing substantially the debates surrounding the "caste" or "tribal" status of the community. Since caste or tribal identity was not the primary aim of the present research, this may have resulted in a diversion from the topic at hand. The village communities were finally selected, therefore, on the basis of empirical factors more relevant to my main research agenda. The chosen communities, described in more detail in the next section of this chapter, were ultimately a mix of caste and tribal communities. They were predominantly Hindu communities, located in rural areas, engaged largely in their "traditional" occupations,[3] were deemed to belong to a relatively lower socio-economic group within the broader scheme of development in their respective states and had, among other non-state mechanisms of dispute processing they take recourse to, a community-based forum specific to their caste or village community.

2.2 The location

In line with the main research question leading this study, I wanted to observe how disputes were confronted, processed and handled in a village community and whether and in which manner this activity engaged with state law and state forums. In light of my own cultural conditioning as an Indian and on the basis of the literature I had read, I had a sense that information about disputes tended to

his study of the Son Koḷī in Mumbai that "the Son-Kolis are concentrated mainly around Mumbai and are almost exclusively involved in fishing. The Mahadev Kolis a scheduled tribe are concentrated predominantly in the hinter regions of Maharashtra and are known for their worship of Mahadev (Shiva). Together these two communities comprise the bulk of the fisher community in Mumbai." The Son Koḷī of Mumbai do not hold a Scheduled Tribe status.

3 The term 'traditional' in relation to occupation is used here to mean a profession or occupation that had been the primary source of livelihood of the members of the said caste or village community for several generations. It is not the intention of the author to use this concept in the sense of "traditional v. modern".

comprise one of the most sensitive and "private" aspects of community life in India, and more so in rural areas, as I was to learn later. People are not willing to speak easily even about the nature of disputes in their community (Nader 1990).[4] The role of "researcher" placed me at once within a community yet at a distance from it. It validated my presence in the communities, but also made space for invisible borders between "the observer" and "the observed". In the rural communities where I conducted my research, therefore, I remained an "outsider" – a stranger – in different contexts. Gaining knowledge about the disputes in a community and being allowed by the community an opportunity to observe such disputes being processed (with the knowledge that a researcher is likely to then engage in discussions about the dispute with people from within and outside the community) turned out to be a precarious task in terms of management as well as research ethics. During my preliminary fieldwork, I realised that norms of hospitality restrained community members from *openly* refusing me permission to view these processes. But at the same, the shared understanding of *izzat* within these different communities, controlled community behaviour, strategically keeping me at bay from exactly these processes.[5]

As part of preliminary fieldwork, I visited close to six villages, five of which were located in the state of Maharashtra and one of which was located in Uttarakhand. In the broader geographical context, I had selected Maharashtra and Uttarakhand as the two states within which I would conduct fieldwork because of their contrasting topographies, levels of development and demographics. Maharashtra lies on the western coast of the Indian peninsula and occupies part of central and southern India. It is home to India's financial capital, Mumbai, and has experienced development at a steady rate. Western Maharashtra, more than other parts, also witnesses a constant flow of migrants from other parts of the country because of the high, though not sufficient, number of employment opportunities the booming private sector in this state has to offer. The state of Uttarakhand lies in

4 Nader (1990, 7–8) in her description of the Taleans presents the analysis that "Talean leaders are intent on believing and having outsiders believe that internal relations are harmonious and in equilibrium," because unless they operate on such a premise "the state would interfere in their business." Indeed, as with the Taleans, even with the village communities in Uttarakhand, this façade of being a harmonious and peace-loving community does keep the state authorities at bay. In fact, according to the analysis of some scholars, the state courts, being over-burdened with pending disputes are constantly trying to avoid entertaining more disputes (Galanter and Krishnan 2004) and this picture of harmonious relations is a perfect reason for non-interference. But in addition to this, maintenance of harmonious relations within the mountain communities is also important for the notions pertaining to honour (*izzat)* of the community. Internal discord within a community is also perceived as a matter of dishonour (*beizzati)*, which certainly cannot be risked in interactions with an outsider. The Koḷī community was an exception to this situation in that they openly admitted to being a quarrelsome community; though despite this it was challenging to find out in detail about disputes in the village.

5 *Izzat* can be broadly defined as honour (see also Virdi 2013, 111–113). For more details about *izzat* in the context of the communities observed in this research study, see page 67.

north India towards the eastern side and borders with Nepal and Tibet. Home to parts of the mighty Himalayas, the state is primarily mountainous, the lower regions of which are dotted with popular tourist destinations and pilgrimage points. Agriculture is the primary occupation in this state. In contrast with the situation in Maharashtra, Uttarakhand has always experienced a trend of out-migration. Until two decades ago most men left their villages because of postings in the army, but now most of the youth population increasingly moves to the "plains" for purposes of education and employment.[6]

Levels of development and education and actual physical location of an area have been argued to have a profound impact on the manner in which people in India "forum shop" (K. von Benda-Beckmann 1981) during dispute processing (Galanter and Krishnan 2004; Sezgin 2013).[7] Preference for non-state mechanisms of dispute processing was observed in earlier literature to be the consequence of inaccessibility both in terms of awareness and infrastructure about state law and its systems. Such inaccessibility was argued to be connected to the low levels of education within a community, lack of development and remoteness of a location, which often went hand in hand. The choice of states, which contrasted greatly with respect to these particular indicators, provided me an opportunity to test this argument. Without denying the value of this contention, I nevertheless pursued it further to verify whether "lack of access" was the only factor that motivated the continued use of non-state forums for dispute processing, and if not, what the other motivations to this end were. Moreover, as the literature overview in the previous chapter highlights, not much research in the sphere of non-state dispute processing has been carried out in Maharashtra and hardly any such exploration has been made in Uttarakhand.[8]

Preliminary fieldwork also allowed me the opportunity to travel across several different locations, enabling several occasions for comparison of different processes and understandings about "law", "what constitutes a dispute", "who or what is the state" and so forth. The perceptions of people from different genders, age groups, economic classes, and education levels, varied starkly. Yet there was scope for observation of similar experiences and therefore common patterns of thought. Forty-five days of continuous travelling across these different locations acted like an eye-opener in terms of the fact that merely witnessing the proceedings of a non-state forum in a community or shadowing non-state actors at the time of dispute processing was not enough to gain an understanding of the complexities that the processing of disputes entailed. "Access", then, meant passage to the

6 "Plains" is the termed used locally in Uttarakhand to refer specifically to the non-mountainous parts of India, but more generally also to all the states and cities that lie beyond Uttarakhand.

7 Benda-Beckmann describes "forum shopping" as the act when disputants make a choice between the different institutions available for dispute processing and base their choice on what they hope the outcome of the dispute will be (1981, 117).

8 References to some of the literature can be found in Chapter 1 and other pieces of literature are cited in reference to the specific scope of their study in the following chapters.

interior dynamics of the community. It meant overcoming the barriers of superfluous narratives *of* a dispute. It meant the opportunity to capture surrounding stories and opinions – in the form of gossip and rumour – about an ongoing dispute, because all these elements had their own impact on the processing of a dispute. Therefore, the ease with which I gained access to these webs of information within the community determined to a great extent my choice of locations for fieldwork. In this broader context therefore, a fishermen's village called Gonjhé in coastal Maharashtra, and four closely located villages in the Dharamgarh valley, spread out across the Bageshwar and Pitthoragarh districts in Uttarakhand, were selected as the final sites for fieldwork.[9]

2.3 Insider-outsider: Asking the right questions

In an earlier section of this chapter, there is a brief reference to being an "insider" and "outsider" (see page 31) within the communities where fieldwork was carried out. Conjectures about the "advantages" of being a "native" ethnographer have been critiqued (Basu 2015; Williams 1996) and rightly so because conducting empirical research in one's home country can be equally advantageous and challenging. Fieldwork reintroduced me to the multiple identities I held and how they placed me apropos my respondents, tore apart any essentialised assessments I held about being an "insider" or "outsider". The several aspects of my socio-cultural upbringing, my marital status, my gender, my profession, my domestic situation and my economic class were different pages of my identity that were read separately and together and sometimes all at once by members of the two communities. I comprised both roles – as insider and outsider – at any given time during fieldwork. But depending on the identities I played out linked to contexts, and also my "need to fit in", one of these roles often outshined the other. At the same time, these positions were very fluid, transforming from one to the other depending on the nature of the relationship I shared with the respondents in that moment and which identities became emphasised as part of this.

An ethnographer's position as insider or outsider is also a reflection of the control the community exerts over the researcher and his or her data collection. Familiarity with the culturally and socially legitimated codes of (behavioural) conduct of the societies studied, and fluency in the language of communication adopted in both these village communities, enabled me to tackle a number of issues that were at least manifestly connected to the initial "adjustment" of living within these communities as a participant observer. Simultaneously, however, for these same reasons, I felt I could not exploit my role as "researcher" to its maximum potential. For instance, as a result of our shared understanding regarding

9 Pseudonyms have been used to replace the names of all the villages (Gonjhé, Mānjai, Gorāi, Pimpaḷgāv, Khasi, Jamkuda, Gangapur, Melatpur, Panchwari, Bilbār, Chilbasa, Nalkhet) where fieldwork was conducted as well as the names of the respondents with whom interviews were carried out. The same is done in order retain the confidentiality of such information exchange.

certain aspects of life and lifestyle, my respondents held a certain disposition with regard to the way in which I conducted myself in relation to the different people I interacted with and also in terms of my responses to social situations. Such expectations I found, sometimes limited my movements as the researcher, thus reducing the scope of my interactions and the extent to which I could ask questions about particular issues.

Narayan explains that: "The loci along which we are aligned with or set apart from those whom we study are multiple and in flux. Factors such as education, gender, sexual orientation, may at different times outweigh the cultural identity we associate with the insider or outsider status" (Narayan 1993, 671). My experience confirmed this observation when "an educated woman from a metropolitan city in India" fixed my initial impressions within the village communities. I was perceived as an outsider in the communities because I had married inter-caste, chosen to continue studying instead of starting a family after marriage, and led a nomadic lifestyle wandering around and living in remote villages.[10] All of this also came about as a subject of surprise, curiosity and some prejudice within the communities.

The contexts, then, in which I was perceived as an outsider, quickly became known to me as a result of the change in conduct that transpired in these situations, not necessarily always to my disadvantage. In Gonjhé, the coastal village in Maharashtra, playing on my identities of having been in an inter-caste marriage and a practising lawyer at one point, the men often dismissed my comments and opinions with regard to social behaviour and labelled them as "very English." The Hindu fishermen's community in Gonjhé perceived people who did not follow (even superficially) religious obligations and caste rules, to have adopted a "Western lifestyle" and they were often colloquially referred to as "English people." As expected, many such "English people" had lived most of their lives in urban centres. Socially, "being English" was not thought of very highly. But in my case, I noticed this labelling also gave men (whose presence dominated most non-state dispute processing forums) liberty to depart from the locally established norms of verbal interaction between men and women. In Gonjhé, men would not hesitate to joke with me or even discuss certain issues, such as women's chastity, which in ordinary circumstances would not be discussed by them (at least openly) with other women who were not perceived to be "English." While this terminology was not used in the villages in the Dharamgarh valley, a similar perception – and therefore code of conduct – prevailed among the men in this region as well. Even as these men remained overtly condescending towards my choice of lifestyle, they would unhesitatingly include me in discussions about property and politics, a domain of male public life. In the given context, this was also out of the ordinary, since men largely believed and openly concurred that "women did not understand" such discussions about legislation, state schemes, and politics.

10 These experiences were in no way unique to me. Srinivas (1976), Kumar (1992), Narayan (1993), Solanki (2011) and Basu (2015) among others who conducted ethnographic studies in their familiar territories in India describe very similar trajectories.

In respect of the women, this positioning was more complex largely because there was more common ground to share experiences about, than with the men. Since I was to "study" dispute processing, all my initial interactions were led by men. Despite (and possibly because) the fisherwomen were known to be "quarrelsome" and to play fairly prominent roles in the processing of disputes, their experiences were not acknowledged as "study worthy" by the fishermen. It was similar in the village communities of Dharamgarh, where for instance the "female *shiyāné*" (see Chapter 4, page 96) from Gangapur were never brought to the forefront because they were mostly involved in the processing of matrimonial disputes, which were disregarded by their menfolk as "trivial disputes."[11] Simultaneously, because of the flexible interaction their men encouraged with me, I sensed the women, both in Gonjhé and the villages in Dharamgarh valley, remained wary of me for a long time. But with time when they realised that my experiences, especially in the domestic sphere, were not so different from theirs,[12] the interaction eased out and I was treated as an "insider" in many conversations. In Gonjhé, the women became my gatekeepers, almost chaperoning me on certain occasions. My host mother, for instance, watched over how I dressed, whether I wore my *mangalsutra* every day,[13] who I spoke to and at what time I returned home in the evenings; making sure that my presence within the community, other than for my research agenda, did not seem out of place. This social obligation of chaperoning me also entailed advising me occasionally. For instance, I was often reminded by several women in both villages to be thankful (to my fate) that I had such a "good husband", who was liberal, who trusted me and allowed me to pursue my dreams. At the same time also cautioning me that I ought not to take advantage of the favourable circumstances in my life and should revert to my role and responsibilities as a "wife" and "daughter-in-law" as soon as my PhD was completed. In the background of all this, of course, was the intimate connection that my relationship with my host family, their conduct towards me and my behaviour within the community generally had with my host family's reputation in the village. By taking me into their homes, in both locations, the host families had probably brought upon themselves, scrutiny within their communities, which as I have mentioned before were extremely tight-knit. My socially appropriate conduct was therefore viewed to be the responsibility of my host families.

11 During preliminary fieldwork, my enquiries about matrimonial or domestic disputes in the village communities of the Dharamgarh valley were put off on the ground that these did not constitute "real disputes". The metaphor of "when two utensils are put side by side, they are sure to make noise" was used to describe the non-complex and everyday-life nature (see Sarat 1995, 3–4 for an explanation of "everyday" nature) of such disputes. Notes from fieldwork, November to December 2014.

12 The way my family was arranged, the reciprocities I shared with my in-laws, and my role in the household seemed familiar to them.

13 This is a necklace of black and golden beads that a woman receives upon marriage. It is a symbolic indication of a Maharashtrian lady being married. See also V. James (1977, 141–142) for importance of *mangalsutra* among Koḷī folk.

An example from a village called Khasi may suffice to explain the nature and gravity of this responsibility. When I first arrived at Khasi in Uttarakhand, everybody in this village of 450 people was polite but refused to volunteer to rent me a room in their homes. Rules around menstruation had to be very strictly followed by married and unmarried women living in this village. Violation of these rules, it was believed, would invoke the ill will of the deities (*devtā*) of the region leading to misfortunes in the village. The tricky part was that these rules were related to very practical everyday matters and therefore such rules could be easily violated if one was not cautious. During menstruation, it was expected that the menstruating woman bathed daily, drank a spoonful of *gomutra* (the urine of a cow) every day, washed her clothes separately from the rest of the household for the duration of her cycle, did not sleep on a mattress, did not engage in cooking, refrained from coming into physical contact with any other person and the main source of water to the household. If she ignorantly, by mistake or due to special circumstances (in the case of breastfeeding mothers), violated any of these rules, the woman had to consume *gomutra* and sprinkle the same around the premises of her house. *Gomutra* was perceived to have (both scientifically and religiously) purifying qualities. The strength of belief in these practices was the primary foundation for their perpetuation in this village community. On the basis of the associations they made with the identities of "being educated" and "a resident of urban areas in the plains", there was enough reason for the local community to believe that I (who also held these identities) was less likely to share their beliefs and therefore less willing to adhere to these practices sincerely. Everyone knew that any family willing to let hospitality trump over their cautiousness would be responsible for ensuring that I followed the code of conduct, and would also be willing to bear the brunt in case of any disturbances occurring as a result of its violation (by me). Eventually, the middle way we found was that I would return to the campus of an NGO located in another village, who I had contact with, during the period of my cycle. It was on this assurance I managed to get a room in Khasi. The most fluid condition of me being an insider on several counts, yet remaining an outsider for different reasons, made such situations, placed on the intersection of these positions, challenging to tackle not just for me but also for these communities. Within the community's sense of order these rules became applicable to me because I was Hindu, and therefore it was obligatory that I follow them. This resulted in the community's insistence of the pursuit of these practices with regard to me. At the same time, they had enough reason to believe (on the basis of reasons stated earlier) that I did not believe in the veracity of these practices and was not likely to follow them. However, the community in Khasi (as I learned later) felt that expressing this insistence openly could have given me the impression of their being "backward", which would not have been good for the reputation of the community. This was of course also important, since I was still a fellow Indian and "one of them" in some broad sense. As a result, they tried to keep under wraps the real reason for their refusal to give me a place to stay for a long time, revealing it only after a certain level of trust and acquaintance had been established.

This dynamic of the insider-outsider identities, brought about by their rather transitional nature, played a crucial role during my fieldwork. As an analytical tool it helped me to identify the spaces that became simpler to occupy on account of any one of these roles. However, since both these positions were constituted in the same individual, in this case me, a lot could change on the basis of the aspects of my identity that the respondents in question chose to emphasise in the given context. I could therefore easily be an insider one moment and an outsider in the next in the very same frame of reference (see also Narayan 1993, 680). I had to remain at all times aware of this positionality, which was part of the context in which I gathered data.

2.4 Everyday life and gaining access

Access in the context of fieldwork for this research study, as I have mentioned earlier (see page 28) was not just about gaining entry to the community and witnessing dispute processing in the non-state forums within the community. Considering the complex nature that processing of disputes assumes within communities that find themselves interconnected for a diverse set of social, cultural and practical reasons; access meant passage into the various threads of information that contextualised such processing. In addition to the insider-outsider dynamic described above, two other factors played an important role in determining the nature of such "access". One of these was my gender and the second was how I established contact with these communities and in what manner I spent my time within them.

In both Gonjhé and Uttarakhand, my gender played a crucial role in the fieldwork. Being a female researcher, women though initially cautious ultimately allowed me into extremely private spheres of knowledge. With no barriers, whatsoever, on the manner of our interactions, my dialogues with the womenfolk unfolded experiences both sensitive and bold. Possibly, and I do not wish to deny this, being a woman myself I could grasp the narratives of the female respondents far more quickly, allowing me to engage with them more intensively.

Practically, at the time of fieldwork in Gonjhé, I lived with a fisherman's family. My host father was a powerful man in local village politics and an active barefoot lawyer (see Chapter 4, page 114). He was often consulted by the village forums active in the administration of village affairs and management of the fishery businesses in the community. In a way, this did restrain my circle of social interaction, as I was viewed to be a member of a particular family. It compelled me to remain aware of the reputation of the male head of this family in the village, his position in village politics, his reputation and his dynamics with other people in the village and to act accordingly. This meant that I could and could not interact openly with certain people. This also determined the type of information about a dispute I would get access to. These are factors that I remained conscious of throughout my analysis of the empirical evidence I gathered.

In Uttarakhand, my access into the village communities in Dharamgarh valley was facilitated by a Non-Governmental Organisation (NGO) working towards creating livelihood opportunities using local resources. Even though my research was not directly connected to the principal objective of this NGO, and the village communities understood this quite clearly, the NGO and its members (also local people) remained the link of the village community's relationship with me. Clearly, this once again determined who agreed to speak with me and what information about village disputes was shared with me. Since I was not located in one village permanently,[14] I remained a familiar visitor for the village communities. This also meant that, unlike in Gonjhé, I did not know of all the disputes in the village and nor did I have the opportunity to witness local everyday discussions about an ongoing dispute as effectively as I did in Gonjhé. However, fieldwork in Uttarakhand was more focused in one way. My main points of connection in any village were presiding members of the local non-state forum, village wisemen, and parties who were or had been involved in specific disputes. As a result, during my time in each village, I could spend several hours discussing the very subjects of governance and dispute processing with these individuals, sometimes being enriched with very deep and focused insights not only on disputes, but also the foundations of dispute processing within these communities.

2.5 A Background of the communities

This section proceeds to give a background of the communities that were studied focusing on descriptions of the caste, their everyday life, gender dynamics and the manner in which they organised and regulated their daily lives. These descriptions are not entirely representative of the general caste, tribal and religious identities these communities belong to. Since this study views disputes as a phenomenon embedded within the broader fabric of society, the sections below are meant to set the context for understanding how disputes were processed within these communities and do not intend to be in any sense essentialising.

2.5.1 The Koḷī community in Gonjhé

Of the two locations selected for study, one was village Gonjhé, which consisted in the majority of Koḷī people. The Koḷī community[15] is primarily occupied with the business of fishing and selling fish.[16] Across Maharashtra this community is found

14 My fieldwork methodology in Uttarakhand could be defined as "multi-locale strategy", where the fieldworker covers a "network of sites that encompass a process which is in fact the object of the study" (Marcus and Fischer 1999, 94; Hapke 2001, 226).

15 For an Indian audience, while the term Koḷī may immediately bring to mind a person connected in some manner with the business of fishing, it is important to mention that there are several other tribal communities in Maharashtra that have the term Koḷī as part of their identity. And these tribal communities may not necessarily be involved in any fishery related trade, in fact many of them do not even reside close to the sea. For instance, there are Mahadeo Koḷī spread out across the mountainous range of the Western *ghats*. Similarly, Agri Koḷī can also be found in the interior areas of Maharashtra.

16 "Fishing is a caste-based occupation – that is, one traditionally engaged in only by particular caste groups." (Hapke 2001, 230).

living in small and large settlements close to the sea in several villages across Konkaṇ (the western coast of Maharashtra) and even in big cities like Mumbai. Gonjhé was one such village located right by the sea in the coastal district of Ratnagiri in Maharashtra with a population of approximately 10,000 people. While Gonjhé does not have any mention in the historical literature, the people of Gonjhé did pride themselves in the folklore that the eminent emperor Shivaji and his soldiers (*māvaḷe*) tethered their horses in Gonjhé before seeking the assistance of the Koḷī from this village to row them in their boats to the neighbouring fort in the middle of the sea.

Characteristically, following Cohn (1965) I would refer to Gonjhé as a "village with small population of a single caste." Though, to what extent Gonjhé with a population of approximately 10,000 people constitutes a "village with small population" is debatable. Close to ninety per cent of the households were Hindu Machimār (or Mahadeo) Koḷī – with the exception of about thirty families being Muslims,[17] two to three families being (Hindu) Agri Koḷī and one Brahmin household. The Brahmin family, I learned later, had moved to Gonjhé from a neighbouring village to fulfil the task of maintaining the village temple. When the present Brahmin retires, another Brahmin would replace him, and it may happen that the family of this successor may decide to relocate to Gonjhé for the period. At ground level therefore, the residents of Gonjhé consequently did not look upon this family as native to Gonjhé.

Almost every family in Gonjhé was dependent on fishing and fishery related activities for a livelihood. There were of course a few families, which in addition to fishing ran convenience stores (*kirāṇā māl*) or plied auto rickshaws between Gonjhé and the neighbouring villages and towns. Between the Hindu and Muslims in the village, while activities related to fishing remained the primary source of livelihood, there were some broad distinctions in the nature of activity carried out by them. This difference was rather obvious during the daily fish auction at the Mānjai *bandar* (the port),[18] located close to Gonjhé. The fishermen being those who went out to sea – who may or may not have owned their own boats – were mostly Hindu. But once the fish was brought ashore, the majority population handling the *māl* (goods) – the auctioneers as well as the *dalāls*, who were middlemen or agents of big companies buying the fish in wholesale (Hapke 2001, 239) – were all Muslims. Clad in crisp white *kurtās*, their *pajāmas* hanging a little above their ankles, skull caps and beards, their distinct attire set them apart from their Hindu counterparts. Having returned from long days at sea, the Hindu fishermen could be seen lugging the tubs overloaded with fish from the boats on to the beach. Clad in shorts, their dark weather-beaten skin and unshaven appearance was conspicuous evidence of their hard work.

17 I refer to the Koḷī community in Gonjhé as Hindu Machimār (or Mahadeo) Koḷī because of the debate about their caste status. For more details see Chapter 4, page 73.

18 The Mānjai *bandar* is an integral part of the lives of people in Gonjhé. It is the place where the fishing boats are docked and the first unbulking of fish takes place. At the daily auction every evening at the *bandar*, twenty to twenty-five tons of fish is sold in crates to small-scale traders and vendors. In addition to this there is also a local market where fish is sold to petty vendors and individual customers (Hapke 2001, 238).

2.5.1.1. The people of Gonjhé: Lifestyle, occupation and the social setup

Gonjhé as I have mentioned earlier was a village comprised largely of the Koḷī community. While I did learn something about the impact of the Hindu-Muslim dynamics on dispute processing between these two communities, in light of the history of interactions between these two religious communities in coastal Maharashtra, the dynamics of their interaction could hold ground as a research subject in its own right. For the purpose of the present book, which is focused more on understanding how disputes were processed as a whole at the village level and to what extent these processes engaged with state law, the impact of religious dynamics on such dispute processing constitutes only a small part of its larger scope. Moreover, since I lived with the family of a Hindu Machimār (Mahadeo) Koḷī during my fieldwork, the disputes I could gain detailed insight into were limited to those within the Koḷī community. Consequently, how the Koḷī organised themselves, regulated, governed and maintained order within their community became the primary focus of my fieldwork in Gonjhé. Accordingly, this section is wholly focused on a description of the Koḷī community.

In my observation, the Koḷī came over as a hardworking, friendly and cheerful community, but also quite "aggressive" in their mannerisms. Men and women both worked within as well as outside the house and therefore this interdependence gave rise to an equality between the sexes, limiting patriarchy from thriving in its gravest forms (Rubinoff 1999, 633; Thompson 1985, 15; Punekar 1959, 65). Formal education was not given much importance among the Koḷī people in Gonjhé. Parents sent their children to school enthusiastically when they were young, but there was no insistence on remaining at school if children chose to drop out eventually, which I noticed was quite a common occurrence. On average, boys attended school till fourth or seventh grade and this was pointed out by people within the community as having been "the pattern" for many years. Punekar (1959, 151) observed a similar trend among the Son Koḷī of Mumbai, about whom she says, the "Son Koli sincerely believe that once accustomed to the easy life of the school, a boy will never succeed as a fisherman, for fishing needs hard work and a strenuous life." Girls, though not a very large number, were increasingly pursuing school to higher grades and many had even completed their senior secondary (10th standard) and higher secondary (12th standard) examinations.[19] Whether as a result of increasing support or plain non-interference on part of the family, the graph of education among girls had steadily risen in this village. "When we were little, even the most liberal families encouraged their daughters to go to school only until the fourth grade; at the most. After that

19 Rubinoff (1999, 636) observed among the Goan fisherwomen that "fisherwomen themselves are very sensitive to this attitude – that there is something shameful and degrading about their work in the markets even though many of them are independent and intelligent businesswomen. … Many of these women encourage their daughters and grand-daughters to pursue higher education, profession careers or office jobs." While such an attitude was not evident among the Koḷī women in Gonjhé, who were in fact very proud of their culture, skills and heritage, Rubinoff's observations cannot be overlooked and may have been partly the reason for increasing education levels among the Koḷī girls.

girls would get so wound up with household chores that there would be no time left for school. And if we showed too much interest in education, our mothers and aunts would tease us: 'What do you want to do with so much education? Do you want to become a teacher?' (*Itka shikūn kāy, bāī vhāycha āhé kā?*), said Hema Pavshe, a fisherwoman now in her early forties. Despite having been brought up in an environment that was cynical towards women's education, Hema appreciated the determination to be educated shown by young girls in this day; this despite the pressure of domestic chores, which had not reduced even since when she was young."[20]

Along with an absence of caste difference, on the whole there was no noticeable class difference between the people in Gonjhé either. While every family did not earn equally well from the fishing business, the general standard of living was comfortable, with everyone having sufficient food and shelter. Many homes even had a television, and two wheelers.[21] As Dr Talathi, the local physician in Gonjhé, practising there for over twenty years now, described, "Largely everyone in the village has enough to eat and is therefore happy."[22] Of course, at the time when power dynamics within different members of the community were brought into play (during discussions in the *Samāj*, for example), the significant connection of power vis-à-vis the "class" of such individuals became quite evident.

Fishing as an occupation was very demanding both physically and mentally. It included not only going to sea to catch fish, but also cleaning and selling it, or salting and drying it for storage. A "sexual division" (Obeng 2014, 35–36) of the labour involved in this business was evident. While the men went out to sea and spent a long time away from the village on the boat actually fishing, the women were responsible for selling the fish and maintaining the household (see also Rubinoff 1999). Drawing from Ram (1991), Hapke (2001, 236) highlights,

> this particular sexual division of labour is at the very heart of the construction of male and female identity, the way men and women in these communities occupy space, and how, in turn, their relationships to the fishing economy and wider society are constructed.

Men remained at sea for several days at a time, ranging from a week to ten days, depending on the quantity of fish they caught. The fishermen had to return to the shore before the ice in the cold storage melted, but at the same time also ensuring that the storage on the boat was closest to, or had reached, its maximum capacity. Working day and many times even in the night, the fishermen came back to the village for a few days between their fishing trips. Where a fisherman had his own boat, he was likely to remain at home for longer periods as he enjoyed the

20 Several conversations with Hema Pavshe between January and June 2015.

21 Even as I mention this, I remain sensitive to the debates about whether possession of television sets, mobile phones and vehicles are/are not substantial indicators of economic prosperity.

22 Interview in Gonjhé (Maharashtra) March 25, 2015.

flexibility of employing others to maintain his boat and go fishing in it. There were many, yet not the majority, who enjoyed this luxury. With more time on hand, the fishermen who owned boats, engaged in other activities – income generating and otherwise – such as brokering in land deals, taking a lead in managing the social and cultural activities of the village and engaging in politics.

Fisherwomen were busy irrespective of the nature of work of their husbands, brothers and fathers (James 1977, 135; Ram 1991; Punekar 1959, 34–35). The key roles of women within the fishing business and the household limited early marriages among girls. The unmarried girls lived with their families helping with household work, child care and those fish processing activities that could be conducted in the *verāndāh*-s, alleyways and backyards neighbouring the house (Edeltraud 1982; Ram 1991; Rubinoff 1999).

Three times a week, days began as early as 3.30 am in the morning, when the fisherwomen had to visit villages away from the coast to sell fish. A woman would cook for the family, leave her child in the care of a neighbour or an aunt and set out with close to 30 to 40 kilos of fish balanced on her head towards villages in the interior parts of the *talukā*. Pushing her way through crowded public transport buses and then walking for several kilometres, her sole objective was to sell all or the maximum possible quantity of her fish. She would rest only in the afternoon for a short while at a home that offered her lunch. "Each fisherwoman has one or more villages allocated to her for business. This is decided mutually amongst us women in the village. I cannot enter the business area of another woman. I have been selling fish in some villages for many years now. And so, we develop a relationship with our customers. Some of them are very kind and offer us food and water. Since our days to go to a village are fixed, the household women are almost expecting us," narrated forty-year-old Leela Pavshe during a conversation one afternoon.[23]

On the remaining days of the week, the day was filled with managing household chores, drying fish that needed to be stored and visiting the auction at the *bandar*. At the fish auction every evening, the Koḷī women bought fish to be sold either at the local market on the same day on the beach adjoining the *bandar* or to be packed and taken to be sold the next day in other villages. Even though the auction was primarily dominated by men, who did a large portion of the selling, women from the households of the fishermen with boats also helped during the auction, either playing the role of auctioneer themselves or standing close to the auctioneer handling the actual money transaction.

This division of labour between the Koḷī men and women seemed to me to be quite strategic; based on skills that are inherent, though of course not limited, to the respective genders. To elaborate a little further; traditional knowledge and experience within the community possibly explained that money remained more secure in a woman's custody, less likely to be frittered away for petty luxuries, alcohol, and gambling. Therefore, it was noticeable at the *bandar* and otherwise as

23 Interview with Leela Pavshe, Gonjhé (Maharashtra) March 23, 2014.

well, that it was the Koḷī women who managed the money earned through the fishing business (Ram 1991, Chapter 6; Rubinoff 1999, 635).[24]

Similarly, "selling" as an activity required certain negotiating skills and more importantly interaction skills. Trained from a young age,[25] the Koḷī women were expert vendors with sharp oratory skills for soliciting customers, efficient bargaining and dealing with their competitors. Being very friendly and talkative, the community perceived that women managed better than men to ensure that the fish got its best price. Hema Pavshe, a lady in her early forties, explained that it is the women who sell fish because they are better sales people. "They can call to the customers – *dādā, māmā, kākā* (brother, maternal uncle, paternal uncle) – inviting them to buy the fish. It doesn't seem out of place. At the same time, women are tough negotiators. It is not easy to bargain with women, even if the customer is a relative. Men give in far more easily to run favours for kith and kin. Women can legitimately use excuses that touch the emotional chord of their customers deterring customers from bargaining aggressively," she said.[26]

Incidental to selling, the Koḷī women ended up interacting with a range of people, from different castes, classes and religions. As a result of this professional activity, the Koḷī women developed strong networks[27] and "accumulation of wealth and economic power in local markets" enhanced their individual sense of pride and identity and also made them very competitive (Rubinoff 1999, 639).

24 Interview with Dr Talathi, Gonjhé (Maharashtra), March 25, 2015. Also see Obeng (2014, 34) who quotes Sakhubai Biru Yidege from the Gowli community, "it is women who keep the family money, disburse it, and perform domestic rituals (*puja*)."

25 Notes from conversation with Hema Pavshe, Gonjhé (Maharashtra), March 23, 2015. Recollecting her own childhood memories, she says, "Our mothers would send us to collect sea weeds by the sea side. Then to keep us busy they [the mothers] would ask us to imitate them. What they would do with the fish we would do with the sea weeds. Separate them clean them and divide them into *vāṭā*-s [small portions the size of a small bowl]. This kept us constructively busy and the mothers could do their work peacefully." As the girls grow older, they accompany the mothers to the fish market. Their practice with the sea weeds has made them familiar with the manner of the trade and they learn to work with fish very fast.

26 Notes from conversation, Gonjhé (Maharashtra), March 23, 2015. Explaining what she meant by "excuses that touch the emotional chord," Hema clarified that the women extend reasons such as "having to run a family" and "paying their children's school fees" to restrain bargaining by customers, especially those who are relatives and friends. Also see Hapke (2001) for a discussion about how among the fisherfolk communities in Trivandrum, Kerala, "women's marketing activities have become crucial in ensuring household survival in a number of fisherfolk communities – in many cases constituting the household's entire income." (Hapke 2001, 221)

27 "The women are very strong and the main decision makers in the household. In fact their opinions are important all the times because they are the ones living in the village." Interview with Dr Talathi, Gonjhé (Maharashtra).

2.5.1.2. Administrative and social structures in Gonjhé

This large Koḷī settlement spread out over a stretch of about two kilometres of the sea coast was divided into *manḍaḷs* and governed by the *Samāj.* Unlike many other villages in this region, Gonjhé did not have a *mohallā* where all the Muslims resided together. In Gonjhé the Muslim households lay interspersed between the Koḷī homes albeit remaining close to the village mosque.

A. THE *MANḌAḶ*

For smooth administration and management of the village, Gonjhé has since historical times divided itself into different *manḍaḷs*. A *manḍaḷ* was a small neighbourhood, which might be comparable to a ward or a hamlet. With an increase in population, the number of *manḍaḷs* grew from five to eight and at the time of fieldwork, there were ten. A *manḍaḷ* did not have a fixed population and a lot depended on the discretion of the local leaders. As a result, there were large *manḍaḷs* and small ones too.

In earlier times, even though everyone belonged to the Koḷī caste, people from one *bhāvkī* (kinship network) settled close together forming one neighbourhood, which later came to be identified as a *manḍaḷ*. A *bhāvkī*, literally translated as brotherhood, comprises families in which the men are agnatic kin of one another. Therefore, when the *manḍaḷs* were first formed, every *manḍaḷ* comprised of members with the same surname. Every *manḍaḷ* had its own temple dedicated to the main deity (*kul daivat*) of the Koḷī. However, with people wanting to move closer to market centres and also issues of property partition between brothers, many members had moved out of their core *manḍaḷs* either towards the village boundaries or to other villages altogether. The social organisation of the village slowly began to change because of this. Gulliver (1997, 27) observed with respect to the Ndendeuli of Southern Tanzania that:

> As increasing number of newcomers join the community, the *indirectness of kinship linkages* between heads of household increases. Men become unable and unrecognised to their linkages with many of their neighbors. They recognise and cooperate with a range of acknowledged kin, cognatic and affinal, and they know of and occasionally cooperate with a range of kin of those kin; but others are merely neighbours. [*emphasis mine*]

A similar phenomenon could be said to have occurred in the newly formed *manḍaḷs* of Gonjhé, where this fabric of social organisation where all males were the agnatic kin of one another had become a rare occurrence. But despite this migration, such migrating families nevertheless continued to identify themselves with their original *manḍaḷs* keeping intact all kinship reciprocities, networks, and responsibilities, particularly on occasions of marriage, death, other ritualistic commitments, and dispute processing. Whether this was to facilitate better administration of village affairs as we shall see in the next chapters or to keep intact the kinship unity in line with Nader's (1990) concept of harmony ideology was difficult to identify.

The village was administered with every *maṇḍaḷ* functioning as a unit of local self-governance. Every year the households in a *maṇḍaḷ* selected or elected two or more *puḍhārīs* for their *maṇḍaḷ*. A *puḍhārī* was a male local leader and came close to the description of a "notable" in Southern Tanzania (Gulliver 1997, 34–35). If a *maṇḍaḷ* was satisfied with the *puḍhārīs* from the previous year, elections were not considered necessary. Likewise, a person once elected as *puḍhārī*, continued to be identified as a *puḍhārī* even if new persons were elected to replace him the following year.

The *maṇḍaḷs* had monthly meetings chaired by the *puḍhārīs*. All *puḍhārīs* did not need to be present at such monthly meetings and much depended on who among the *puḍhārīs* was in the village and not away at sea at the time of the meeting. Unlike some of the other caste group meetings in the Konkaṇ region,[28] attendance at such *maṇḍaḷ* meetings within the Koḷī community was not compulsory. However, remaining absent from meetings did not excuse any income-earning adult male within the *maṇḍaḷ* from payment of the monthly contribution. While only adult males who had an income were supposed to contribute, adult males reaching an age of earning were also expected to contribute irrespective of whether they were actually earning or not. Payment of contributions legitimated the contributor to have a say in all the decisions made by and for the *maṇḍaḷ*. The amount of such individual contributions varied from *maṇḍaḷ* to *maṇḍaḷ*. It was usually decided by the *puḍhārīs* in consultation with the members of the *maṇḍaḷ* and it depended on the average earnings of the majority of members and their willingness to cooperate with community affairs. I also learnt that where a family in the *maṇḍaḷ* did not have an earning member (for instance old women, disabled persons) or was relatively poor compared to the others, such family was not expected to contribute to the *maṇḍaḷ*. Reasons of management of the *maṇḍaḷ* temple, village temple and organisation of various social and cultural activities were used to justify the collection of this fixed minimum contribution in the *maṇḍaḷ*. *Maṇḍaḷs* fixed within themselves a treasurer and secretary, who handled the accounts and maintained records. The money most often remained in the safe custody of such treasurer.

Earlier, when *maṇḍaḷs* consisted of a single kinship network related by agnatic kin, the *bhāvkī* and *maṇḍaḷ* were almost coterminous. However, with the population of *maṇḍaḷs* becoming unrelated or related very distantly, the family became the most basic unit of social structure in Gonjhé followed by the *bhāvkī* and then the *maṇḍaḷ*.

B. THE *SAMĀJ*

The highest forum of authority in Gonjhé is the *Samāj*. At the level of the village, it was the *Samāj* that regulated, administered, and managed the village affairs. The

28 For instance, within the caste groups meetings of the Kuṇbi community in Konkaṇ (some of which I had a chance to attend), it was compulsory for one member from every household to remain present for the monthly meeting. In some instances, even a penalty was levied for non-attendance.

word *samāj* in Hindi or Marathi means community or society at large. In Gonjhé the word *Samāj* was however used to also refer to the group of people who had been entrusted with the responsibility to govern and regulate village affairs.[29] Each *manḍaḷ* is represented by two individuals in the *Samāj*. These two individuals were usually from the *puḍhārīs* elected by the members of each *manḍaḷ* annually. Comprising of twenty such *puḍhārīs*, the *Samāj* also convened monthly for a meeting popularly known as *gāvki* in coastal Maharashtra.

The *Samāj* regulated several social and cultural issues in the villages. It intervened to settle intra- and inter- village disputes, if it was called upon by the community to do so, usually through an application to this effect. It corresponded with the state body of the Grām Panchayat (or what stands of it) on issues concerning road works,[30] setting up of electricity poles and progress of the public school in the village. It also coordinated occasionally (if it was so requested) with the locally formed Fisherman's Credit Society on behalf of fishermen. Additionally, the *Samāj* was also responsible for management and maintenance of the village temple and coordination of the celebration of village festivals.

Like the *manḍaḷs*, the *Samāj* also had a treasurer, a secretary and a chairman. While the members of the *Samāj* may or may not have changed every year, the chairmanship of this body did change annually. Thus, the body came into force every year on one of the most important festivals in the calendar of Gonjhé – *Rām Navamī*. According to the Hindu calendar, this festival falls on the ninth day of the bright fortnight of *Chaitra*, which according to the English calendar falls in April or May. The celebrations in Gonjhé began four days before the actual festival. A grand village carnival, several cultural programmes, and exchange of gifts and money between families and friends, marked the entire celebration. While the *Samāj* ensured that all festivals, including *Rām Navamī* were celebrated peacefully and in an orderly manner, the actual organisation of this festival was undertaken every year by each *manḍaḷ* in rotation. The ceremonious handing over of the responsibility of leading the *Samāj* and overseeing the social, cultural, and administrative activities of the community took place on the occasion of *Gudī Padwā* every year, which fell eight days before *Rām Navamī*. At this time, all responsibilities related to the upkeep and maintenance of the village temple, the temple equipment including the jewellery of the deities and the temple donation box (*dānpeti*) were handed over by the *manḍaḷ* then in charge to the forthcoming *manḍaḷ*. What also transpired at this point was the transfer of chairmanship of the *Samāj*, from a member of the previous *manḍaḷ* to a member of the new *manḍaḷ*. This process had a rather formal tenor with several villagers – mostly men – witnessing the handing over ceremony, records being made of the items being handed over and felicitation of the new committee.

29 The usage of this term in this manner is not unique to the Koḷī. Obeng's work (Obeng 2014, 24) shows that the Lambani, a nomadic community, categorised as "Scheduled Tribe" under the Constitution, also refer to their community based social, political, and administrative structure as the Samāj.

30 The community in Gonjhé has been boycotting Gram Panchayat elections for several years now (see page 81).

In theory the *maṇḍaḷs* were accountable to the *Samāj*. At the meetings of the *Samāj*, the representatives of each *maṇḍaḷ* were to report or could be asked about any important events in their neighbourhood by the *Samāj*. Part of the monthly contribution collected by every *maṇḍaḷ* was also handed over to the *Samāj*. This was then used for organisation and management of the village festivals through the year and other administrative or social activities undertaken at the level of the village. In addition to this sum, expenditure for any other purpose, which may be decided upon by the *Samāj*, was met through a spontaneous collection of contributions in the village. The *puḍhārīs* from each *maṇḍaḷ* took the lead in motivating and encouraging people to make generous contributions, as neither was this payment compulsory nor was the amount fixed.

The *Samāj* of Gonjhé held importance beyond the territory of this village too. It was an important decision-making body not just for the residents of Gonjhé, but for the Koḷī community that is presently dispersed across four neighbouring villages. Gonjhé has since historical times been considered the basic place of origin (*mūḷa gādī*) for the Koḷī in these villages. While the Koḷī communities residing in each of these villages had their own decision-making and regulating bodies, important decisions that were likely to impact on the Koḷī community as a whole had to be made in consultation with the *Samāj* of Gonjhé. An example of modifications in local marriage customs that occurred a few years before fieldwork the present study conducted provides a good example. Traditionally, according to an age-old marriage custom the wedding rituals for every marriage between parties, one of whom resided in Gonjhé, had to be conducted in Gonjhé. Practically, with the list of invited persons growing beyond the family, and rising marriage expenses, it became increasingly difficult for the family of the spouse not residing in Gonjhé to keep up with this custom. “They had to actually shift to Gonjhé for a few days before the marriage, because the custom required that all the ceremonies of *haldi* (turmeric), and henna had to be conducted in Gonjhé,” explained Ravindra Pavshe, a *puḍhārī*. However, this custom could not be altered without a consensus of the *Samāj* in Gonjhé. This finally happened towards the end of 2014 when the entire community and their representatives from different villages convened together to alter the custom to its present state. At the time of the fieldwork, only if the bride-to-be was a resident of Gonjhé was the actual wedding ceremony expected to be conducted in Gonjhé. In the case where the prospective bridegroom was from Gonjhé, the marriage could be conducted in the bride’s natal village or anywhere else depending on convenience of the marriage parties. Similarly, the *Samāj* in Gonjhé was also at the centre of the discussions surrounding the debate of whether the Koḷī of the coastal region should or should not be recognised as Mahadeo Koḷī and be granted the status of Scheduled Tribe (see page 27).

2.5.2. The Pandit, Thakur and Bhotiā of the Kumaon

Turning around the bend from the Dharamgarh market and following the long and winding road into the valley, one is greeted by a picture of communities living fairly solitary lives in this mountainous terrain surrounded by dense forests. The broad tar road, which is viewed as the bearer of connectivity and development in rural India; here in the Dharamgarh valley witnessed only a few jeeps that passed in the morning and evening; and besides that, lone shepherds with their animals, woodcutters knocking at the trunk of pine trees, and school children frolicking back home, were its only occupants. This was very different from the village environment in Gonjhé where the road that cut across the village was bustling with activity from morning to night. The fisherwomen in their shrill tones called to one another across it, buses, jeeps, and scooters ferried people from the port and neighbouring villages, children played cricket in the temple courtyard alongside the road, and adding to all of this, the sound of the sea waves crashing against the rocks that lined it left no room for solitude, silence or monotony at any point in the day.

Towards my second location for fieldwork, I moved from the animated and lively scenes of the Koḷī community to live within what appeared as a relatively quiet, peaceful and demure vicinity in the lower Himalayas. In stark contrast to the Koḷī community settled at the seaside in one of the most developed and flourishing regions of Maharashtra, the communities in the Kumaon Himalayas were located in villages nestled in the folds of these young mountains, sometimes accessible only by foot or on mule. Mostly agrarian, dependent either on farming, animal husbandry or related activities for a livelihood, these communities – like the Koḷī – were also settled in groups in which the men are related through agnatic kinship. Some villages comprised entirely of descendants from a single male, in which case everyone belonged not just to the same caste, but also the same sub-caste (*gotra*); or there were others that were mixed-caste villages consisting of different groups, each connected within themselves through agnatic kinship. In mixed-caste villages, every caste group then comprised a separate cluster. Typically, all these villages were either "villages with a small population of one caste" (Cohn 1965, 83) or "multi-caste villages with or without a dominant caste" (Cohn 1965, 86–98).

The Kumaon Himalayas range across the Eastern side of the state of Uttarakhand, with Pitthoragarh district, where most of the fieldwork for this book project was conducted, lying at the north-eastern end of the state bordering with the neighbouring countries of Nepal and Tibet. The people of this region spoke Kumaoni, a language with a melodious rhythm drawing some of its vocabulary from other Indian languages such as Marathi, Gujarati, Rajasthani and Hindi.

In Uttarakhand, as I mentioned earlier I did not focus on one specific village or a particular community. The villages, as compared to those in coastal Maharashtra, are much smaller in size and population. Additionally, as a result of constant out-migration, villages, located far away from major town centres, were largely comprised of old people and young women – both daughters and daughters-in-law. While people belonged to different castes and sub-castes, on the whole because of the topography of the region, the lifestyles of most people were similar. And therefore, I chose to observe a number of villages located in the same valley in close proximity to one another. This also allowed me to compare and verify whether, and the extent to which, dispute processing mechanisms between different castes differed despite the similarity in economic and practical conditions of living.

2.5.2.1 The mountain people: Ways of life

A. THE DIFFERENT CASTE GROUPS

In the villages in the Dharamgarh valley there were three predominant castes – the Pandits, the Thakurs, and the Bhotiā. In some villages there were small clusters of people belonging to Scheduled Castes, locally referred to as Harijans.

The Pandits were Brahmins and were traced back to having migrated to the mountainous regions of Uttarakhand from the states of Maharashtra and Gujarat during pre-colonial times. They engaged in conducting ritualistic ceremonies connected to birth, death and purification in their own and other villages, as and when they were called upon. This being their primary source of livelihood, they also owned land, which until more recently was still given to Thakurs for tilling. At the time of fieldwork, many Pandits were enrolled in government jobs related to teaching, banking and forestry. In the social hierarchy, they were considered the highest caste.

The Thakurs, who were perceived to be below the Pandits in the local social hierarchy were also the largest community in the villages in the Dharamgarh valley. Most of the data collected during fieldwork in Uttarakhand is largely based on ethnographic research within this community. The Thakurs traced their lineage to the Rajput caste in Rajasthan,[31] which was from where they originally migrated to Uttarakhand in times of the Mughal rule in India. The Thakurs were the main agrarian community in the Kumaon region of Uttarakhand. They owned large fields and had a local reputation of being very hard-working. Men and women both worked in the fields, but migration since earlier times had always led the men away from the villages to jobs, first in the army and later even in the private sector.[32] Maintenance of the household and farms consequently was left to the care of the women. From March to November, the people worked in the fields tilling the land, sowing the crop and harvesting it according to the season. In villages further away from the head of the road in the Dharamgarh valley, many households owned cows, buffaloes, and sheep, and agricultural practices were still very traditional in the manner they were carried out. The women woke up early to bring fodder, some of which was fed straightaway to the animals and the rest was kept aside to be dried and stored for the winter months. If there was more than one woman in the household the chores were divided, with one looking after the

31 The information about the migration and other history of the caste groups is gathered mostly from oral narratives with village elders and the District Gazetteer report for the district of Pitthoragarh (Government of India 1967, 8–9).

32 On migration trends of people from rural agrarian and other communities to urban areas see Dhar (2014).

household and caring for the animals, while the other tended to farm-related activities. Similar to Palriwala's (1991) observation in Panchwas village in Rajasthan, women in one household in the Thakur community were not in relations of equality, particularly mothers-in-law, and daughters-in-law, and older and younger daughters-in-law (*jethāni-devrāni*). Even in spheres designated to be under female control, younger women remained subordinate to senior women for varying lengths of time. In the months of harvesting, the workload increased tremendously. In these months it was common that relatives and neighbours helped one another and men who migrated for private jobs to cities were seen returning to the village to help with harvest-related activities.

The Bhotiā community was characteristically a nomadic tribe, but under the state list of Uttarakhand, it is included within the list of "Other Backward Classes" (OBC). Within the Bhotiā community, there were further subdivisions of social hierarchy, which determined the nature of their social interaction with members of other castes as well. The Bhotiā were considered the original inhabitants of Uttarakhand. Traditionally they were salt traders who brought salt from Tibet and traded it in exchange for food grains and other resources with the settled communities. Being well-versed with the terrain, climate and paths in the higher mountain areas thick with forests, the Bhotiā community moved from salt trading to rearing large herds of sheep, which were taken into the higher mountain areas between the months of May to October. In this time, the families that travelled along with the sheep settled in small hamlets in these glacier areas (*johār*) and collected herbs believed to have medicinal properties. Today, these herbs have found a market not only locally but are also are in great demand in the pharmaceutical industry. The Bhotiā women were expert spinners and weavers and the products they created found a consumer base, which had slowly grown beyond just local areas because of the interventions of several national and international NGOs making an effort to support this traditional art. Of course, like in other castes, besides engaging in their traditional occupations, employment opportunities in the army and in the private and government sectors in the bigger towns had become popular for this community as well.

Most of the Harijan communities in the Dharamgarh valley held a scheduled caste status and did not own any land. Any wage-earning activity therefore was crucial to their survival. Traditionally this community comprised castes that were engaged in providing specific services in the villages, for example, playing of the *dhol*, a musical instrument played during religious ceremonies and weddings. They received grains, vegetables, fruits, and other returns in kind for these services. In time, however, members of castes that comprised the Harijan community became involved in a variety of income earning activities ranging from running restaurants in the market areas to teaching in government schools. Government schemes and the system of reservations (or affirmative action) were perceived to have alleviated the economic status of many from this community; this however had not dramatically influenced the nature of social relations between Harijans and other castes maintained in the villages.

B. THE SOCIAL STRUCTURE AND FACTORS INFLUENCING IT

Caste factors are salient in shaping responses to social norms and community values. Consequently, the social structures within each caste differ considerably. Like in Gonjhé, a shared division of labour characterised the caste communities in the Dharamgarh valley as well. While the nature of tasks may have differed in every caste, men were mostly responsible for many of the activities, income earning as well as others, that required engagement with the public sphere beyond the village. Matters in relation to the village networks, the household, and the farm were largely within the control of the women.

In the Pandit community, since earlier times, women received education up to higher levels. Also, the absence of farming-related activities in this community meant that women confronted less physically strenuous tasks compared to their counterparts in the Thakur community. In the Thakur community women single-handedly attended to all farm and animal husbandry related activities in addition to household chores. Both within the Thakur and Pandit communities, the forces of patriarchy were rather evident. The "male-breadwinner" (Grover 2009, 9–10) ideology prevailed widely and in most of the households, husbands and/or sons were engaged in some sort of income-earning activity in addition to agriculture; wives were restrained from taking up paid work outside the household as this was seen to detract from family respectability and male honour. In my own experience, despite offering even a substantial stipend, it was very difficult in Khasi, a single caste village belonging to Thakurs, to find a female translator. Many of the young college going girls who volunteered initially then retracted under pressure from their brothers, father or uncles, who reasoned with me that if their girls were seen "moving around freely in the village" it "would be considered dishonourable (*beizzati*)" for the family.[33] The reason for their moving around in the village, in this case for the purpose of facilitating my interviews and interactions, was irrelevant. Since all these girls were of marriageable age it was believed that such "loitering" (*idhar-udhar ghumna*) would impact their prospects of finding a suitable match for marriage. On the basis of my participant observation in this village though I learnt that the notion of *beizzati* was perceived to be pronounced more strongly when women and girls engaged in paid work as against "moving around freely in the village," as was the excuse offered to me by the men for restraining their girls from "working" with me. This, of course, was directly related to the "male-breadwinner" ideology that was prominent in this community. Interactions with a local NGO, which aimed at creating employment for women within the precincts of their villages further confirmed this. The NGO shared that it was very difficult to convince women to take up even a few hours of work outside of their farming routine. Experiences of the women working with the local NGO revealed that it was justifiable for a woman to take up paid work only when they were compelled by circumstances, such as husbands being unable to fulfil their provider role because of excessive drinking, personal shortcomings, or failure to find a

33 Notes from conversations in Khasi (Uttarakhand), January 2016.

stable job. The young girls learning to weave at the centre of this NGO in Khasi smiled as they confessed that their parents had been made to believe that they were attending a "course in weaving" at this centre, which is how they managed to get permission to come here from their households.

In addition to the detraction from family respectability and male honour, as Grover (2009) analysed in her fieldwork, I observed that participation in the process of earning money enhanced the confidence level of women, making them aware of their own skills and power beyond the household. This development was undeniably connected, in part, to the increasing stress and consequential value of cash incomes, the advantages of which, of course, were largely enjoyed only by men till now. In light of all this, women's participation in paid work was probably viewed as a "threat" by men. The capacity building of women that resulted from such participation may have been perceived by men to enable such women to question or challenge established social (and power) structures, which were then unarguably more favourable to the freedom men enjoyed (see also Sen 1990; Agarwal 1994; Kabeer 2001). And men had enough reason to believe so, since the confidence that paid work lent to women was evident not just among those who joined the NGO, but also among women who traditionally, as part of their caste-based occupations, contributed to the family income. The Koḷī women in Gonjhé, mentioned in the earlier part of this chapter (see page 38), are one example, but also the Bhotiā women in the Dharamgarh valley.

The Bhotiā women were expert weavers and spinners and it was this skill on which the husbands depended to bring a cash income into the household. While it was the men that would go out to sell the products, their wives and daughters did the weaving. And with retail culture fast replacing door-to-door sales, it was easy to spot several shops in and around the market areas being run by Bhotiā women selling their own products. Consequently, it could be observed that the gender balance within Bhotiā communities tilted in favour of the women, who as a result enjoyed far more freedom than the Thakur and Pandit women in how they led their lives. My fieldwork did not allow me the opportunity to interact extensively with the Harijan community; but from what I observed, I would say that the position of the women in Harijan communities was similar to the Bhotiā women. Not being owners of land and with loss of monopoly over the services they traditionally offered, Harijan families had to engage in different types of income earning activities. As a result, men as well as women were often seen seeking employment in paid work, which, in accordance with my earlier observations, reformulated the power relations between men and women in these households. Interestingly, an overview reveals that it was the women from the lower castes (Bhotiā and Harijan) that were far more involved in paid work, traditionally as well as because of financial necessities. And to this extent, the argument of some scholars that scheduled caste women are exempt from (upper-caste) notions of patriarchal honour where higher status is contingent on withdrawing women from work outside the household (Kabeer 2001 citing Deliege 1997; Searle-Chatterjee 1981) stands confirmed.

Along with caste, another factor that was beginning to significantly influence the social structure of villages in the Dharamgarh valley was education. Whether it was the inherent nature of the people or, as many locals narrated, due to the abatement of agriculture as the primary occupation, the people of this region had gained an identity of being fairly reclusive. Explaining this transition, Jagdish Kumar, a young engineer from a neighbouring village working on solar technology with an NGO in the area, said: "agriculture compelled people to remain connected to one another. When seeds had to be sown in one person's farm, all the community members helped knowing that even their farm work would require others to contribute their labour. Therefore, people were very close to each other, there was a unity."[34] However, in the newer generations fewer people were dependent on agriculture and related activities as their primary source of livelihood. The returns were not perceived to be proportionate to the amount of hard work that farming required. Changing weather conditions, the nuisance of rodents and wild animals, and absence of relevant technological know-how were used to explain how farming had become an unsought activity. This combined with the lack of private or public enterprises offering non-agriculture related employment opportunities in the area resulted in high levels of migration from this region. In earlier times, it was mainly men who migrated as a result of enrolment in the army. The army provided a secure job, social prestige in the village, an additional income, and a substantial pension after retirement. But today, the younger generation found education as its ticket to urban centres (Samal and Dhyani 2007). Unlike in Gonjhé, youngsters in the villages in Dharamgarh – more men than women – were willing to, and did, invest large amounts of money and time in higher education pursuing courses right up to post-graduation levels, where possible.[35] While entry into the army still remained relatively high, many youngsters also vied for teaching jobs in the government sector and some even ventured into private jobs. At the time of fieldwork, the proportion of men in migration was still higher than that of women, although the number of women willing and wanting to migrate either on their own or with their husbands was also increasing tremendously. "In search for jobs that would match their degrees, people migrate to bigger towns and city centres. Those who are unable to find jobs and have remained bound to the villages are a frustrated lot. They keep to themselves most of the time and all of this in totality has led to disintegration of the village system,"

34 Interview, Melatpur (Uttarakhand), April 18, 2015.

35 Samal and Dhyani (2007), however, note in the official statistics that female literacy in the Indian Central Himalaya has increased from 4.78 per cent in 1951 to 54.16 per cent in 2001. The overall increase in women's education in the Dharamgarh valley is noticeable. But see what Derrett (1978b, 83) notes, "girls were sent not only to school but even to college to occupy them during the enforced waiting period and to lower the amount of their dowry or give their fathers more time to accumulate it." This was also true in the context of the girls in the Dharamgarh valley, where it was not uncommon to find girls enrolling in graduate and post-graduate courses and unhesitatingly admitting to doing so in order to improve their prospects in the "marriage market".

said Jagdish Kumar, who felt that education had sown the seed of individualism in the younger generation.

2.5.2.2. *Village ways: Administration and regulation in the hill villages*

Similar to the Koḷī community in coastal Maharashtra, the communities in the villages of the Dharamgarh valley were very conscious of their caste-based identity and the rules of conduct arising therefrom. Following this, there were certain matters that were discussed, administered, and regulated at the village level, and certain other matters that were first handled at the level of the caste group and thereafter brought before a group of village wisemen (*shiyāné*) only if necessary.

Unlike in Gonjhé, there were no community or even caste-based structures of self-administration in the villages of the Dharamgarh valley. In fact, the very term "*pancāyat*" did not imply for the local people a specific body with particular tasks (see Chapter 4, page 84). In mixed caste villages, every caste group comprised of one *birāderi*, which as Blunt (1931, 104–31) described is an "exogamous segment of caste in India, in which boys and girls are considered brothers and sisters and hence cannot be marriage partners." Usually, they traced their lineage to one common ancestor. Within a *birāderi* there were *shiyāné*. The word *shiyānā* (singular of *shiyāné*) is literally translated as the "wise one" or the "learned one". When men and women crossed a certain age, they referred to themselves as *shiyāné* with respect to their own families. The term could be confusing, as it was also often used synonymously with "having aged" ("*Ab mein shiyānī ho gayī*"). In the case of men, one became a *shiyānā* in his family on becoming the eldest surviving male. In case of women, they tended to refer to themselves as *shiyānī* (female version of *shiyānā*) on becoming grandmothers. As a result, there was no fixed number of *shiyāné* in a village. Every family, in any case, granted the status of *shiyānā* privately to the eldest (usually male) member(s) of their household. Some of these elders were however considered *shiyāné* in the context of the entire *birāderi*. Some *shiyāné* from within a *birāderi* also doubled up as *shiyāné* for the entire village. If a village consisted of many *birāderi*-s from one or different castes, the village *shiyāné* may have comprised of *shiyāné* from all or some of these *birāderi*-s. Traditionally, and to some extent even today, wisdom was attached to age and so the elderly men and women of the village who had a good social reputation were looked upon as the *shiyāné* at the level of their *birāderi* and sometimes even at the village level. At the *birāderi* or village level, the title of *shiyānā* was earned with one's deeds and was often closely related to the roles one played at the community level. Therefore, *shiyāné* were often found to be active in the regulation of village affairs especially those related to the village temple and its administration. *Shiyāné* often took the lead in activities related to welfare of the village community. Such activities often concerned civic issues that depended on personal contributions of community members such as construction of a road or renovation of a school and social things like arrangement of marriages, division of property between family members and processing of disputes in the village. *Shiyāné* were sometimes consulted in the meetings of the statutory body of the Gram Panchayat as well. In the previous years it was usually an individual who had been actively involved in helping the village acquire a road, a school teacher, the priest of the village temple or even a person known to be very fair in his or her conduct with others who was likely to be identified as a village *shiyānā*. With time, the *shiyāné* also came to include men and women who had some exposure to an urban life.[36] At the time of fieldwork, the village *shiyāné* included a broad variety of people. While age and the experience that came with it still remained important, factors such as education and a city-based job also contributed to an important status in the village.

In the villages in the Dharamgarh valley, village *shiyāné* took regulation of village affairs upon themselves. The issues they primarily dealt with concerned management of the village temples, inter-caste disputes (in mixed caste villages), protection of village forests and assisting state supported bodies such as the Grām Panchayat and the Van (Forest) Panchayat in carrying out tasks related to their village. At the *birāderi* level, the *shiyāné* of their *birāderi* were primarily concerned with issues relating to marriage, birth, divorce, partition of property within individual families, and ensuring maintenance of (adherence to) caste rules. A meeting of *shiyāné* would fall within the description of a *pancāyat* (see Chapter 4, page 81). If such a meeting concerned a matter of the *birāderi* it would be a *birāderi pancāyat*, whereas if the matter concerned the village, the meeting would be considered a village *pancāyat*.

One of the village *shiyāné* was usually the *Grām Pradhān*. Before the state government introduced the rule for appointment of a *Grām Pradhān* through election, it was common for villages to have a village chief or village head, then known as the "*pradhān*". He was usually selected by the villagers from among those who were considered *shiyāné* for village issues. More often than not (and possibly to avoid controversy) the oldest village *shiyānā* was given this post. Female *shiyāné* were not common in any of the villages except for one and even in that village there was no experience of a woman being selected for the post of *pradhān*. The *pradhān* presided over the *pancāyat* meetings comprising the *shiyāné* at the village level that were meant to settle village disputes or issues of village administration. He also maintained records of marriages, births and deaths in the village. He would also be at the forefront of any activity, which called for engagement of village residents with state actors, be it a visit to the police station, the government office issuing a ration card or the tehsil office for procurement of a caste certificate.

The *Grām Pradhān*, a post that was created by the state government as part of Panchayati Raj institutions (see Chapter 1, page 9, footnote 22), was supposed to head the Grām Panchayat – a state body for local self-governance – and represent the village at *talukā* (sub-district) and district levels. In the initial years after this

36 See also Obeng (2014, 100–103); the case study of Anjali Salu Siddi who gauges that her "experience outside of Ugingeri however might have been considered an asset for the post" of *budavanta*. "That Anjali had lived in Mumbai a cosmopolitan city and worked for non-Siddis were no doubt perceived as assets she brought to the position."

post was introduced, older villagers remembered that the village *pradhān* would be recommended to take up this post, which however became contested for on the basis of elections in the village. At the time when research was carried out there were no *pradhān*-s in the villages. Additionally, the state government has introduced specific eligibility criteria for this post, which like other government posts is also subject to reservation clauses as part of affirmative action initiatives. Therefore, a *Grām Pradhān* may not necessarily have been a *shiyānā* of the village; this post could be held by fairly young people, members of the Scheduled Caste, and even women, which was not very common when the *pradhān* was traditionally selected.[37]

In practice, the role of the *Grām Pradhān* as described under the Uttar Pradesh Panchayat Raj Act 1947 (*The Uttar Pradesh Panchayat Raj Act, 1947 (Uttaranchal Amendment) Act, 2002*) and how it was understood locally was not very different from what the former *pradhān* did. But the process of state regulated elections and the opportunity to allocate (and appropriate) a state-sponsored budget for village administration had changed people's perception of and expectations from the *Grām Pradhān*. Elections brought with it the segregation of the village community into factions based on the different candidates everyone chose to support. While the repercussions of such factionalism were not very grave in the Dharamgarh valley, elections nevertheless commonly led to a certain section of village residents discounting the capabilities of the elected *Grām Pradhān*, which was something that was claimed to be rarer when the *pradhān* was selected in consensus by the entire village. The motivation for being elected through voting remained high because of the small monetary honorarium that a *Grām Pradhān* received from the state, and also the opportunity to handle the funds allocated by the State government for village administration and development works. As per the regulations of the Uttarakhand State Government, female candidates and individuals from the Scheduled Caste and Scheduled Tribes are required to hold the post of *Grām Pradhān* once every few years.[38] In the designated years, a person from the prescribed category was to be elected as *Grām Pradhān*. Even though women in the villages in Dharamgarh valley were more educated and consequently more confident and outgoing in comparison to earlier years, there tended to be very low expectations from such candidates themselves. A woman, whose husband seemed an appropriate candidate, usually came into power and it was her husband (*Pradhān-patī*) who ultimately carried out all the bureaucratic tasks and responsibilities assigned to such a posting. The experience with elections when the seat of the *Grām Pradhān* was reserved for a member of the Scheduled Caste or Scheduled Tribe was similar, particularly in mixed caste villages. Voting for such elections was considered symbolic, if the

37 Of course even today, though the government attempts to bring about a sense of equality by entitling women and members of scheduled caste to hold the post of the village head, candidates belonging to these categories are selected only in the years when the eligibility criteria set by the government for holding the post requires it.

38 Such measures are a consequence of the 73rd Amendment to the Indian Constitution aimed at according "powers and authority to women and marginalized Indians" (Pal 2004, 134).

population of persons from a Scheduled Caste or Scheduled Tribe in the village was very low. Unless the individual himself/herself or his/her family, had a long-established reputation of stability or capability and goodwill in the village, chances of such a person in the post of *Grām Pradhān* being taken seriously were fairly low.

As a result, the present day *Grām Pradhān* appointed through election did not hold the same prestige and importance of the *pradhān* from earlier times. S/he nevertheless commanded some respect because of their role as the official representative of the village for state-related matters. The post on the whole was treated as a political one, though there remained close cooperation between the state body of the *Grām Pradhān*, his ward members, and the village *shiyāné*, from whom advice was often sought with respect to internal issues of the village. In regard to such internal issues, a generous part of which involved processing of village disputes at inter and intra-caste levels, the *Grām Pradhān* may or may not have had a voice depending on his/her cooperation and rapport with the *shiyāné* of the village and in the village community at large.[39] In consequence thereof, what was observed in some villages, was that village *shiyāné* would be appointed as ward members to assist and advise the *Grām Pradhān*. This in many instances went a long way in reassuring the villagers of the credibility of this post.

2.6 Conclusion

In the above sections I have set out the socio-economic and cultural contexts in which the present research study is set. I have also mapped the methodology I used and the manner in which I carried out fieldwork. This concluding section of Chapter 2 is devoted to an explanation of how the two geographical locations selected for fieldwork compare to enhance our understanding of the phenomenon of dispute processing as a whole, within these communities.

Besides the practical consideration of being able to gain access to the rich narratives of experiences with dispute processing that these two locations so generously enabled, there were certain other factors that prompted me to proceed within the communities set in these two locations. The manner in which I gathered data was significantly different in both locations. While in Gonjhé I was located in one village, in the villages in the Dharamgarh valley, I remained in circulation between several villages. Additionally, in Gonjhé I focused on a specific caste, the Koḷī, whereas in the Dharamgarh valley, my data is gathered from the experiences of people belonging to different castes and tribes, although their ways of living – as a result of the topographical situation they were placed in – were very similar. But despite these differences, there were points of similarity within these communities that allowed scope for comparison and a more diverse understanding of non-state dispute processing mechanisms within Indian society.

39 See also Holden (2003) for similar observations about co-operation between the "*buzurg*" members of the caste community and candidates of statutory Gram Panchayat in Piparsod village in central India.

Firstly, in both locations I observed predominantly Hindu communities. These communities were, either by reasons of their caste or their location, or because of their socio-economic circumstance, and in certain contexts because of all three factors, perceived to be deprived of measures for social justice that the Indian government puts in place as part of its development agenda. Communities like the Koḷī from Maharashtra and the Harijan community in Uttarakhand were within the lowest rung of the caste hierarchy. The Koḷī find a mention within the state list of Other Backward Classes (National Commission for Backward Classes), while the majority comprising Harijan belonged to the state list of Scheduled Castes. The Bhotiā were categorised in the list of Scheduled Tribes of Uttarakhand (Ministry of Tribal Affairs, Government of India). Exception to these categories are the Pandits and the Thakurs of Uttarakhand, which communities have also been observed but are from what is known as the "Open Category". Nevertheless, their higher caste is not a necessary marker of their improved socio-economic position within the broader scheme of "development" within the region and further within the state in which they are located. They, along with the Bhotiā and Harijan, remain at the margins of development and access to social justice as a result of their "remote" (Mathur 2015) location. Observation of these communities and the manner in which they confronted issues that interfered with the smooth governance and maintenance of peace and order within their communities, sometimes fell within the scope of "public law", bringing forth the influence of factors such as religion and caste on the actual processes of dispute processing and the varied understandings of concepts such as "justice" and "rights".

Secondly, the geographical situation of both locations provided a comparative context. Gonjhé lies in the economically flourishing and well-developed coastal belt of Maharashtra. Besides high levels of economic and education opportunities, calamities such as famines, water scarcity, epidemics, and food scarcity are lesser known in western Maharashtra compared to the rest of Maharashtra. In closer connection to the research question of this study, is the fact that Gonjhé is located 12 kilometres from the nearest *tāluka* court (sub-district court) and three kilometres from the police station in Mānjai having jurisdiction over the area.[40] There were several types of transport facilities to and from the village operating with dependable frequency. The Mānjai *bandar*, was a popular tourist point with a flow of visitors from Mumbai, Pune, and other large town centres, keeping alive the connection of Gonjhé's community with the urban world. Contrastingly, the villages in Dharamgarh valley were set pretty much, in what might be referred to as "the back of the beyond". Neither close to a tourist centre, nor in a region with a noteworthy rate of development, the villages in the Dharamgarh valley find themselves at a distance of about 36 kilometres from the nearest *tālukā* court and not less than 22 kilometres from the closest police station. Distances seemed longer and traversing them was made more challenging because of an almost complete absence of public transport in this valley, leaving people to depend upon the energy in their feet or

40 *Tālukā* courts are the courts of first instance for majority civil and criminal cases in India (see also Krishnan et al. 2014).

the intermittent appearance of a private vehicle plying between market centres. The position of the Koḷī community enabled it smoother access to the state forums, unlike the position of the villagers in Dharamgarh valley for whom accessing state forums was a challenge that began with basic proximity. However, in both field locations, non-state forums were acknowledged, encouraged and supported in playing an active role in the processing of disputes, including those concerning land, matrimony, and forest resources. This situation allowed me a) to explore the factors that legitimated non-state forums to exercise jurisdiction and b) to examine the connection between physical proximity to state actors and the influence of state law and its systems on individuals and communities thus located, a connection that is strongly emphasised in "access to justice" debates.[41]

Thirdly, a substantial part of the communities in both Maharashtra and Uttarakhand continued to engage in their traditional occupation, being pursued for generations. Even as this remains true, both communities were also being influenced by the spread of formal education. Levels of formal education in the Koḷī community were however low compared to those among the people in Dharamgarh. This contributed to understanding the connection between education, changing nature of occupations, and choice of dispute processing forums. It also helps us understand the manner in which non-state forums may be evolving as a consequence of the change in these surrounding factors.

And fourthly, in both locations women formed the crucial link between the household and the community at large. Among Koḷī folk, the nature of their occupation kept men away at sea for extended periods. Similarly, in Uttarakhand, for reasons of education and jobs, men migrated to the urban centres. As a result, among the Koḷī as well as the communities in the Dharamgarh valley, managing the household, maintaining local kinship reciprocities, and sustaining village networks became entirely the responsibility of women, which in turn made them important decision makers. I observed in both field locations, how women's agency structured and activated through this distinct social set-up, came into play during the processing of disputes.

In the following chapter, I present an understanding of how disputes are perceived in the dynamics of community life. The chapter explains the different legal orders that may govern dispute processing, the actors that comprise these legal orders, and how disputes move between these various spheres.

41 Refer Chapter 1, page 23, footnote 42 to understand how I use this term.

3 Many laws, many orders

Disputes and their processing in the non-state arena

This chapter focuses on the manner in which disputes were processed in the village communities in Gonjhé and the Dharamgarh valley. Dispute processing is marked by different "layers of legality" (see page 68) in these communities that witness an interaction and struggle of different types of law, and the postulates underlying them, that seek to govern and regulate the lives of people in these communities. People's instinct for self-preservation then reveals the, often furious, engagement between the spheres of religion, state and everyday life practices within these processes.

The first part of this chapter describes how a dispute is perceived by the communities in Gonjhé and Dharamgarh valley. This part delves into understanding the location and significance of a dispute in the backdrop of an intricate web of relations defined by kinship, gender, and power. The second part of this chapter is more conceptual and explains the manner in which disputes move through various layers of legality as they are processed. It examines what such processing ultimately means for the disputing parties themselves and their communities at large.

3.1 Disputes within the context of everyday life

Disputes, as a type of conflict, are "essential to society and not necessarily, anti-social to be utterly removed" (Coser 1956; Sandole 2011). Disputes were perceived by the communities in Gonjhé, and the Dharamgarh valley like "hiccups" in the order of everyday life.[1] They did distract the disputing parties, and other community members, for brief moments of time, but rarely to the extent of interfering with the overall progression of an individual's or community's life. Similar to hiccups, some disputes got cured instantly whereas certain types of disputes tended to persist. However, as Felstiner, Abel and Sarat (1981, 639) highlight, "people never fully relegate disputes to the past, never completely let

1 The intention here is not to equate disputes with an "illness" of any sort by referring to this perception of the community, but in fact quite the opposite. Disputes were largely viewed as minor breaks in the everyday order of things, and not too important to receive a lot of attention and energy, but nevertheless some disputes could not be ignored entirely.

bygones be bygones: there is always a residuum of attitudes, learned techniques, and sensitivities." An interesting consequence of this was that disputes leave impressions, which many times remain like vivid memories (Nadel and Sinnott-Armstrong 2012) recollected on many occasions as part of reflections of interpersonal relationships or in order to emphasise those relationships that were either undermined or fortified in the process.

Given that the relationship of Hindu and Muslim communities in India is known to be fraught with communal violence at times, in response to a query (made by different visitors to this village) regarding the relations between the two communities in Gonjhé, the Koḷī always made reference to a marriage that occurred between a girl and a boy from these communities. Clarifying their own position, the Koḷī said, "One of our boys even got married to a Muslim girl. We accepted the match, but the Muslims were the ones who became angry and ostracised the girl and her family."[2] In the Koḷī community, inter-caste marriages, though not encouraged, were not unheard of. But an inter-religious marriage had never been witnessed by the residents of Gonjhé. This, despite the fact that Muslims, Christian, and the Hindu Koḷī lived in close proximity to one another in this village and region. Common to all the narratives about the incidence of this marriage were two facts that were always prominently highlighted. One was that, even though the Koḷī community was doubtlessly not pleased with this match, they did not impede the marriage when the couple and their families decided to proceed with it. The second fact concerned the response of the Muslim *jamāt* (community forum of the Muslims) to this marriage. I was told that the *jamāt* decided that if the couple proceeded with the marriage, the girl and her family would be ostracised from the Muslim community in Gonjhé for a period of two years. When the couple finally did get married, regardless of the deterrence from the Muslim community, they – along with the girl's family – were ostracised by the *jamāt*. Nevertheless, the couple received a generous share of money from the same *jamāt* towards marriage expenses. "This was the first such Hindu-Muslim marriage in the village," said Naru Chogle, an old fisherman. "And look what luck the girl brought; soon after their marriage, the boy even got a good job with the naval dockyard in Mumbai. The girl's family who is ostracised had to leave the village. Even the girl and boy live in Mumbai. But the girl visits her in-laws often. She is present at many Koḷī weddings and she is just like us. We don't even feel she is Muslim," added Hema Pavshe, a fisherwoman with whom I visited the home of this couple for a religious ceremony one evening. The ostracism of the bride and her parents by the Muslim community was criticised by the Koḷī in comparison to the tolerant response of their own community. At the same time, the emphasis on the money that the Muslim *jamāt* extended to the couple was an appreciation of the Muslim community having duly fulfilled their responsibility towards a member

2 From a conversation between a group of men and women while watching an India-Pakistan cricket match in Ravindra Pavshe's house. The term "India vs Pakistan" is also often metaphorically used to indicate the postulated rivalry between Hindus and Muslims, Gonjhé (Maharashtra), February 2015.

of their community. Of course, this example was also narrated to exemplify that the relations between the two communities were fairly peaceful, possibly because the (Hindu) Koḷī – as the narration of this example hints – were more generous than the (Muslim) Koḷī in Gonjhé; but not necessarily – as we shall see in a later section (see Chapter 4, page 111) – more accepting of inter-religious marriages.

3.2 Gossip: The dialogue about disputes

Disputes constituted an important element of gossip in both these communities (see also Ishwaran 1964, 238–239). Gossip, as a mechanism of "information management" (Paine 1967) often led to disputes being discussed at great length. On a rainy day, or when the men would return from several days at sea, a group of men would often gather in *puḍhārī* Ravindra Pavshe's living room to chat and catch up over cups of tea. After brief conversations about the fishing business that week, the best sale at the auctions, and the state of each other's boats and businesses, conversations would linger on to discuss the troubles or disputes (*bhāngaḍi*) in the village in the days gone by. It was usual that the *bhāngaḍ* most discussed would involve or pertain to an individual someone or everyone in the gossiping group knew very closely or was even related to (see also Punekar 1959, 34; Gluckman 1963, 312).

What was common to both field locations was that a dispute would come into the limelight, only if it became a *tamāshā*. The performance of a dispute (Kokal 2018) is often crucial in determining whether a dispute will become the focus of community gossip and attention. Like all performances, those concerned with disputing and dispute processing could also have a theatrical element, one that is exaggerated, either in form or content or both, to the extent of being almost unreal. In Hindi or Marathi language such theatrics are referred to as a "tamāshā". The term *tamāshā* does not find a direct translation in English but could be generally understood as an act or series of acts that result in the creation of a spectacle or a dramatic scene. The act may become a spectacle because of the "actual physical performance" the actors might undertake or because of the content and style of dispute processing that sets it apart from the "ordinary."[3]

Disputes were often perceived to turn into a *tamāshā* when there had been a necessarily *public* exchange of verbal abuses and insults, or some physical assaults, or when either party may have approached the police station or a local leader in the event.[4] In other words, the dispute had become more public rather than being only a matter between individuals. For instance, it was known in Melatpur village that Kamla's husband was a drunkard and often became very violent towards her.[5] But the story about Kamla's husband that became a subject of community gossip was the day on which he appeared drunk outside her workplace and began hurling

3 The term ordinary here is placed into quotes because what comprises the "ordinary" may differ in every community and context.

4 Here "*public*" is italicised to add emphasis.

5 Kamla's case study is described in further detail in Chapter 4 – see page 102.

abuses at her boss. "*Dadda* (big brother, here referring to her employer) filed a complaint in the local police station against him and Kamla actually slapped her husband to bring him back to his senses before she dragged him back home," recollected Kavita Bhauriyal, a weaver at the NGO – who had witnessed this *tamāshā* – during an early morning chat with her neighbour. The subject of Kamla had casually come up, and the reference to her plight because of her alcoholic husband had almost immediately been touched upon. The recollection of this particular incident remained common to many narratives in Kamla's workplace campus.[6]

On the whole, because of their expatiated form of expression and fairly flagrant style of communication, *tamāshās* arising from disputes were perceived to bring *beizzati* or damage social standing and were often equated to "washing one's dirty linen in public." Therefore, the more respectable a person or household was, the more cautious they were of being associated with a dispute-related *tamāshā*. And consequently, people creating a *tamāshā* or those involving themselves in it were rarely looked upon favourably.

A dispute could become a *tamāshā* for several reasons; sometimes to bring the issue into "public" space, or because it was the intention of one of the parties to the dispute to "make a statement or a point," or merely to test boundaries and see how far one could go. For instance, in Gonjhé, a dispute turning into a *tamāshā* was quite common and I observed this to be more a defence mechanism than anything else. Fisherwomen more than men were well-known for creating a scene, which typically included the hurling of obscene verbal abuses and a whole lot of shouting and screeching and sometimes threatening with the scythe (*koytā*). A prominent consequence of these *tamāshā*-s was that the men in the community always remained wary about getting into an argument with the fisherwomen, and even if they did, accusations or the show of power was often retracted at the slightest hint of a *tamāshā*. It secured the fisherwomen from being taken advantage of – emotionally, financially or physically – by customers, relatives and competitors. With their men in particular, this worked to counter-balance the gendered power equations.

The bigger the *tamāshā*, the more vividly gossip sessions recollected it throwing light on (and allowing me an insight into) the cause of the dispute, its history, the general reputation of parties involved in the dispute and sometimes even that of their families. Additionally, these discussions also elucidated the manner in which the disputing parties, their responses to a dispute and the method by which the dispute may have been resolved (if at all) were perceived by the community members. Gossip as a catalyst of social process may work to avoid a disputing situation or exacerbate it; either way it sets into pattern a range of issues that may have until then been perceived by people in a rather blurred or vague form (Paine 1967, 283). All of these factors in a discussion of the nature of gossip, therefore, had a crucial impact on the manner in which a dispute was processed or advised to be settled by acquaintances of the disputing parties as well as the local leaders in

6 Fieldwork observations, Melatpur, Uttarakhand, December 2014.

the community, if their help had been sought or authority had been stimulated (see also K. von Benda-Beckmann 1981, 131).

3.3 Dispute processing in the communities of Gonjhé and Dharamgarh valley

That dispute processing in the non-state arena was extremely prevalent in both the fieldwork locations examined in this study is now confirmed by the evidence in the previous sections – see pages 42–55. Additionally, given the vastness and diversity in India, the very character of non-state dispute processing, and the variety of actors involved, is extremely varied depending on the geographical location and the contexts in which a community sanctions such processing. And therefore, this book argues that any claims about the methods of non-state dispute processing in rural India that are based on an alleged uniformity in their nature and form are totally misleading (John 2013; Ingole 2015; *The Hindu* 2014).

This section introduces the different types of "layers of legality" that a dispute, in the communities observed, often passed through in the course of being processed. It provides an overview of what the author identifies as the "postulational values" (Chiba 1984) of the various laws governing such processing, the dynamics of which, disputing parties and non-state actors must tackle in order to preserve community solidarity on the one hand and protect the interest of individual members of the community on the other.[7]

3.3.1. The nature of community solidarity and its impact on dispute processing

> The dispute processing practices prevailing in any particular society are a product of its values, its psychological imperatives, its history and its economic, political and social organisation. (Felstiner 1974, 63)

And therefore, "cumulative relationships (social organisation)" (Felstiner 1974, 64) are important in order to understand why individuals within particular communities resort to certain types of the forums and mechanisms for dispute processing. In order to understand the nature of engagement between non-state forums and actors and state law, it is necessary to develop an understanding of the religious and cultural backgrounds, and social structures of the communities within which such non-state forums and actors exist. In both fieldwork locations, these religious, social and cultural contexts nurtured values that were fundamental to the cultivation of a community's sense of order, which in turn regulated the nature and extent of their engagement with state law. These backgrounds and structures were not transfixed in time and were rooted as much in the order

7 In his later work (Chiba 1986), Chiba refers to "postulational values" as legal postulates (Chiba 1986, 6). But I have selected to retain his earlier terminology as I think it allows me broader scope for describing the values identified without impinging on a discussion about their "legality".

arising from everyday life practices as they were in the order originating from a divine or supranatural source.

The ethnographic research for this book, which was carried out in two predominantly Hindu communities, indicated that the influence of state law was best evaluated through an understanding of its operation in the context of a community's own sense of order, of which non-state law and forums were only an expression.

In both Gonjhé and the villages in the Dharamgarh valley, it was observed that maintenance of self-preservation and an experience of interconnectedness lay at the root of all dispute processing interventions, whether at the level of the community or at the level of the self as part of the community. In the two communities, I observed community solidarity to be an expression of the interconnectedness that members of these communities experienced – partly on account of their religious and sociocultural identities, and partly as a consequence of their everyday life practices.

3.3.1.1. Interconnectedness as a religious and sociocultural experience

The interconnectedness that these communities experienced on the basis of their religious and sociocultural identity facilitated the emphasis and preservation of the postulational values that the community identified with (*dharma, izzat*), which in turn cultivated the community's sense of order. Both communities studied in this case were Hindu.[8] Both these communities were extremely conscious of and sensitive to their religio-cultural identities and caste affiliations. An understanding of "order" in the context of being Hindu was therefore necessary to gain an insight into this experience of interconnectedness.

Hindus are not bound by any one single religious, moral or legal code as a matter of dogmatic belief. A Hindu understanding of order, as Menski (2003, 78) explains, emerged first, in the concept of *rita* or *rta* (pre-existent macrocosmic order) and later *dharma* (self-controlled microcosmic order). He further suggests that:

> This old Vedic conceptualisation reflects and signifies the early awareness of people ... that there is a superhuman, macrocosmic form of order in the world which is not directly subject to human influence, but to which mankind in its quest for a good life should relate and, to an extent, submit. ... Hindus as a collective appear to assume that one cannot expect one particular named

8 Hinduism has often been described as a "family of culturally similar traditions" (Lipner 1998, 6) or "a potpourri of religions, doctrines and attitudes towards life, rites and cults, moral and social norms" (A. Michaels 2004, 3). It is therefore difficult to define "Hindu" or "Hinduism" and thus the reference to being Hindu not just as a "religious", but equally a "cultural" experience. For a description of more complex expressions of being a Hindu in India, see Derrett (1968, 57–61) who describes religious affiliation in India not as "question of individual's belief" but one of "social belonging."

> superior God to take care of everything, thus all individual beings – god, humans, and others – should try their best to partake in this superhuman Order, contributing as much as possible to its sustainability. (Menski 2003, 87)

Within this Hindu conceptual system, every Hindu, not only those who are in power, perceive themselves as guardians of this *rta/dharma* complex – the superhuman order – which remains at the core of this self-maintained order system. Seen from this plurifocal and multi-perspectival view, the maintenance of order at the micro level – in the villages of Gonjhé or the Dharamgarh valley in this case – through the exercise of agency at the level of the self (see Chapter 5), through the working of *pancāyat*-s (see Chapter 4, page 80) at the level of the community and/or through strict adherence to caste rules and customs, became some of the ways in which every person, individually or collectively, participated in sustenance of the superhuman order.

The absence of a methodological tool in Hinduism specifying what code of conduct constitutes appropriate participation in the sustenance of such an order makes space for tremendous flexibility in responses to a particular situation. But this does not mean that "anything goes", as above all individual behaviour is the superior element of cosmic interlinkedness derived from the *rta/dharma* complex. Its relevance may be understood in terms of a Hindu perception of life, which:

> is seen as a complex experience, in which everybody and everything has a role to play and is visibly and invisibly interconnected in a giant systemic network of cosmic dimensions, a kind of universal spider's web. (Menski 2003, 90)

The awareness, arising from this cosmic interlinkedness, is that every action is part of a cosmic network of interrelationships that may have potentially wide-reaching consequences for oneself as well as others, thus having its implication on people's understanding of "self-preservation". Therefore, while there is no universally prescribed list of "what is appropriate behaviour", every individual must constantly assess the appropriateness of his or her actions in light of the consequences that are likely to arise in the context of the perceived interlinkedness of all things in this world (of which s/he is very much a part). This explanation contextualises, in part, the manner in which members of these communities chose to process their disputes.

3.3.1.2. Interconnectedness as a result of their everyday life practices

Complementing the interconnectedness that these communities experience on the basis of their religious and sociocultural conditioning was the interconnectedness that arose as a result of the interdependency created by practical life situations. As Gulliver (1997, 30–31) highlights: "a more realistic explanation to why people are willing to help one another and be involved in collective action is because of the help they themselves have received and expect in the future to receive from the party then in a disputing situation." This held true for the Koḷī and the communities in the villages of the Dharamgarh valley. Collective action was required by people for several activities, which went beyond the means of their own household, for example, in any type of constructions, agricultural activities, for ritual performances, during marriages and funerals, etc. and jural support is only a part of this (Gulliver 1997, 30, 1963, 119).

In both communities, the community members shared the same means of livelihood. In Gonjhé, every family was involved in the fishing business or some activity closely related to it. In the villages in the Dharamgarh valley, every family was dependent on agriculture as the primary source of livelihood. Every fisherman's household was connected to and dependent on other fishermen's households for several reasons ranging from the support fisherwomen required from one another at the time of sorting fish and handling issues related to selling the fish, to the dependency that fishermen experience in connection with building boats, fixing fishing nets and collaborating for a joint fishing business. Likewise, in the villages around Dharamgarh, families were dependent on each other for activities arising from the type of farming practices that were common to all households. Women would visit the forest together to collect firewood and girls would take their cows grazing together. It was common for women to help each other at the time of harvesting and for weeding. Additionally, families sought each other's support during the delivery of a child in the household, preparations for marriage and fulfilment of funeral responsibilities. The absence of service providers in any of these categories made interdependence inevitable. As a result, the unrest in relationships caused by disputes had to be tackled in these contexts of interconnections and need for one another (thus, preservation of the self) that everyone knew would continue to exist despite the disputing situation.

Community solidarity and the need to remain within this circle of solidarity therefore became one pragmatic expression of this experience of cosmic interlinkedness and practical interdependence. Its maintenance therefore was perceived to be crucial. Preservation of values the community identified with was linked to maintaining this community solidarity and strengthening of community solidarity in turn reinforced community values. Any dispute tends to disturb social concord thereby threatening community solidarity and interlinkedness. Thus, despite the provision of an alternative state machinery, the authority held by non-state forums such as the *Samāj* in Gonjhé or Goddess Kokiladevi and the *Birāderi* in Uttarakhand have not broken down in present times because such authorities in their nature were "undifferentiated dispute institutions," which "tend to preserve and strengthen multiplex, affectual, enduring social relations" and were perceived to symbolise "values which come to be strongly held by society" (Abel 1974, 298).

3.4 The movement of disputes

In both Gonjhé and the villages in the Dharamgarh valley, dispute processing cut across different layers of legality. These layers should be imagined in the form of concentric circles, with dispute processing mechanisms involving only the individual or self, located at the core. In the diagrams – see Figures 3.1 and 3.2 – I show the actors that play key roles in the dispute processing within each "layer of legality". In my experience in the field, the "self" was usually the first stage of dispute processing, where an individual considered for himself/herself the dispute s/he might be involved in, weighing the precariousness of their choice of response in light of all the other elements in the surrounding circles. Every semi-circle in the diagram represents a different layer. The layers are arranged in a manner to represent each community's perception of the different levels at which successive attempts to process the dispute and finally settle it, ought to be made. Dispute processing mechanisms involving the family and then the community stood closest to the self and were followed by those involving the state machinery. The layer involving religious and supernatural elements such as deities and goddesses stood the furthest because, in both communities, dispute processing in this sphere was popularly expected to be resorted to usually after the dispute had passed through several other mechanisms of dispute processing. However, this was not always how things proceeded. Similarly, according to the scheme of dispute processing that the communities deemed appropriate, the processing of a dispute that was presented before the state machinery should have seen it pass through all the intermediate layers. However, in practice, this did not necessarily always happen. There were disputing parties that chose to process their disputes in any of these layers without necessarily having it pass through the intermediate layers. Similarly, a dispute could be simultaneously processed in two or more different layers; but usually in such situations processing would temporarily come to a halt in all but one of the layers. Therefore, in the diagrams the yellow dotted lines make way for such possibilities denoting flexibility. The dotted lines also indicate that elements from one layer may flow freely across other layers, thereby remaining present in the processing of disputes outside their specific layer. Such instances would include a *puchiāri* (see Chapter 4, page 85) from the outermost layer acting in her capacity as a *shiyānī*, becoming part of the third layer in Figure 3.2. Or a policeman participating in the *Samāj* meetings as part of the presiding committee, thereby becoming part of layer four in Figure 3.1.[9] These layers are referred to as "layers of legality" because from the perspective of the community, each of these layers comprised of a certain type of legality involving the play of different types of laws. A certain nature of dynamics between the "postulational values" underlying these laws characterised every layer of legality.

The notion of *izzat*, human rights, *dharma*, and the values of state law highlighted in the ring that runs around these semi-circles are the "postulational values" identified as underlying or "providing justification" (Chiba 1984, 17–18) for the various state laws, caste rules and customs prevalent in Gonjhé and the villages in the Dharamgarh valley.[10] Postulational values are "diffused and

9 Interview with police constable S. Kolad in Mānjai outpost, where Kolad narrated his experience of sometimes being invited by the villagers to participate in the meetings of their pancāyats, Mānjai (Maharashtra), February 3, 2015. See also Jauregui (2011, 378) on how the police in India have the ability to "cross lines" and reside at "the margins" of the state and non-state spheres.

10 But see, Davis (2007) who argues that *dharma* is a reference to law in the Dharmaśāstra.

apparently vague, although some of them are ideologically emphasized as vital values in religion, politics or social structure" (Chiba 1984, 18). Postulational values set a normative standard for conduct and cut across all layers. They were used as tools of self and social ordering. They underscored individually or jointly with other values the several different types of laws that governed the lives of these communities. *Dharma, izzat*, the values of state law and human rights were in no way the only postulational values that underscored the laws regulating the lives of people in the village communities of Gonjhé and Dharamgarh valley. The four types of postulational values that I highlight in the diagram were however selected in order to explain the argument presented in this book, as they featured most prominently in the patterns of dispute processing within both the communities I observed – thus, making scope for meaningful comparison. "*Dharma*" can be broadly explained as an abstract form of righteousness that finds its roots in the Hindu way of learning.[11] The notion of "*izzat*" relates to honour and social reputation, which develops for individuals, families and communities in consequence of respectable behaviour carried out consistently. Since the idea of respectable behaviour may differ from community to community, the indicators of *beizzati* (loss of *izzat*) also tend to differ. These values were reinforced by the communities not just in their own capacity but also through an insistence on maintenance of power equations within the community and adherence to caste rules. The values of state law in India include the value of human rights.[12] This is however also highlighted as a separate postulational value because it finds a pronunciation within Indian society at large, and these communities specifically, as a value of state law, but also of international law (F. von Benda-Beckmann 2006; Schiff Berman 2009).

Fieldwork showed that dispute processing in any and every layer was influenced by such values. As we see in Figures 3.1 and 3.2, postulational values (including those that are not mentioned) surround the layers of legality, in a way as though encompassing them. The postulational values are free floating, cutting across and at work in every layer of legality. They did not however exert the same amount of influence on dispute processing within each layer, thereby explaining partly the differences in the outcomes of dispute processing in every layer. Nevertheless, merely because a value exerted less importance within a layer did not imply that it was ignored or remained absent from the processing of disputes within that layer.

In every community, whether determined on lines of caste, religion or territory, the layers of legality may be fewer or greater, so also the values. The number of layers of legality in a community, I argue, had a direct connection with the competition between the values of what were perceived as "community laws" and "state laws" or the "values of others." This is explained in more detail in the next chapter, and it suffices here to mention that the greater the competition between

11 See Khare (1972), Derrett (1982, 1978a), Menski (2003), Ishwaran (1964) for more detailed explanations about *dharma* in the context of law and social normative.

12 To understand how the term "human rights" is understood for the purpose of this book, see Chapter One, page 13 footnote 28.

these two types of values, the more the number of layers of legality. As we see, in Gonjhé there were more layers of legality than in the villages in the Dharamgarh valley. Every layer had a set of actors who acted as gatekeepers, working to limit the processing of disputes from going further beyond their layer in both directions.

3.5 The layers of legality in Gonjhé and the villages of Dharamgarh valley

In Gonjhé, non-state dispute processing would usually occur within the layers involving the self at first stage and then the roles of the family, the *Bhāvkī*, the *Maṇḍaḷ* and the *Samāj*. The *Bhāvkī*, *Maṇḍaḷ*, and *Samāj* were social and administrative divisions in the village as described in the previous chapter (see pages 42–45). Dispute processing at the level of the *Bhāvkī* could involve any of the agnatic kin of the parties to the dispute. For administrative purposes, the workings of the *Maṇḍaḷ* and *Samāj* were regulated by groups of *puḍhārī*-s selected annually; members of these groups of *puḍhārī*-s were necessarily engaged in the processing of a dispute that happened at the level of the *Samāj* or *Maṇḍaḷ*. The Police Patil and the Dispute Free Village Committee (DFVC) were state-supported actors. They consisted of people selected from within the community to control or settle petty disputes at the village level. In Gonjhé there was considerable overlap between the members of the Samāj and the DFVC.[13] See Figure 3.1.

The DFVC was another attempt of the Indian government, this time through the channel of a specific state government (Maharashtra State Police 2007), that of Maharashtra in this case, to channelise the dissemination of official norms and procedures at the village level (See Galanter 1972, 58–67 on judicial panchayats). The Police Patil and the DFVC as a committee received nominal honorariums to carry out their tasks. In case the police were to investigate the circumstances of any dispute they had received a complaint about from the village, the Police Patil was the first point of contact for the police machinery. The converse was also true. Many people would first approach the Police Patil in order to have a complaint filed in the police station. Even though they had no judicial sanction and were partially voluntary posts, both the DFVC and the Police Patil were viewed within the community

13 In my time spent at Gonjhé, I did not witness even one DFVC meeting since none were conducted. Two years before I began my fieldwork Gonjhé had received the award designated under this scheme for being "dispute free". Since a majority of the members of the *Samāj* were also members of the DFVC, I would presume that it may have been difficult for disputing parties to know which forum exactly was processing their dispute, if at all they sought some clarity in this regard. From Ravindra Pavshe, who was a former chairman of the DFVC in Gonjhé I learnt that in order to fill the government registers provided under this scheme many matters processed by the *Samāj* were shown as processed by the DFVC. Since the constitution of both bodies was the same this was only fair according to him (Interview, Gonjhé (Maharashtra), January 2015). Such an overlap of members however must have made the working of this forum very different from what it was imagined to be under the scheme set up by the Maharashtra state government.

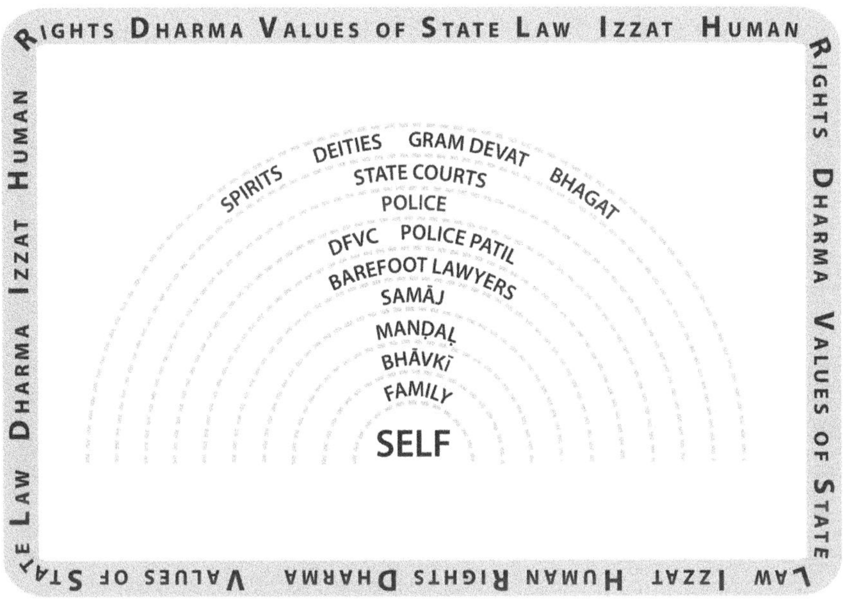

Figure 3.1 Layers of legality, Gonjhé (Maharashtra)

in Gonjhé as agents of the state. The role of the barefoot lawyers, as we shall see in the next chapter, and those of the DFVC and the Police Patil, tread on territory that involved both state and non-state procedures, norms, and systems.

In the Dharamgarh valley non-state dispute processing involved the self, the family and the *Birāderi* and individual *shiyāné* – see Figure 3.2. Many times, one *Birāderi* comprised the entire village and at other times a part of the village. The *Birāderi* in the villages in the Dharamgarh valley and the *Bhāvkī* in Gonjhé were comparable units of their respective societies. The *Grām Pradhān* was the elected head of the village and its representative in the state body of the *Zillā Parishad*.[14]

The *Grām Prahari* was appointed by the police machinery to remain an informant to the police about incidences of public-nuisance and criminal offences that had taken place or were likely to take place in their villages.[15] This made the roles of

14 Cohn (1965) referring to the works of Beals (1962) and Dube (1955) describes villages where "a single, most important and powerful individual, who because of his status is in a commanding position to settle disputes." The post of the *Grām Pradhān* finds its roots in the concept of "pradhān" who was an individual as described by Cohn and unanimously recognised as such by the village. The state introduced the concept of democratic elections in the villages by making the post of the *Grām Pradhān* an elected one.

15 The provision for appointment of a *Grām Prahari* is made under Section 47 of the Uttarakhand Police Act 1861. He is to be under the authority of the District Magistrate and District Superintendent of Police. Section 56–58 of the Uttarakhand Police Act 2007, also provides the appointment of a "Village Guard" who is locally called the *Grām Prahari*.

Figure 3.2 Layers of legality, Dharamgarh Valley (Uttarakhand)

the *Grām Pradhān* and the *Grām Prahari* similar to that of the barefoot lawyers and Police Patils, who acted involving both the state and non-state machinery.

A dispute that found itself embroiled in the layers involving the police machinery and the state courts was processed with the procedures that leaned more in favour of what was laid down in state laws and rules. There was also an attempt to lay greater emphasis on the postulational values embodied in state law and notions of human rights, although impossibility of ignoring the values of *dharma* and *izzat*, and local customs and caste rules, sometimes resulted in the lower rungs of state actors processing disputes in intriguing ways (Menski 2003).[16] In both locations the communities perceived that once a dispute entered the sphere of state courts, the dispute became the issue only of those party to it and community actors, and thereby the pressure of community mechanisms, lost control over it.[17] Interestingly, disputes that

16 Curious instances of such type included policemen processing disputes within the "space" of the police station as a location of dispute processing, but through language that appealed to the values of the community. Fieldwork observation, Mānjai Police Station (Maharashtra), March 2016.

17 There have been other studies that reveal a similar formulation of dispute processing taking place in different layers within a community. Comaroff and Roberts (1981, chap. 4) describe it with reference to the Tswana community, Gulliver (1997) with reference to Ndendeuli in Southern Tanzania, Nader (1990) with regard to the Talea, and Chaudhary (1999) with reference to a Pakistani Punjabi village. However, any substantial study providing an overview of dispute processing in a village community is absent in the Indian context. Hayden (1999) and Srinivas (2009b) provide insights into the working of one particular non-state forum, the caste *pancāyat*. Cohn's (1965,

invoked the intervention of Kokiladevi in the outermost layers of the villages in the Dharamgarh valley, drew a similar sentiment from within the community.

The formation of legal layers in the villages in the Dharamgarh valley and those in Gonjhé was not drastically different, although the authorities exerted by the different layers differed greatly in the two locations. For the people of Gonjhé, the *Samāj* was the highest and most influential authority in non-state dispute processing (see Chapter 2, page 43). Once a matter was placed before the *Samāj*, it could not be heard concomitantly by any of the other non-state forums, unless specifically directed. Furthermore, decisions of the *Samāj* were considered final. Within the Koḷī community the values of their caste rules and those of *dharma* and *izzat* were revered. The *Samāj*, therefore, made maximum efforts to ensure that the dispute was processed in such a manner that these values remained honoured, emphasised and balanced. In the villages of Dharamgarh valley, there was no fixed village or caste-based *pancāyat* that met regularly or even occasionally to discuss caste or village related issues. *Pancāyat-s* consisting of *shiyāné* from a *birāderi* or the village (see Chapter 2, page 52) were formed spontaneously to discuss issues that a disputing party thought needed imminent attention. Unlike in Gonjhé, such *pancāyat-s* could consist of different members each time. Maybe for these reasons, but not only, it was the realm of the religious and the supernatural that held most authority in non-state processing of disputes in the Dharamgarh valley. As we shall see in more detail in the next chapter, when a disputant invoked the intervention of goddess Kokiladevi located in Pitthoragarh district, all other mechanisms of dispute processing came to a halt. Not necessarily, but often enough, once a dispute entered this layer of legality, the disputant would stop pursuing the said case in a state forum and even the *birāderi pancāyat* would not entertain the dispute further. The goddess was perceived to have exclusive jurisdiction. Dispute processing in these village communities of Dharamgarh valley was always carried out in a manner such that the community's notion of *dharma*, most importantly, remained honoured. The values of their caste rules and notions of *izzat* followed this in terms of eminence.

Chiba observed that it was necessary to study the historical context of every society in order to understand the struggle between received law, in this case state law, and indigenous law, in this case the laws of the community such as caste rules and customs. He proposed that people endeavour throughout their history to preserve a cultural identity in law on the basis of one or more basic legal postulates that:

> provide the people with the criteria with which they are enabled to determine, from among many possibilities, what kinds of law they should develop selectively and, … what foreign law and to what extent it should be received or rejected in order to preserve their cultural identity in terms of law. (Chiba 1986, 390)

1959) and Khare's (1972) work provide a beginning in this direction, which never seems to have been followed up.

He termed these basic postulates as the "identity postulates of indigenous law". In light of their religious and cultural backgrounds as Hindu and a sense of interdependence arising from the functioning of everyday life practices connected to the performance of traditional occupations and customary rituals, both communities studied here experienced a similar awareness of interconnectedness. This study proposes that this historical experience of interconnectedness within these two communities nurtured the values of "*dharma*" and "*izzat*", which following Chiba, could be viewed as the identity postulates of the caste rules, customs and practices that cultivated the sense of order guiding the lives of the people in Gonjhé and the Dharamgarh valley.[18] Without claiming that *dharma* and *izzat* were the only identity postulates of the laws within these communities, I will show through the next chapters how these two identity postulates nevertheless played a prominent role in regulating the manner in which the dispute processing forums and actors in these communities engaged with state law.

18 This book will refer to the "identity postulates" as "postulational values" or "values" through the next remaining part of this book.

Preparing for the auction. Fishermen seek each other's help in offloading their fish from the small boats onto the beach adjacent to Mānjai bandar near Gonjhé in Maharashtra.

Some fisherwomen sold their fish immediately after purchase at a spot on the Mānjai beach. They had customers from the local neighbourhood, but also from towns as far as Mumbai and Pune.

Rām Navamī celebrations in Gonjhé.

The road to Khasi in Uttarakhand, mostly deserted with one private jeep plying people to and from the market in Chilbasa when the weather conditions were good.

A ‘branch’ of Kokiladevi’s temple in Melatpur, Uttarakhand.

The main temple of Goddess Kokiladevi in Pankhu, Uttarakhand.

Written petitions to goddess Kokiladevi in her temple at Pankhu, Uttarakhand.

A session in Draupadevi, the *puchiāri's* attic in Gangapur village, Uttarakhand. Draupadidevi interprets the cause of a party's misfortune by reading her fingernails.

4 The legal landscape

Forums and their experiences of engagement with state law

The availability of a wide range of state and non-state actors and forums ensured institutional plurality in the sphere of dispute processing in the village communities of Gonjhé and the Dharamgarh valley. Within the state machinery, it was the state courts, police stations, and the several local level quasi-judicial authorities that the people in Gonjhé and the Dharamgarh valley could seek grievance redressal from, whereas in the non-state area, people had the options of *pancāyats*, notables, barefoot lawyers, and priest magicians (Ghurye 1957, 48). In addition, the communities in both locations could also look towards state-supported actors such as the Dispute Free Village Committee and Police Patil in Maharashtra, and the *Grām Pradhān* and *Grām Prahari* in Uttarakhand.

Institutional plurality resulted in competition within these different types of forums in their pursuit for retention of power, but also their legitimacy. It was within this pursuit for power and legitimacy that disputants navigated the best possible manner of tackling their dispute. This chapter presents empirical evidence to illustrate the conceptual explanation offered in the previous chapter.

4.1 *Sarkār*: Community perceptions about the State

The *sarkār* is a word common to both Hindi and Marathi languages and is used to refer to the government, the ruling party, the state, and bureaucracy. In both Gonjhé and the villages around Dharamgarh valley, the *sarkār* was not a very popular entity. In Gonjhé, the Koḷī community has been locked in a tussle with the Maharashtra state government for grant of a Scheduled Tribe (ST) status instead of the Other Backward Class (OBC) status that had been granted to it (see Chapter 2, page 27 footnote 1). The community in Gonjhé had therefore decided to boycott all Gram Panchayat elections until such time as the government adheres to this demand. The gravity of this resolution taken by the community is such, that five years ago, a member of the Koḷī community from Gonjhé, who tried to contest elections despite this understanding within the community, was ostracised by the *Samāj*.[1]

In the villages in the Dharamgarh valley, the reasons for not holding a favourable view of the *sarkār* had more to do with the nature of government

1 Notes from fieldwork, *Samāj* meeting Gonjhé (Maharashtra), May 22, 2016.

interventions in the villages, the introduction of which according to the communities worked towards disintegrating community solidarity. In Khasi, a former *Grām Pradhān* of the village, Mohansingh Meher, felt that the biggest bane introduced by the *sarkār* was the insistence on appointment of *Grām Pradhān* through elections.[2] Until elections were made compulsory, the village head, then known as the *pradhān*, was selected by the people unanimously. His appointment did not depend on votes, but upon his goodwill, wisdom, and experience with social issues and state-related issues. With the introduction of elections, several people contested for this post. Mohansingh alleged that elections caused brothers to turn against one another, and the village had broken up into factions.[3] Similarly the appointment of a *Grām Prahari*, an appointment made by the police machinery to expand their reach in the village, was also viewed suspiciously for the same reasons. The police expected the *Grām Prahari* to report criminal offences occurring within his jurisdiction to the police, which meant that one member of the village – merely as a result of such a posting – felt compelled or allured into complaining against his own community members, many of whom were his kith and kin.[4] As a result of such experiences, people in Gonjhé and also in the Dharamgarh valley remained cautious of the state.

At the same time, an increase in the type of legislation regulating social and family life has contributed to a certain extent in blurring society's sense of the boundaries between public and private domains, resulting in an unequal, yet notable engagement between state and non-state institutions through what Solanki describes as processes of "centralisation of law" (Solanki, 2011, 172–173). The values of state law are seen to compete more and more explicitly with the other values that exert their influence at the community level. A considerable share of authority and "sublime qualities" (Hansen 2001, 35) are attributed to institutions such as courts, as well as state court judges and bureaucrats (see Krishnan et al. 2014, 537–39). While people are less in awe of state systems today, the state still continues to be regarded as "indispensible for public order and for recognizing communities, leaders or claims as legitimate" (Hansen 2001, 37). Thus, the engagement between the state and non-state arenas viewed from the perspective of non-state forums and actors in the village communities studied led to several interesting modifications in their practices and procedures including the creation of a new set of service providers within the non-state arena. In this context, Merry's (2004, 571) observation about "the interconnectedness of social orders and the vulnerability of location to structures of dominations far outside their immediate worlds" became evident.

2 Sundar's (2009, 199) data from an Adivasi community in Jharkhand on preference for traditional structures over elected representatives reveals similar reactions.

3 Interview, Khasi (Uttarakhand), March 11, 2016.

4 Interview with *Grām Prahari* Puransingh Meher, Khasi (Uttarakhand), February 1, 2016.

4.2 Dispute processing in the communities of Gonjhé and Dharamgarh valley: Understanding value dynamics

The usual course that disputes were popularly expected to follow (particularly by those in power within the community) was to proceed from the layers of legality where non-state actors were active to those layers where state actors were active and finally, if the party(-ies) remained dissatisfied with the dispute processing in all these layers, they could turn towards seeking the intervention of religious and supernatural elements in the outermost layer. Observations in the field showed that following this course was not a rigid rule. Therefore, it was not necessary that every party that chose for his/her dispute to be processed in an outer layer, would have necessarily seen it pass through all the intermediate layers of legality (see Chapter 3, page 68).

In every layer of legality, the postulational values that were emphasised were different. In the layers that consisted of dispute processing by non-state actors, the postulational values that the community, and the self as a member of the community identified with, were emphasised the most. The concepts of *izzat* and *dharma* were often described by the community as foundations of their methods of dispute processing, which was primarily described to be governed by caste rules, customs, and local practices (*ritī-riwāz*). At the level of self in the communities of Gonjhé and Dharamgarh valley, following the caste rules and *ritī-riwāz*, and a popularly accepted behavioural code – that amounted to maintaining one's *izzat* and fulfilling one's *dharma* – were important markers of an individual's identity. One prominent example of this was people's hesitation to go to state actors for dispute processing, as going to court was perceived as bringing *beizzati* upon one's family and community. As Chandrasingh Rathore, a retired policeman and a *shiyānā* from Gangapur village explained: "People usually understand. When the community mediates between disputing parties, relations will most likely be restored sooner or later. But if a person goes to the court or the police station, the party which was dragged to the state forum will always hold a grudge against the petitioning party."[5] Of course such circumstances came with their own set of nuances. While practices of behavioural codes (in some instances only superficially) were crucial facilitators in helping an individual exercise agency, preservation of behavioural codes and caste rules also worked towards reinforcing the established power structures within the community.

Interviews with respondents revealed adherence to these positive expressions (Chiba 1984, Chapter 1) of the postulational values the community identified with, which were perceived to be interconnected with self and social ordering within the village communities in Gonjhé and the Dharamgarh valley and constituted what could be termed as the "laws of these communities." Customary law, as Ishwaran (1964, 229) also found in Shivapur was an "integral part of the normative system, deeply rooted in the concept of Dharma." Here lay the connection of adherence to positive laws embodying the postulational values that the communities perceived themselves to identify with to the religious and cultural

5 Interview, Gangapur (Uttarakhand), April 21, 2015.

conditioning of these communities as Hindu. Since the *rta/dharma* concept, discussed earlier (see Chapter 3, page 63), is so flexible and there are no binding guidance rules as to what constitutes "appropriate behaviour towards sustenance of the superhuman order," there always remains scope for havoc and chaos. Very much aware of this, the village communities in Gonjhé and the Dharamgarh valley sought guidance for appropriate behaviour by following standards of conduct devised by them as falling in line with the broader notions of *dharma* and *izzat* further related to their awareness of interconnectedness. These standards of conduct were devised in the context of everyday life circumstances such as marriage, parenting, and so forth as well as social situations, such as use of temple premises or a dispute between an older and younger brother. Insistence on adherence to the positive expressions of such values in the form of caste rules and *ritī-riwāz* was only an extension of this. These practices and customs, it must be understood, were merely positive rules that ultimately embodied postulational values that the community identified with, thus explaining why embracement of local laws was perceived as following one's *dharma*. Consequently, all efforts to process disputes at the community level were marked with an inevitable emphasis on community values themselves and the laws that accentuate them. "We work on the parameters set by *dharma* (*hum dharma maryādā se chalte hain*)," said Hayatsingh Bhandari, the former *panch* of Panchwari village, when he described the type of rules that were prioritised during dispute processing.[6] It is obvious that this can mean a lot of different things. Likewise, in Gonjhé, when Bhagwan Chogle, the secretary of the *Samāj*, explained what rules dictated dispute processing by this body, he said that people were very much aware of the state law, but – referring to the working of the *Samāj* – he said: "We lay more emphasis on custom."[7] In this background, the threat of ostracism from the community's circle of solidarity or fines imposed by *pancāyat*s for non-adherence to these values may have been perceived by those imposing these as a reminder for individuals to follow *dharma* of their own accord rather than anything else (Menski 2003, 109). As a result, caste laws, customs, and prescribed behavioural codes took prominence over state law in the maintenance of social order in these communities. This situation was clearly not unique to Gonjhé and the villages in the Dharamgarh valley alone. Ishwaran (1964, 234) concluded from his observation in Shivapur that "in all such societies, peace and order are maintained in such a way that norms and values inherent to its social structure are preserved."

Within the layers of legality where community actors played a key role, caste rules, customs, and behavioural codes in accordance with notions of *izzat* and *dharma* were used as tools to maintain social order; social order also reinforced community solidarity, which in turn strengthened these postulational values. Thus, these postulational values could be said to be a condition as well as a consequence of community solidarity (Ishwaran 1964, 234), the maintenance of which was necessary for self-preservation (see Chapter 3, page 62). Hence it was important

6 Interview in Bhagwati temple, Melatpur (Uttarakhand), April 2, 2016.
7 Interview, Gonjhé (Maharashtra), February 14, 2015.

for these values to be retained and remain emphasised and balanced in everyday occurrences and particularly during the processing of disputes, when community relationships and structures were threatened with disturbance. As Bhagwan Chogle articulated it, while processing disputes the aim of the *Samāj* was to change the attitude of the disputing parties, "otherwise the wheels of the community get disturbed (*nahitar samājācā chakra baighaḍto*)."[8]

Characterised as Derrett (1982, 138) explained, by the "reverence for order and balance in the universe, which must be kept and sustained afresh with every solution to problems which arise in the guise of legal disputes," within those layers of legality where non-state actors were active, the postulational values of *dharma* and *izzat* were used as tools for maintaining social order and cohesion. In both communities, state laws comprised the category of "received laws". The postulational values of state laws, including human rights and individual choice, held relatively less gravity in their individual right and more importantly, they were identified with "others" (see also Chiba 1986, 378–389), which included people who were from outside the village, the more educated, the state, and anyone who chose not to be a part of the community circle of solidarity.[9] In contrast to caste rules, customs and practices embodying values such as *izzat* and *dharma*, the laws embodying the values of state law and human rights were perceived to be "formulated, controlled and enforced by those unfamiliar to the community and therefore suspected feared and often avoided" (Ishwaran 1964, 241). However, both types of postulational values – those that the community identified with and those that were identified as belonging to others – coexisted, though not necessarily harmoniously in all instances, as also identified by Chiba (1998), who uses the word "conflictingly".[10] It might appear here that certain values are ascribed to underlie state law, whereas certain others are identified as values of community laws (see page 75) resulting in the pre-emption of a type of dichotomy between these different sets of values. It is useful to remain aware at all times that values are neither static nor fixed categories, but rather extremely fluid in nature often underscoring different types of laws at the same time. The above distinction between values of state law and values of community laws is nevertheless retained through the remaining part of this book as analytical categories in order to evince the nature of engagement between non-state forums and state law.

8 Interview in Gonjhé (Maharashtra), February 14, 2015.

9 Without delving into this very deeply, it is sufficient to mention here that respondents identified many postulational values embodied in the positive rules of state law and human rights in the religious and social norms they were currently practicing. Possibly, therefore the need to identify them independently did not seem to arise.

10 Cohn, one of the earliest scholars to study dispute processing in India, makes a reference to this clash of values in the context of procedures of dispute settlement. He observed, "In attempting to introduce British procedural law into their Indian courts, the British confronted the Indians with a situation in which there was a direct clash of values of the two societies." (Cohn 1959, 90) My reference to the clash of values in this book differs slightly, in that, it is made in the context of the content of state laws more than just processes of their implementation (which is what Cohn speaks about).

4.3 Engaging with state law: Of resistance and embracement

von Benda-Beckmann (1981, 142) in her study in Minangkabau observes, that state forums "through their mere availability, form a threat to the authority of village institutions." I argue that one of the threats that state forums pose, is in the form of competition between postulational values of state law and the laws of the community. Fieldwork revealed that the greater the competition between the two types of values, the greater the perceived threat that postulational values of "others" posed to community values. The empirical evidence highlights that the efforts to counter this competition were greater in the villages that had more proximity to state institutions and urban areas, as for example in Gonjhé. Thus, revealing that it was in areas that were closer to state institutions, urban centres, and "development" that the perception of threat to community values was stronger. Consequently, greater efforts were made to reduce the impact of such postulational values identified as belonging to others, indiscernibly resulting in resistance of the state.

Within the sphere of dispute processing, specifically, this resulted in communities – like the Koḷī in Gonjhé – working towards retaining the processing of disputes within the layers that laid greater emphasis on the postulates that were important to the community.[11] One of the efforts that the key actors, acting as gatekeepers in every layer of legality made, was to limit the processing of a dispute to the layer of legality they were active in or to those before them. When asked about the nature of dispute processing in her village, Anandibai Mehra, a female *Grām Pradhān* said: "Everything gets resolved in the village. When a dispute gets extended then it will go to court. We don't allow it to extend. Egos should be kept under control."[12] Similarly, Draupadidevi, a *puchiāri* from Jamkuda, a key actor in the outermost layer of spirits and deities said: "The police," (while shaking her head disapprovingly), "is not a good thing for the village. It brings defamation (*badnāmi*)." In fact, this *puchiāri* even went on to clarify that in her own caste of Bhotiā, even involving the *Grām Pradhān* in the processing of dispute within members of their own caste group was considered as a "matter of *beizzati*" (loss of *izzat*).[13] Moore (1993, 532) observed a similar trend during her fieldwork in Rajasthan, but she does not explore the reasons for it in much detail and attributes the practice by the *panch* only to the monetary benefits that *panch* gain from processing disputes. On the one hand, as Moore also highlights, this is a part of the power play for those in power, but on another hand – and that is explored further in the next sections of this chapter – is that this limiting of dispute

11 There are several mechanisms that the Koḷī community adopted to thin down the impact of the postulational values identified with others. For example, disallowing youth to watch Hollywood films, was one. But since this book is meant to focus on dispute processing, I limit myself to the efforts made in this sphere to achieve this end.

12 Interview, Bilbār (Uttarakhand), March 18, 2016.

13 Interview, Jamkuda (Uttarakhand), April 25, 2015. At the time of fieldwork, the *Grām Pradhān* in Jamkuda belonged to the Thakur caste. It is difficult to know whether Draupadidevi would have had the same reaction with respect to the *Grām Pradhān*'s involvement in their caste disputes, if the *Grām Pradhān* belonged to the Bhotiā caste.

processing to community actors is also an indication of the community acting upon its sense of order that is cultivated on the basis of the identity postulates of their laws, which determine the extent to which state law should be received or rejected in order to maintain their cultural identity in law. Consequently, several mechanisms were brought into play in order to attain this objective.

One such mechanism was the existence of many actors and the very creation of a pattern of several layers of legality involving the key participation of non-state actors in dispute processing.

A second mechanism that came to light in this regard was the effort by non-state actors to increase their credibility. In my observation, most of the efforts by the non-state actors in this mechanism worked towards increasing their resemblance in form (and not necessarily content) to their counterparts in the state machinery. Interestingly, this was done more often through the adoption of structures borrowed from the state systems. One structure that dominated the scene was the practice of written documentation. I propose that this was probably in order to seem as "professional" as the actors within the state machinery, thereby reducing some of the reasons for people to choose dispute processing within the layers where state actors are involved over dispute processing by non-state forums and actors.

A third mechanism was the structural change that seemed to have developed in order to limit dispute processing from going into the state machinery. This was the adaptation of customs, practices, and perceptions of the key actors in dispute processing to better suit changing social circumstances activated through the propaganda surrounding promulgation of state law. In this case, the postulational values of state law were interwoven into the discourse of dispute processing by non-state actors. This effort complemented the above in some ways. Adaptation in certain substantive parts of dispute processing once again gave people less reasons to choose state actors over community ones in dispute processing.

And the fourth mechanism was the creation of new spaces that acted as buffers on the boundaries of the state and non-state machineries of dispute processing, where postulational values identified with "others" and those the community identified with, held equal prominence.

These structural modifications that non-state actors had developed have contributed to their evolution. Far from resulting in these village communities living in a bubble insulated from the effects of state law, these mechanisms were nothing less than evidence of an intense engagement with state law because as Pirie (2013, 38) highlights (about Sally Falk Moore's study of semi-autonomous social fields) the "possibility that someone could invoke" state law and its regulatory systems and "appeal to its enforcement agencies, shaped the context in which informal norms were developed and played out."

The following section discusses in more detail, though not necessarily in this order, how these mechanisms worked to reinforce the postulational values the community identified with and the changing nature of non-state actors in this light, revealing thus an engagement of non-state forums with state law and its systems. It begins with the description of the various types of non-state actors and forums that people in Gonjhé and those from the villages in the Dharamgarh valley took recourse to in the processing of their grievances and disputes. Here, I also examine the nature of impact the interaction between the different layers of legality has on dispute processing within the layers where non-state actors and mechanisms are predominant.

4.4 Resisting the state? The working of community-based mechanisms to emphasise postulational values of the community

The very creation of several layers of legality that a dispute is expected to pass through before reaching the arena where state actors are active was one of the ways in which the community tackled and countered the threat posed to postulational values of the community laws. In Gonjhé as we see from the diagram (see Chapter 3, Figure 3.1, page 69), there are a number of layers of legality involving the key participation of non-state forums and actors, which were more than those in the villages of the Dharamgarh valley. The type of non-state actors and forums akin to a *pancāyat*, or a body of community members – usually wisemen or elders – holding authority in dispute processing, were far more evident in Gonjhé than in the village communities of the Dharamgarh valley. In the village communities of the Dharamgarh valley, there was only one layer of legality between the family and the state actors, and this was shared by the authorities of the *birāderi* and individual actors such as *shiyāné*. In Gonjhé, contrastingly, there was a layer of legality where the *Bhāvkī* was prominent, another where it was the *Mandaḷ*, and a third in which the *Samāj* played the key role. Individual actors such as the barefoot lawyers held space in an independent layer of legality.

I observed that a greater number of layers of legality had two impacts on engagement with state law. The first was that if a dispute within the community followed the popularly expected method of processing, that is, proceeding from processing by the self to the community governed layers, and then to the layers involving state actors; the more the number of layers, the more the attempts to process the same dispute. Greater numbers of layers of legality involving non-state actors meant that the dispute processing would remain for longer within the ambit of the community's control with emphasis on community laws. Simultaneously, there was also the likelihood that several attempts at processing would diminish the gravity of the disputing situation, with time consequently decreasing the motivation of disputants from proceeding further into the state arena. As a result of this, in Gonjhé, either the actual processing of the disputes never reached the layers involving state actors, or some insignificant aspect of it invoked the authority of state actors in order to improve bargaining positions in the non-state sphere of processing. The second impact of more layers was the consequence this had on the flow of state law from the legislature to the individual. Moore (1973) explained how state law is impacted on by different forces as it travels through different semi-autonomous social fields. Likewise, the more layers of legality a state law travelled through, the lower the likelihood of its prominence in dispute processing at the level of the self and the family.[14] Concurrently, this would also lead to what I term as "thinning" of the significance of the postulational values identified with "others", including those of state law, thereby reducing their threat to the thrust of the values of community laws.[15]

It must not be forgotten, however, that the converse of this situation was also true and evident in the village communities of the Dharamgarh valley. Since the village communities were located very remotely – away from the market area, tourist destinations, and urban centres generally – the threat to community laws from the laws of the state was perceived to be far less. Fewer layers of legality involving non-state actors were one element of evidence of this. But fewer layers of legality meant stronger competition between the postulational values of state law and community laws that coexisted in each layer; resulting often as we see in Chapter 5 in the postulational values of state law having more significance during dispute processing at the level of the self and the family in such situations. Here we see therefore, that the identity postulates of law of the village communities in Gonjhé and Dharamgarh valley did in fact regulate the extent and manner in which state law would be engaged with in dispute processing within the community.

The following sections will elaborate how the various non-state forums and actors that were active in dispute processing actually functioned in order to retain dispute processing within the community's control, which in turn will shed light on the nature of their engagement with state law.

4.4.1 Demystifying the Pancāyat*: About layers of legality engaging the* Birāderi, Bhāvkī, Mandaḷ, *and* Samāj

Pancāyats, a council of five men engaged in regulation of caste and/or village affairs, were often referred to as "Panch-Parmeshwar".

> *Panca* means five, and *Parmeshwar*, God; so that *Panca-Parmeshwar* means Council (of five) which is equivalent to God. The magical figure five has some special symbolic significance in India. The Universe is made up of five elements, earth, water, fire, air and [a]ether; five senses are at the disposal of man, the hand with which we work is made up of five fingers. So that the magic figure five represents "wholeness". (Bose 1960, 11)

A group of elderly men – usually from the same caste, sub-caste, village or religion – gathered under a tree or in the village square to decide the fate of certain parties to a dispute is the typical picture that shoots back into the mind

14 The opposite situation would also hold equally true according to this proposition. In that, in the case where there is a greater number of layers of legality, community laws and their postulational values, including *izzat* and *dharma*, hold less significance in the processing of disputes in the layers involving the engagement of state actors.

15 The term "thinning" here is used to mean "diminishing impact or influence"; in the context of the postulational values of certain laws.

when the term "*pancāyat*" falls before one's eyes (see also Headley 2015). This picture was further calibrated by the media, which relies on pictures of moustached men with elaborate turbans to complement their updates about the arbitrary use of power by "*pancāyats*" to serve nerve chilling diktats (Lemons 2010, 64–65). Even a fresh researcher like myself could not escape these images, particularly because the last pieces of writing providing any in-depth insight and analysis of dispute settling by *pancāyats* – state and non-state – appear between the 1960s (Cohn 1959; Bose 1960; Ishwaran 1964; Cohn 1965) and the 1980s, a period that saw the hopeful introduction followed by the hasty suspension of the "Nyay Panchayats" (Meschievitz and Galanter 1982; Galanter 1989).[16] But today, more than twenty years later, on the basis of my fieldwork, I argue that the above stereotypical image does not fit entirely the picture of every *pancāyat*. While, in essence, the role of a *pancāyat* in dispute processing may be broadly similar, there is tremendous heterogeneity in their nature and form, as also in their constitutions, and as a consequence their methods and perceptions about what constitutes "*nyāy*" (justice) (see Sen 2009, 20–22 for the concept of *nyāy*).

In Gonjhé, the *Bhāvkī*, the *Mandaḷs*, and the *Samāj*, and in Uttarakhand, a meeting of *shiyāné* or the *birāderi*, all constitute *pancāyats*. More specifically, since members of such *pancāyats* belonged to the same caste,[17] they would fall within the category of what are today more popularly known in India as "caste (*jāt) pancāyats*". The jurisdiction of caste *pancāyats* extends mostly to issues related to their specific caste and no further. Moreover, there may be different levels of such caste *pancāyat*. The decisions of some caste *pancāyat* hold force only within their caste group residing in a particular village or region, while in certain other cases *pancāyats* (usually higher than the village or regional ones) are able to make decisions that hold force over members of the caste irrespective of their location. The *Samāj* in Gonjhé belonged to the second category, where, along with regulation of caste affairs in Gonjhé, it was also responsible to decide issues for the entire Koḷī community living in a region spread over five villages along this coastal strip (see Chapter 2, page 45). The *pancāyats* observed matched the essentialised image to the extent that these were mostly gatherings of

16 Exception to this are the works of Solanki (2011) and the edited volume on non-state actors in the north-eastern states of India by Pereira et al. (2018).

17 Hayden (1999) argues that there is no such thing as a "village panchāyat". The data collected in Gonjhé coincides with Hayden's argument, in that, since Gonjhé was predominantly a one caste village (excepting the few Muslim families), the caste panchayat of the Koḷī was not distinct from the village panchāyat. The *Samāj* was thus a caste *pancāyat* as well as the village *pancāyat*. In the villages in the Dharamgarh valley, my experience was different. In multi-caste villages, there were certain issues that called for the attention of the village as a whole and in such instance *shiyāné* from different *birāderis* (caste groups) came together. Power dynamics, however, did result in the *shiyāné* of a dominant caste (in terms of social hierarchy or number) holding sway over the discussions in such meetings. But unlike Hayden's observations, such a *pancāyat*, irrespective of the manner in which it worked was understood as a "village *pancāyat*" within these communities.

men in a public space,[18] the village or neighbourhood temple. But that is where the stereotype met its end. These gatherings, as is alleged in several media reports and litigation claims, were not always ad hoc and sporadic. The *Samāj*, for instance, met very regularly on the tenth of every month and on the occasions that this meeting could not be held on the said date, a circular announcing the date to which the meeting was postponed was circulated among the presiding members and prospective applicants, whose issues were to be heard at such a meeting.[19] Much unlike the setting of a court, applicants and presiding members of the *Samāj* – some dressed in the traditional Koḷī attire and others in white shirts and pants – all sat in the temple premises in a continuous circle. This made it fairly challenging for an outsider to decipher the applicants from the witnesses (if any) and the presiding members.[20] It was neither compulsory nor common for people, other than those who had something to say before the *Samāj* or the *Manḍaḷ*, to attend these meetings. To this extent meetings of the *Samāj* were quite different from the "village panchayat" meetings that Moore (1993, 527–528) describes from the Meo village in Rajasthan, which was usually a large gathering of over seventy or more men comprising several individuals who appeared only to witness the dispute processing. During the meetings, emotions and enthusiasm both ran high and as a result decorum was difficult to maintain. The *Samāj*, one type of a *pancāyat*, was the highest body of authority in Gonjhé. Ideally, parties that sought their dispute to be processed by the *Samāj* should have already attempted to negotiate their difference before their respective *Mandaḷ* and the *Bhāvkī*, as well, if such parties were related to one another as agnatic kin. Only when the parties remained dissatisfied with the processing by these bodies could they make an application to the *Samāj* to hear them.

The *birāderi* meetings in the village communities of the Dharamgarh valley, were caste *pancāyat*s having jurisdiction only over issues arising within their caste group in their village. While the word *birāderi* refers to the kinship group (see Chapter 2, page 52), the term was also used to refer to the group of people who met to decide caste issues or disputes. Their meetings were not as regular and formalised as those of the *Samāj* or *Mandaḷ*s in Gonjhé. An application to the *birāderi* to process a dispute could be made in writing or orally. The *shiyāné* (see Chapter 2, page 52) gathered at the initiative of either one or all the disputing parties, who then had to also be willing to share the expenses involved in such a meeting. "If the party wants the entire village to preside over the issue, the parties must pay 100 or 200 Rupees along with the application. The money is given to

18 But see Strathern's (1985, 118) observation in the context of a community in Papua New Guinea, highlighting: "formal dispute settlement in which men alone are prominent, although the character of their transactions here cannot be fully understood without appreciation of the adjustment of relations among kin of both sexes and in the domain of domestic production where women are as significant as men." My own fieldwork in both village communities revealed insights similar to Strathern's observation. See section on female *shiyāné* on page 96.
19 Interview with secretary of the *Samāj*, Gonjhé (Maharashtra), May 1, 2015.
20 Field notes of *Samāj* meeting, Gonjhé (Maharashtra), February 10, 2015.

the man who delivers the circular to the villagers. Whereas if the party only wants the *Grām Pradhān* to make a decision, an application is made accordingly and the *Pradhān* can select some people and even go to the *verandah* of the parties and decide the issue," explained Mohansingh Meher, the former *Grām Pradhān* of Khasi village, which was a single caste village.[21] Unlike the *Samāj* in Gonjhé, the constitution of the body that gathered to hear a dispute in the village communities of Dharamgarh valley differed, depending on the party's preferences and the nature of dispute or grievance at hand. "In fact when there is a dispute to be decided, if it is an old dispute that is still being processed, the *Pradhān* and *panch* in whose term the dispute had arisen will be called to discuss a possible settlement or solution to the problem that has arisen," explained Mohansingh Meher.[22] This helped the new group of *shiyāné* who were to decide the dispute, understand the history and the contexts in which this dispute may have arisen, and possibly even the commitments the parties had made to one another in previous meetings. The meeting would comprise *shiyāné* from the *birāderi* who were commonly acknowledged by the entire caste group as reputable knowledgeable, and fair. In mixed caste villages, if the dispute concerned the entire village, then the *pancāyat* that met was a village *pancāyat*, which comprised *shiyāné* from the different caste groups (*birāderis*) in the village. The *Grām Pradhān* of the village, however, had the privilege, depending on his rapport with the *birāderi*, to participate in both the *birāderi pancāyats* as well as village *pancāyats*. Popularly perceived as an agent of the state, his presence was often strategically ensured, lest the parties decided to pursue the matter in a state forum in which case he would, if required, be the only individual (expected and allowed) from the village to appear in the court as "witness".[23]

The above data shows that the form of *pancāyats* in both locations was very different. The impact of institutional plurality in the arena of dispute processing was evident in the changing nature of the forms – the manner in which presiding members dressed and held themselves – but also in the very manner in which these *pancāyats* functioned. While in Gonjhé, the term *pancāyat* was still used sometimes to refer to the meetings of a *Bhāvkī* or the *Samāj*, in the villages of Dharamgarh valley I was confronted with the difficulty of making members of certain communities understand what I meant by the term "*pancāyat*". In Uttarakhand, the *pancāyat* was spoken about as a "thing from the past", often with references to the "Nyay Panchayats" that were introduced under the Uttar Pradesh Panchayati Raj Act, 1947 (Kushawaha and Singhvi 1977, 21–22), which no

21 Expenses could include organising tea for the *shiyāné* individuals and buying stationery such as paper and ink for documentation, if any. Interview, Khasi (Uttarakhand), March 11, 2016.

22 Interview, Khasi (Uttarakhand), March 11, 2016.

23 Being an agent of the state, village communities understood that participating in bureaucratic procedures whether of the state or otherwise was part of the *Grām Pradhān's* "professional" duty. Generally, however, people were not encouraged to appear in court as witnesses since this meant taking sides between members of their own extended family, that is the *birāderi*.

longer applies to Uttarakhand since its separation from Uttar Pradesh.[24] Despite this, though, what remained common to the bodies in both locations was the approach, which is best explained in the words of Felstiner, Abel and Sarat from their article *The emergence and transformation of disputes: Naming, blaming and claiming* (1981):

> some types of dispute processing seek to narrow the disputes with which they deal in order to produce a construction of events that appears manageable. Others are alive to context and circumstance. They encourage a full rendering of events and exploration of the strands of interaction, no matter where they lead (Felstiner, Abel and Sarat 1981, 642).

*Pancāyat*s in the village communities of Gonjhé and the Dharamgarh valley exemplified this latter type of dispute processing. They examined disputes in background of the social and circumstantial milieu in which they arose. The metamorphosis in the nature of *pancāyat*s, however, seems to have been part of their competition with other non-state actors to retain authority, credibility and power. There was a variance in authority of the different non-state actors on the basis of individual preferences, their socio-cultural conditioning, and the context of the dispute. So, for instance, if it was the *Samāj* that held highest authority in Gonjhé, it was goddess Kokiladevi and the system of spirits, deities and *puchiāri*s that commanded maximum authority over dispute processing in the villages of Dharamgarh valley, ensuring once again to balance out the tension between the postulational values in favour of those the community identified with. The next section describes this mechanism of dispute processing activated in both locations; however, it was manifested to a lesser extent in Gonjhé than in the villages of the Dharamgarh valley.

4.4.2 Seeking out the supernatural

A mechanism that people in Gonjhé and in the Dharamgarh valley popularly resorted to, sometimes contemporaneously with other dispute processing mechanisms, if not as the "only" or the "last" resort, was to seek out the guidance and intervention of the religious and supernatural elements for processing of their disputes. The Koḷī people accessed a *bhagat* and the mountain folk met with a *puchiāri* for this purpose. Ghurye (1957, 48) describes the *bhagat* as a "priest magician" and Punekar (1959, 169) describes the *bhagat* as "spiritual heads" and further distinguishes between the *Bāvā Bhagat* (the religious priest) and the *Bhutāchā Bhagat* (the one who deals with spirits) (Punekar 1959, 170–171). In the villages of Uttarakhand, a *puchiāri* was commonly consulted to know if a misfortune (social, financial, health related or otherwise) was caused by the

24 Notes from conversations with advocate Bora and deed writer Mahesh Pant in Chilbasa (Uttarakhand) and former *Grām Pradhān* Ramchandra Joshi, Devali (Uttarakhand), December 2014.

intervention of spirits or deities (*devī* or *devtā*). The *puchiāri* would inform the individual if the misfortune was a result of the intervention of Kokiladevī or any other deity or spirit; the disputes that caused such an intervention and the likely solutions to their problems. While literature in India describing dispute processing mechanisms involving supernatural elements and actors such as the *bhagat* and *puchiāri* (Harper 1957; Gough 1960, 50; Baxi 1976, 60; Agrawal 1992; Suzuki 2008; Malik 2016) is limited, fieldwork in both Maharashtra and Uttarakhand, however, revealed that there was extensive reliance on dispute processing mechanisms that involved supernatural and religious elements.

As explained in an earlier chapter (see Chapter 2, page 38 and 47), both the Koḷī and the village communities in the Dharamgarh valley had a very intimate connection with their natural surroundings. The Koḷī were dependent on the sea for their livelihood and lived in close proximity to it; the people in the Dharamgarh valley also had a complex connection with nature because of the topography of the region – a mountainous terrain thick with forests and extreme but also sometimes unpredictable and hazardous weather conditions. Agriculture as the primary source of livelihood in these villages also compelled an intimate connection of the hill-folk with their natural surroundings. As a result, a large part of the manner in which these communities planned their day depended on what the weather and natural conditions permitted. This I gather, had a profound influence on their belief system and their inordinate faith in the power of "nature" and the supernatural (see also Doye 2015), which in turn precipitated into the manner in which these communities tackled dispute situations as well.[25]

In Maharashtra, the prevalence of the Maharashtra, Prevention and Eradication of Human Sacrifice and Other Inhuman, Evil and *Aghori* Practices and Black Magic Act, 2013 had become well-known in most communities at the time of my fieldwork. A fair amount of propaganda by the media and activists who campaigned for this law surrounded the enactment of this legislation. Police officers in the local police outpost at Mānjai or even in the *tālukā* headquarter of Gorāi were observed to often make a mention of this law and its penal consequences in their interactions with disputing parties from the Koḷī community, especially when allegations included practice of "witchcraft", "black magic", and the involvement of *bhagats*.[26] All of this contributed to propelling the exaggerated implications of this state law to travel fairly quickly among the Koḷī people. While people in Gonjhé stated that they did not know the exact content of the code, they were aware that this law criminalised "all" practices that were based on superstitions and blind faith (*andhaśraddha*).[27] Interestingly, however, this legislation prohibits only

25 See Ghurye (1957, 48) and Punekar (1959, 23) with reference to further description about the religious life of the Mahadev Koḷī and Son Koḷī. The customs of the Koḷī in Gonjhé overlap considerably with the customs of these groups.

26 Notes from several interactions with the police constables at the police station and observation of a dispute being mediated by police personnel at the police station, Gonjhé (Maharashtra), February 3, 2015.

27 Notes from fieldwork in Gonjhé (Maharashtra), January to June 2015, and May to June 2016.

a specific list of practices. Nevertheless, this knowledge among the locals had a particular impact on my data collection. Firstly, the Koḷī people were reluctant to endorse this mechanism as a method of dispute processing prevalent in the community. This made any conversation about their experiences with the employment of this mechanism rather challenging. That I was a lawyer added to their prejudice, and people remained very cautious. Most experiences that were related to me were either "hearsay" or that of "someone the respondents knew well", but never admittedly "their own". Secondly, consequent to the enactment of this law, practitioners of rituals – primarily a *bhagat* – that facilitated access to this mechanism of dispute processing had gone underground, making it extremely difficult to even identify such individuals, let alone interview them.

In Uttarakhand, in contrast, the mechanism invoking the intervention of spirits and deities, besides being well-established, was also accepted and acknowledged widely. "We would be finished, if this practice was prohibited! (*Hum mar jayenge, agar idhar aise ho gaya toh)*," was Hira Meher's reaction when I shared with him information about the law against *andhaśraddha* in Maharashtra.[28] "Finished" was his expression to explain the fact that the village communities in his region would find themselves at a complete loss in certain situations if they were prohibited from taking recourse to supernatural and religious elements. Hira was a young man from Khasi who after spending several years of employment in Delhi had returned to live in his village. He worked as a security guard for a small private establishment close to the Dharamgarh market. The absence of a state law regulating any aspect of the mechanism of invoking the intervention of spirits and deities for dispute processing definitely made people more comfortable and expressive in discussions about their perceptions and experiences with this system. This allowed me to explore the mechanism far more widely in the Dharamgarh valley compared to Gonjhé.

This mechanism of dispute processing also operated quite differently in Maharashtra and Uttarakhand. What was common though was the presence of religious norms, ritualistic practices, and supernatural elements to the way these processes unfolded and were understood. In both locations misfortunes related to finances, health, social situations, and general turmoil (*aśānti*) in the household were considered a sign of such elements being at play.[29]

In Gonjhé I learned that the *bhagat's* help was sought very often in order to balance out the disproportionate bargaining positions between two disputing parties. Such an unevenness in bargaining positions may have been the result of the hierarchy within kinship relations, power dynamics within the community or just differing economic conditions. Even though the intervention of a *bhagat* was widely sought by several people in Gonjhé for different kinds of disputes, the disputing

28 Conversation with Hira Meher, Dharamgarh market (Uttarakhand), March 2016.

29 The term *śānti* means "peace and stability", *aśānti*, the opposite means "unpeaceful" implying unsettling circumstances either due to a troubled state of mind or troubling situations in one's close surroundings leading to general disturbed state of mind of one or more individuals claiming the existence of *aśānti*.

party that resorted to the services of a *bhagat* was likely to draw public disapproval (possibly in consequence of the law as well) and as a result, these activities were conducted in a fairly clandestine manner. However, since the belief in the power of these practices was shared by the entire community, alleged repercussions of such consultations were nevertheless evident to the disputing parties themselves.

In the Dharamgarh valley, the avenues for seeking out the intervention of the supernatural in the processing of disputes were many and more diverse. In times of trouble, when an individual felt that s/he had been unjustly treated, such an individual "called out" to his or her family deity or Kokiladevi (also known as Goddess Bhagwati or Bhagwati *Mātā*) to seek such deity's intervention in helping him or her settle the dispute favourably. Kokiladevi is one of the many local deities in the Kumaon Himalayas that is not strictly a part of the more popular Hindu pantheon. One of the significant differences between these local deities and gods of the Brahmanical patheon was the very territorial nature of these gods. These deities were very much linked to the land and a particular area, and they often required their followers to perform rituals and celebrations in particular ways (Baindur 2016). Since acquiring information in Gonjhé had been a challenge, the case studies in this section focus on experiences with seeking out the intervention of Kokiladevi for dispute processing from the village communities in the Dharamgarh valley (and also beyond).[30] While the experiences of people from the villages in the Dharamgarh valley remain central, interviews carried out at the various temple premises extend to areas in other parts of this region.

The practice of invoking the intervention of the goddess was brought into play not just simultaneously with other dispute processing mechanisms, but also as locals described it, more commonly when an individual had already exhausted all other mechanisms or because s/he could not afford to access any or some of them (www.jagran.com 2016). "A person who has been unable to find *nyāy* in any other forum will ultimately come here," said the young priest (*pundit*) Joshi, one of the priests at the main temple of Kokiladevi located in Pankhu in Pitthoragarh district.[31] While describing this mechanism and reasons for its appeal, respondents explained to me how Kokiladevi was the "*nyāy ki devtā*" (goddess of justice) or "Supreme Court" referring to her jurisdiction and powers as being more extensive than the highest state court as well.[32] Local replicas of the temple in the form of shrines existed in nearly every village or group of villages in Pitthoragarh district.

30 Kokiladevi is one of the many deities looked upon as "Gods of Justice" in this region of Pitthoragarh district and Bageshwar as this region is believed to be primarily within her "territorial jurisdiction". "Goludev", whose main temple is located in village Chittai of Almora district (Uttarakhand) has also been written about in this context (Agrawal 1992; Malik 2016).

31 Interview with temple priest, Pankhu (Uttarakhand), March 30, 2016. There is one main temple of the goddess located in Pankhu. However, smaller shrines dedicated to the goddess can be found in almost every other village or cluster of villages across the district.

32 Baindur (2016) and Malik (2016) make similar observations about the manner in which "Goludev", another deity of justice in the region is perceived.

Thick bunches of petitions, appeals, and settlement deeds in English, Hindi, and Kumaoni hung from nails near the main entrance into the inner quarters of the main temple in Pankhu and other smaller temples dedicated to the goddess in different villages or *tālukās* of Pitthoragarh and Bageshwar district. There were appeals to the Goddess from those seeking justice in land disputes, those seeking revenge for the ill health or death of their close ones, and even from those seeking to settle scores in matrimony related disputes, to name a few. There were also written records of settlement deeds, where the parties expressed the peaceful settlement of their dispute and the removal of all ill feelings and doubts that they bore against one another. Then there were people who appealed to the goddess for fulfilment of their wishes – birth of a male child, success in finding a job, and marriage into a respectable household. It was impossible to read all the petitions for the sheer quantity of their number as well as for reasons of lack of legibility in handwriting.[33]

While narratives about how Kokiladevi's intervention was sought, marked all types of disputes, a majority of the narratives as well as my observations at the sessions of a *puchiāri* revealed that the goddess's help was sought most popularly in property-related disputes. Typically, anyone who was frustrated with a land-related dispute, either due to arbitrary encroachment by another individual or due to unequal partition of property between family members or for any other reason, would in vain "call out" to the Goddess seeking her help. The "call" to the goddess was in the form of a *manauti* or individual pledge to make an offering to the goddess when an appeal to her had been fulfilled (Agrawal 1992; Malik 2016, 206).[34] In the case of Kokiladevi, this involved the gifting of a brass bell to her and the sacrifice of one or more goats to her assistants (*ān-bāṇ)*. In all probability, as was narrated, this would cause some misfortune to fall upon the opposite party against whom the help of the goddess was sought. It was explained by *pundit* Joshi that the goddess made a decision on how to punish the wrongdoer and her *ān-bāṇ* (assistants), such as Golu *devtā*, carried out the punishments.[35] "The Goddess is like the

33 For more details about such written documents, see Agarwal's (1992) study based on an analysis of all the written petitions and settlement deeds he found in the temple of Goludev in Chittai near Almora.

34 Like Kokiladevi there are other deities in other districts of Uttarakhand who are worshipped for the same reasons. C.M. Agrawal (1992) and Malik (2016) have done a study on the worship of Goludev, another deity who is also believed to mete out justice. While Kokiladevi remains most popular in Pitthoragarh district, Goludev's temple in Chitai village near Almora town is accessed more by people in Almora district. My fieldwork in the Kokiladevi temple coincides with the data provided by Agrawal with respect to the worship of Goludev revealing that the manner of invoking the intervention of both deities is identical.

35 Kokiladevi has several *ān-bāṇ* (assistants). According to mythological folklore, Goludev in one of his forms (*avatārs*), known as Bhandāri Golu, is the leader of Kokiladevi's assistants. Malik (2016) who has written about "Goludev" also writes about this *avatār*. It is in another *avatār*, however, Goludev is worshipped as a deity in himself and characterised locally in the same manner as Kokiladevi (footnote 34).

judge: she will hear the parties and make a decision about the type of punishment. Her assistants will then implement her order," said *pundit* Joshi.[36]

Presiding members of *pancāyats* also clarified that the Kokiladevi held exclusive jurisdiction over the disputes in which she received a plea for intervention. Speaking from his experience as a member of several *pancāyats* (*panch*) for nearly thirty-five years, Hayatsingh Bhandari, a former *Grām Pradhān* from Panchwari village said that in disputes where the *Mātā* (mother) had been called upon,[37] the *pancāyat* did not have the right to preside. "If the *panch* nevertheless preside over such a matter, even the *panch* will be penalised by the goddess," he said.[38] In addition to this, there are strict rules of conduct that followed the intervention of the goddess in a dispute. Gopilal Rawat, a *panch,* who had accompanied the heirs of some disputing parties from his village for a *pūjā* to mark the settlement of their differences, said "When there is a dispute and the goddess is called upon to intervene, some rules of conduct must be followed [between the parties]. In a dispute involving the goddess, the disputing parties must not interact with one another or eat with one another. They must not celebrate festivals and occasions together and generally there should be very little interaction with one another. This is to continue even among the heirs of the disputing parties. And if good relations are restored then the disputing parties or their heirs, depending on in which generation the relations are restored, must jointly conduct a *pūjā* before the Goddess. Otherwise, all parties and/or their heirs will be victims of the goddess's wrath [and will face unfortunate circumstances]."[39]

Misfortunes that were an expression of the deity's penalisation were either in the form of grave monetary loss (death of cattle, loss of gold, etc.) or deterioration in health of the opposite party or one of his/her close family members. This was usually discovered when an individual was unable to find a "logical" cause for his/her the economic loss or failed to be cured by "a doctor's medicines" in case of a health issue.[40] A *puchiāri* was then consulted to know if such misfortune was

36 Interview with temple priest at Pankhu (Uttarakhand), March 30, 2016.

37 The term *Mātā* (mother) is often used to refer to any Hindu goddess. In this case, since the discussions were about Kokiladevi, it was with reference to her that this term was used.

38 Interview with Hayatsingh Bhandari, Panchwari (Uttarakhand) April 2, 2016.

39 Interview with Gopilal Rawat from Chaubati (Uttarakhand), March 30, 2016. He had accompanied the heirs of three brothers who had a dispute over land. While the original disputants had died, over generations the relationship between the heirs had improved, so much so that the present heirs conducting the *pūjā* did not even know the exact cause and gravity of the dispute. However, since they had not done a *pūjā* before the goddess, despite improvement in relations, members of all three families had been falling ill constantly.

40 When I asked Kismetsingh Rawat from Chaubati (same case as referred to in above footnote 39) how he and his cousins had come to know that Goddess Bhagwati was revealing her wrath, the heir of one of the brothers said that they had gone to the *puchiāri*. "There was illness in our respective families. Illnesses that no doctor's medicine could cure" said Rawat, who along with his cousins had conducted a *godān* at the temple in Pankhu in settlement of a dispute that happened five generations ago. Interview with Kismetsingh Rawat at Kokiladevi temple in Pankhu (Uttarakhand), March 30, 2016.

caused by the intervention of spirits or the goddess. The *puchiāri* would inform the individual if the misfortune was a result of the intervention of Kokiladevi or any other deity or spirit; the disputes that caused such an intervention and the likely solutions to the problem.

Practice had it that aggrieved parties were less likely to visit a *puchiāri* within the vicinity of their village. A *puchiāri* in close proximity was likely to be aware of local friendships and animosities and kinship ties, and it was therefore apprehended that she was likely to base her interpretation on the basis of such knowledge. Therefore, a *puchiāri*, like the one whose sessions I observed was usually unaware of the background, networks, and connections of those who consulted her because the majority of people who visited her came from very far off villages. Similar to Epstein's (1974, 362) description of how an exorcist functioned in a Mysore village, the *puchiāri* would usually point out the category of people between whom the dispute may have occurred, sometimes even narrowing down to how many men and women the dispute involved, and in which generation the dispute had occurred. Unequal distribution of property being the cause of many disputes in this region, it seemed to be highlighted most often as the cause of disputes. Such an interpretation left the actual choice of accused to the victim, and an opportunity to reinstate relations of discord with whosoever the victim chose.

The period between the first consultation with a *puchiāri* and the aggrieved party being relieved of the misfortune they were faced with, was interspersed with a series of rituals, sometimes involving only the immediate family of the aggrieved person, and many times extending to involvement of the entire *birāderi*. Speaking with reference to *jāgar* rituals, but also true of all the other rituals such as *ghaṇiyāli* and the various offerings made to the spirit or deity, Malik explains that "the participant's return to health or integrity is contingent upon the intervention of divine power that is made present during these rituals". At the beginning, the *puchiāri* advised the aggrieved party to carry out certain simple rituals to confirm the specific deity whose intervention had caused the misfortune. The *puchiāri* of course provided a general idea but it had to be confirmed before proceeding further. For the *puchiāri* this of course meant a repeated visit from the aggrieved individual and an additional donation. Confirmation was usually achieved through making an offering of specific foods to the specific deities the *puchiāri* had discerned to have intervened. In the case of Kokiladevi, for instance, such an offering consisted of a rice and lentils preparation (*khichaḍi*) and sweets. If the severity of the cause for grievance, usually health or financial issues, reduced upon making such an offering, the intervention of the said deity(-ies) could be safely assumed and more elaborate ritualistic procedures to process the dispute and appease the deity (-ies) could then be pursued. Such procedures involved the aggrieved individuals, either on their own or along with the party on whose *manauti* the goddess had intervened, performing a *jāgar* or a *ghaṇiyāli* to awaken the deity followed by a *sthāpanā* and a proper *pūjā* to appease the deity and seek his or her forgiveness.[41] In the case of

41 *Jāgar* means "waking" or "staying awake". "The *jāgar* can therefore be described as an intense ritual of "awakening" for both the deities and devotees" (Malik 2016, 204). For more details on this ritual, also see Krengel (1999) and Fanger (1990). In the

Kokiladevi, the goddess being vegetarian had to be pleased with a *godān* and a *prasād* of sweets.[42] Rituals for her *āṇ-bāṇ*, however, required the sacrifice of a goat.

On the question of whether invoking the intervention of Kokiladevi in dispute processing was competitive with pursuing a case in court, there were mixed responses. Especially, with regard to the duration of dispute processing and the financial expenditure that accompanied it, some respondents like Shankardutt Bhatt felt that dispute processing involving Kokiladevi was simpler than going to court. "A person might die, but he may still not get justice in a court", remarked Bhatt, referring to generations of heirs of the disputing parties having to face the penalisation by the goddess if a dispute in which her power had been invoked lay unresolved. At the time of the interview, Bhatt was visiting the local shrine for Kokiladevi near his village to conduct a *godān* to appease the goddess. He claimed to be experiencing some sort of disquietude (*ashānti*) in his home, which he believed was an expression of the goddess penalising his deceased father for having treated his deceased aunt (father's sister) unjustly with regard to some land issues. With regard to the financial expenditure incurred, Bhatt explained that expenditure all depended on how a person chose to appease the goddess. "What I did today – a *godān* – was not expensive. It cost me only Rs. 300. But yes, if the *pūjā* involves sacrificing a goat, it can be expensive. Even a little goat costs nothing less than Rs. 1,200 to 1,300," he said.[43] Taking a broader view of "expenditure", Deewan Pant another *pundit* (temple priest) at the main temple of Kokiladevi in Pankhu felt that dispute processing before the goddess was in any case less expensive than going to court. "One has to have the capability and courage (*sāmarthya*) to go court, isn't it? You need to make documents, appoint a lawyer (*vakīl*)." Then, referring to the conciliatory *pūjā* between another group of cousins who were the heirs of three brothers involved in a dispute over partition of family property, he remarked, "Today, look they have settled the matter and conducted this *godān* in Rs. 79. In court, not even an application can be made in

villages where I conducted fieldwork, the processes of conducting a *ghaṇiyāli* or *jāgar* were almost identical, though the recipients were different. A *jāgar* was primarily conducted to "awaken" a deity, usually a household deity, to exorcise the aggrieved person off the ghost (*bhūt*) that has possessed him or her. Whereas a *ghaṇiyāli* was conducted to "awaken" a deity usually to seek a solution to the grievance the person sponsoring such a ritual may be facing. Many times, however, a *ghaṇiyāli* was conducted only to please a family deity or in fulfilment of a vow. The *sthāpanā* involved building a shrine as a symbolic dedication to the *bhūt* or deity. It was usually putting together a mound of stones in the field (in case of a *bhūt*) or in an allocated area in the village (for deities), which was then worshipped from time to time.

42 *Godān* literally means donation of a cow to the temple or the Brahmin. However, since temples and Brahmins are no longer keen to rear the donated cows, a symbolic *godān* is carried out by conducting a *pūjā* of the permanently established marble statue of a cow in the temple premises. The priest receives a sum for carrying out this *pūjā* (Interview with Sharkardutt Bhatt, March 29, 2016 and observation of his *pūjā* before in the Bhagwati temple at Melatpur (Uttarakhand)).

43 Interview at Bhagwati temple, Melatpur (Uttarakhand), March 29, 2016.

Rs. 79. Forget application, not even a form will be filled for you in this amount."[44]

But then there were other respondents who felt that the court was a one-time solution to settling issues, whereas once the goddess was involved, dispute processing could go on for generations; with expenditure of time and money to be incurred even after the relations were restored. "Seeking the help of the Goddess can sometimes be more expensive than pursuing the case in court," related Janak Bhauriyal, a construction supervisor in a local NGO.[45] Bhauriyal continued to conduct a joint *pūjā* with the heirs of a man his grandfather had a dispute with. "Once the conciliatory *pūjā* is performed, there is a short game where three chits are folded and placed in a pot. On each chit is a number – usually one, three or five. The chit you pick decides the schedule of the *pūjā*s you must continue to conduct together. If the chit has the number one, you will have to conduct a *pūjā* every year, if it contains the number three, you will have to conduct the joint *pūjā* every three years and if it is five, then the ritual must be conducted every five years," he explained (see Chapter 5, page 129).

Like the *pancāyat*s in Gonjhé, this rather well-organised system in Uttarakhand that invoked spirits and deities also compelled the parties to negotiate their differences in order to restore peaceful relations. Experiential narratives revealed that Kokiladevi did not accept a dispute to be fully settled until the disputing parties performed a joint *pūjā* before her and ate together a meal of the *prasād* that was an offering to her or her assistants. According to the *puchiāris* and temple priests, a dispute was considered fully settled only when both the parties to the dispute, that had been the cause of the goddess's intervention, negotiated their differences and jointly performed a *pūjā*. Describing his experience with two (of the three brothers) who performed a conciliatory *pūjā* before the Kokiladevi temple in Melatpur village with regard to a dispute concerning the alleged unequal partition of family property between the three brothers, *pundit* Rajendra Upadhyay, the temple priest, said that he told the brothers that "rather than sacrificing this goat, it would have been better if they resolved their differences peacefully and did something good." The brothers who had come to conduct the *pūjā*, however, felt that *pundit* Upadhyay was speaking in favour of the brother who had not participated in the rituals. "But for me all three were equal and so I would speak fairly. Which brother was going to give me gold, just because I spoke in his favour," narrated *pundit* Upadhyay rhetorically.[46] According to *pundit* Upadhyay these rituals were of little use until all the three brothers resolved their differences. That would be the ultimate redressal to all their grievances. So long as each party continued to conduct their individual *pūjās*, it merely meant the incurrence of more expenditure in sacrificing goats and feeding *pundits*. However, an ideal situation like the one *pundit* Upadhyay favoured did not always occur. In most instances, where one of the parties to the dispute refused to participate in the joint

44 Interview with second *pundit* Deewan Pant, Pankhu (Uttarakhand), March 30, 2016.
45 Several interactions, Melatpur (Uttarakhand), December 2015 to May 2016.
46 Interview with *pundit* Rajendra Upadhyay, Melatpur (Uttarakhand), March 27, 2016.

conciliatory *pūjā*, the affected party proceeded to perform an appeaseable *pūjā*, which was believed to alleviate the unfortunate circumstances s/he was facing and supposedly cause the goddess to castigate the other party as well.

In this context, Bhauriyal's information about the continuation of this ritual of joint *pūjās* by the parties, even after their dispute was "settled", seemed like a mechanism to ensure that continued peace and order was maintained between the parties. So long as the *pūjās* continued, the parties were compelled at least once a year to have a meal together, which situation automatically facilitated cordial interaction extending to subjects beyond the dispute. Any further disputes that these parties may have engaged in were likely to be put to rest by this act of joint *pūjās*. Additionally, since the goddess was believed to have exclusive jurisdiction, the party(-ies) that invoked her intervention, in this moment, usually stopped pursuing their dispute in other forums.

Even though this mechanism was based on religious and other beliefs, factors that were closely connected to the daily lives of the people in the Dharamgarh valley; there was enough evidence to show that non-state actors within the other layers of legality, particularly the *birāderi* and the family, made utmost efforts to restrain disputes from being pursued within this outermost layer. One possible reason could be that just like in the case of disputes that reached the layers involving state actors for processing, matters where the goddess's intervention was invoked, then went "beyond the control" of the community and also the self. In both cases, there was the risk of chaos as a result of someone not taking a balanced approach and/or making excessive claims. As stated earlier in this chapter (see page 78), *pundit* Upadhyay felt that disputes were best resolved among the parties themselves either through intervention of families or the *birāderi*. Despite being a temple priest, he often dissuaded people from invoking the intervention of the goddess, as "it is easy to call upon the goddess, but quite challenging to ensure that she is ultimately pleased. And until this happens, a lot of money and time can be spent. Bhagwati is known to be pleased only when all disputing parties with a clean mind conduct the *pūjā*. But until then the financial or physical misfortunes will keep befalling either or both of the parties," he remarked.[47] Whether under the garb of the excessive financial expenditure this might invoke or the length of time that might pass before the dispute is processed, family members, *shiyāné*, and the *birāderi* always responded saying that it was better for parties to negotiate their differences within the layers of legality that involved them than seek out the intervention of the goddess. As *pundit* Upadhyay said: "One can get a decision in court, but justice by Bhagwati takes time. She can reveal her wrath on the opposite party over generations. And as far as expenditure is concerned, both are equally expensive. In both forums somebody has to be paid, and somebody has to be bribed."[48] Even though the postulational values that were reinforced through the mechanism involving religious and supernatural elements were those that the community identified quite closely with, it remained unclear as to why – besides of

47 Interview at the Bhagwati temple, Melatpur (Uttarakhand), March 27, 2016.
48 Interview at the Bhagwati temple, Melatpur (Uttarakhand), March 27, 2016.

course the need of those in power to retain their power – there was a social control to limit the processing of disputes from extending to this layer of legality involving the invocation of supernatural and religious elements. For people from the villages in the Dharamgarh valley, this mechanism (invoking the intervention of the Goddess Kokiladevi) held foremost authority and close to every dispute involved a part of its processing in this layer. Almost everybody who had experience with this mechanism disclosed that processing of a dispute (though at times delayed) was always fair and satisfactory within this layer of legality. What mattered was that the parties could have a situation of discord tackled in a respectable manner (*izzat se*) without power equations, caste rules and commitments towards their *dharma* being disturbed. Moreover, it was claimed that such processing did not draw them away from their communities, in a way that pursuit of a dispute engaging state actors was perceived to do.

4.4.3 Guides, mediators, advocates: Individual actors with the non-state machinery

In the different layers of legality we see in the diagrams in Chapter 3 (see page 69 and 70), besides community based bodies, there were also individual actors who played crucial roles in limiting the dispute processing to sphere(s) within the community. The existence of some of these actors, such as the "barefoot lawyers" (see page 114) in Gonjhé, led to the creation of a separate layer of legality, whereas some of these actors, like the *shiyāné* in the Dharamgarh valley, shared space with others in a particular layer of legality.

Pancāyats were as much about the collective conscience of a group of community members as they were about the individuals who comprised them. The examples below illustrate how the personal views of individuals bestowed with the titles of *puḍhārī* and *shiyāné* also intervened in and impacted at a certain level on the strategies people adopted in the processing of their disputes. While *puḍhārīs* and *shiyāné* formed part of *pancāyats*, they were also in their own right important focal points of power. In their view, a consistent thread of learning could be observed, and it was this capacity of theirs that made them popular as independent actors. Power here emanated from a combination of charismatic personality and the specialised knowledge they possessed, mostly as a result of personal experiences, increasing the appeal of these individuals as competent leaders and advisors (see also E. Moore 1993, 523).[49]

Puḍhārīs and *shiyāné*, in their individual capacities, were important actors in the processes of how people decided to tackle their disputes. In many ways, they were also responsible for shaping people's experiences with state forums, thereby becoming effective gatekeepers. In Gonjhé for instance, *puḍhārīs* played an

49 Foucault's (1979) description of the intertwining relationship between knowledge and power by pointing to the strategies used by some people to shape or change realities for others becomes fairly relevant to understand this dynamic of power.

important role in determining the process of forum shopping by an individual. On asking Ravindra Pavshe, a *puḍhārī* and barefoot lawyer from Gonjhé, whether people consciously made a difference between the various forums available to them for dispute processing, he said: "No. People come to a *puḍhārī* for advice and then the *puḍhārī* tells them where to place their dispute – before the police, before the *Samāj*, or then before the *Tanta Mukta Samiti*."[50] According to Pavshe, the common disputant was "ignorant". "They don't know anything. We tell them whom to approach," he summed up.

The role of these non-state actors varied from case to case. In some instances, they only acted in an advisory capacity, at other times they took on a role similar to that of an attorney – representing the individual who approached them, and in still other situations *puḍhārīs* and *shiyāné* assumed the position of a mediator, or even an adjudicator, deciding how best the parties should or could resolve their disagreement.

I argue that perceptions and opinions of individuals such as *puḍhārīs* and *shiyāné* in a community were an equally important indicator of the nature of non-state dispute processing as were *pancāyats*, consequently making a study of their biographies, and the manner in which they exercise power, crucial. It is for this reason that when I referred to the evidence from individuals I interviewed during fieldwork, I have tended to provide also some biographical background of their respective social situations and personalities.

4.4.3.1. Women's era: The female shiyāne *of Dharamgarh*

In Gangapur village in the Dharamgarh valley, which may in itself have been an exception, and therefore deserves mention, it is a fact that in addition to men, many of the *shiyāné* in this village were women. While wives of the *puḍhārīs* in Gonjhé were known to play an important role – although acting in the background – in determining the course of several initiatives their husbands took in their role as *puḍhārī*; in Gangapur, in many instances it was the woman who was at the forefront playing *shiyānī*.[51] The fact that women did not find a place in the public gatherings of *shiyāné* individuals (in the form of *pancāyat* or otherwise) or were taken less seriously in their positions as *Grām Pradhān*, did not undermine their potential as a *shiyāné* in their individual capacity. Here, too, we see that the formal-informal binary in assessing legal processes does not produce meaningful distinctions. Advice and help from female *shiyāné*, as I learned, was sought more often, but not only, in matrimonial and domestic disputes. Chandradevi Rathod, a *shiyānī* in Gangapur, related her experience when she was called upon by an errant husband, to intervene in a domestic dispute with his wife: "Just next door is a couple. The husband drinks a lot and always returns home in a state of

50 Notes from conversation with Ravindra Pavshe, Gonjhé (Maharashtra), January to June 2015. The *Tantā Mukta Gāv Samitī* is the Marathi name for the Dispute Free Village Committee (see page 127).

51 The term *shiyānī* is the female version of *shiyānā*.

intoxication rising to fight at the slightest instance. Finally, his wife said she would not eat or drink until he gave up alcohol. Last week she was in bed for three days continuously, she had neither eaten nor drunk anything. When the husband became worried, he came to call me requesting me to speak to his wife. I went with him to their home and spoke to his wife. I knew why she was doing this, and so I scolded the husband too. I said that he was the only one to blame for this state of hers. "Behave yourself. By drinking so much you are not only ruining your family's happiness but also harming your own body. It is okay to drink occasionally in small quantities, but such excessive consumption is unacceptable" I told him. It would only cause him trouble and lead his health to deteriorate. Eventually, I managed to make him promise to his wife that he would improve his ways. I also advised the girl that such extreme behaviour was not advisable, even though I sympathised with the reasons for her conduct" related Chandradevi, without disclosing the names of the parties.[52]

In disputes related to the domestic sphere, female *shiyānī* were often *suo motu* interveners and acted like other non-state actors to limit disputes from proceeding into further layers for processing. Khastidevi Rathore, another *shiyāni* from Gangapur, said that people from all castes in her village approached her. "Men and women both come to me. And if the situation turns very grave, I ask my husband to intervene," she said, giving the example of a matrimonial dispute from the neighbourhood.[53] The issue concerned the grievance of Vimla Rathod, a young wife, whose husband was addicted to alcohol and spent most of his days away and in a drunken stupor. This often led to the couple having arguments, which ended with the husband beating his wife, who had approached Khastidevi for help. "One day she arrived at my home saying that he had beaten her so badly that she had decided to go to the police station. I intervened and calmed her down. I explained [*samjhāyā*] to her that approaching the police station would only worsen her situation. "Her husband would get beaten and probably be kept in jail for a few days. Was that going to bring her any peace? Ultimately he was her husband and that she did have some relationship with him." And what good will going to the police station bring? It would only lead to gossip. Instead, I requested my husband to intervene and sound him out," said Khastidevi. Chandrasingh Rathore, Khastidevi's husband, was a retired police officer. His intervention had possibly brought to the notice of Vimla's husband the fact that his wife had begun "speaking" with other members of the community about his violent behaviour towards her and made domestic issues "public" (also see Chapter 5, page 133). "He beat her less after my husband intervened, but it has not stopped completely," she said. Here we also see the potential power of gossip in the community as a form of informal punishment or deterrent, and the husband's reaction shows that avoidance of negative publicity is an important consideration in such cases, which could easily spiral into more serious disputes (See Chapter 3, page 60 on gossip).

52 Interview, Gangapur (Uttarakhand), April 17, 2015.
53 Interview, Gangapur (Uttarakhand), April 21, 2015.

Khastidevi's prominent position as a *shiyānī* was attributable to a combination of factors. That she belonged to a relatively wealthy family was one part of it. Another factor for her respected position was the profession of her husband. Khastidevi's husband – Chandrasingh – used to be a police officer, a prominent actor in the sphere of dispute processing in the layers involving the state.[54] Khastidevi travelled to many places in the district with him, as he got transferred fairly often. While Chandrasingh had the reputation of being a fairly reclusive man and his work kept him away from the village for long periods, Khastidevi soon came to be acknowledged as a *shiyānī* because of her experience from having travelled extensively and that too in the company of a police officer, an actor in the judicial machinery of the state. The community attributed her wisdom and aptitude for fair judgment of a situation to this experience that she had gained. Her outgoing nature was a further bonus and encouraged people to reach out to her.

Chandradevi on the other hand, had not travelled far and wide like Khastidevi, but in fact had to her credit the long experience of having been an active member in one of the Mahilā Mangal Dals run by an *āśram* near Gangapur.[55] "We did a lot of work. Saved money and also opposed the production, sale, and consumption of alcohol in the village. On one or two occasions all of us women in this Dal went and destroyed the *dārū bhaṭṭi* which was located nearby. Every time drunken men created trouble on this road, it was us women who handled them – scolding them and even giving them a beating sometimes," said Chandradevi.[56] When I asked Chandradevi about her husband, she and Khastidevi, who had by then joined our conversation, giggled quietly. "Oh, he is a drunkard. He does nothing. She is the one who is always at the forefront," shared Khastidevi, praising Chandradevi as "the strong woman". Chandradevi was no longer a part of the Mahilā Mangal Dal. But the manner in which Chandradevi had exercised her agency, being at the forefront of its activities for many years, and also her prominent role in leading the protest against the *dārū bhaṭṭi*, was what she felt moulded the community's acknowledgement of her as a "*shiyānī*".

The strong intra-village networks of female *shiyāné* helped them remain informed and updated about how daughters-in-law, sisters-in-law, wives, and brothers in their village were getting along. This position of knowledge that

54 Notice here that Chandrasingh Rathod, though now a retired police officer, still held a reputation for knowing the law and possibly being able to implement it. The involvement of Chandrasingh in dispute processing in the non-state arena is an example of the free floating of elements belonging to one layer in other layers of legality.

55 A Mahilā Mangal Dal is a local women's group that functions like a self-help group. Primarily, these Mahilā Dals in the Dharamgarh valley were the initiative of a local NGO. Simultaneously though, the state body of the Grām Panchayat had also begun to promote the foundation of such Mahilā Dals. Through the platform of the Mahilā Dals, women are motivated to come together to make savings contributions and create a common fund, from which the women can then take loans for different purposes. Depending on the agenda of the institution instrumental in establishing the Mahilā Mangal Dal, a Dal may also engage in other social and welfare activities and work as a support group for other women from within the Dal and outside it.

56 A *dārū bhaṭṭi* is a place where alcohol is locally brewed.

female *shiyāné* held challenged traditional understandings of the "public" and "private". What was known by them was information that belonged to the internal sphere of the most basic social unit – the family. Men, by the mere virtue of being men in a highly patriarchal set-up, legitimately remained aloof from the domestic dynamics of all other families except their own. But it was socially acknowledged and accepted that women, particularly if they were *shiyāné*, would know of the happenings in this internal sphere, even if they were not actively a part of it. This unique position that the social set-up itself bestowed upon them caused the blurring of boundaries between the public and the private and possibly, as Khastidevi rightly articulated, "obligated female *shiyāné* to sometimes intervene *suo motu* to settle a dispute", something the male *shiyāné* admitted having rarely done.[57]

This entire section therefore shows how several layers of non-state actors acted and were coordinated in different capacities in the processing of disputes. What remained common to all of them was their emphasis on enforcement of community laws, incidental to which was their effort to retain as far as possible the processing of disputes within the layers involving community actors.

4.5 Structural adaptations: Learning from the State?

Another strategy to resist the state was the effort of nearly every non-state actor engaged in dispute processing to organise himself/herself, itself or themselves in a manner that had striking similarity to their counterparts in the state machinery. Bureaucratic practices like these, as Kirsch (2008, 185) explains are often enacted to exert power. I propose that this attempt by non-state forums to bureaucratise their performance was strategically made in order to seem overtly as "professional" as the state actors and forums. State law and its regulatory systems were viewed by the village communities as something external to their social contexts and often many community members (mis-)used this popular belief to their advantage in dispute processing. In the words of Kirsch (2008, 239), this practice of bureaucracy by the non-state forums, however, made the "absent present". Bureaucratisation by non-state forums resulted in integration of the practices perceived to belong to state actors into the local context. This was perceived to endow the affairs of a non-state forum with a tone of seriousness, but also meant to override some of reasons that seemed to induce community members to take their dispute to a state forum for processing.

57 "There is no good faith in society any more [*bhalāi kā zamānā nahi rahā*]. There is no point intervening in another person's dispute, unless s/he approaches you for advice. What happens in present day is, that the *puḍhārī* may enter in good faith to settle a matter and ultimately the parties turn around to blame the *puḍhārī* for the dispute itself; all this solely because he intervened of his own initiative," is what Ravindra Pavshe, a well-established *puḍhārī* from Gonjhé told me. This was his word of caution to overenthusiastic *puḍhārīs* wanting to "do good". Similar risks of intervening in disputes *suo motu* in the spirit of "social work" were echoed by men in Uttarakhand as well.

Meeting on a fixed day in the month; processing disputes only in the presence of a minimum number of *puḍhārīs*, which meant practising a method of quorum; the process of insisting on written applications from disputants, and the appointment of a chairman, secretary and treasurer were formalities that marked the working the *Samāj* and *Manḍaḷs* in Gonjhé. Complementing modifications in form, one also found variations in procedure that mimicked dispute processing methods in the layers involving state actors (see also Srinivas 2009a). For instance, the process of maintaining written records held importance in dispute processing whether at the level of families or within the layer involving the *pancāyats*. In addition, there was also an issue of whether or not to adopt the practice of following precedents, which stirred several discussions among non-state actors.[58] All these variations in form, however, seemed to make the non-state actors ostensibly look more and more similar to the state actors, though on closer inspection it became evident that the manner in which processing of disputes was carried out by non-state actors continued to remain alive to local sensitivities, community values, and indigenous approaches. Structural adaptations were thus another form in which non-state forums engaged with state law and its systems.[59] This guise of structural similarity, as the following sections show, was meant to increase the appeal of non-state forums and simultaneously draw members of the community away from dispute processing in the layers of legality involving state actors.

4.5.1 Written documentation: Lending the formal touch

Galanter (1968, 73) observes the elevation of "textual law over lesser bodies of customary law" as one of the "most remarkable and unanticipated results of the British administration of Hindu law." This may have been a beginning, but the elevation of all things in "text" over anything oral or customary was perceived as one of the most distinct characteristics of dispute processing by state forums and actors. "Lawyers turn the fate of cases on the basis of documents," said Ravindra Pavshe, a *puḍhārī* reputed for his familiarity with the state courts and police station, to Alka, a fisherwoman who had come to seek his advice in a matrimonial dispute.[60] Alka had eloped with her husband and had no marriage certificate. She now sought a separation from him and a share in his property as her maintenance. "But I have two children from him," she persisted, drawing Ravindra into launching into his favourite story of how a dead man was once made "alive" for the benefit of the court in the absence of a death certificate. In Gonjhé, as in the villages of the Dharamgarh valley, written documents were perceived to wield

58 Derrett (1961) highlighted in his study of Hindu law that regard for precedents was foreign to the system and observed that the rule of *stare decisis* diminished the flexibility of Hindu law. The debate in the Koḷī community over whether or not to follow precedents becomes totally understandable in this light. See also the *pudhari's* statement on page 108.

59 See van Binsbergen (1993) on bureaucracy as a result of interaction with state agencies.

60 Notes from a meeting between Ravindra, Alka and her sister in Ravindra's office, Gonjhé (Maharashtra), February 6, 2015.

tremendous power in state forums as evidence of what may (and may not) have transpired. To what extent this is actually true can be verified from case law and court room ethnographies.[61] But state and non-state actors, such as Ravindra, made no less effort in reinforcing this belief, particularly in contexts where activities were very unlikely to be recorded in writing. In a society where traditionally there has been no practice of written documentation, such beliefs worked to create illusory epicentres of power and keep people in awe and fear of authorities insisting on such procedures. Ravindra, a barefoot lawyer, was one such authority, who always asked people seeking his advice in the processing of a dispute, to bring along all the documents they had in support of their claim. "*Arey*, only documents speak in court. Even a thousand witnesses are not effective," said Ravindra, in another dispute, to a man who had been duped by his brother in a land dealing. Ravindra was an actor in the links that led a dispute to be pursued in the layers of legality involving state actors. His own experience as a litigant in the local *talukā* court, and the networks with state actors that he cultivated as part of being a *puḍhārī*, strengthened people's faith in the precision of his knowledge in this sphere, making him one of the key actors on the layers of legality that fell on the borders of the state and non-state machinery. Ravindra's experience had taught him that documents could turn the fate of a case in state courts. State actors, Ravindra stated, were unable to verify the actual contexts of a dispute. If at all, they were dependent on non-state actors to facilitate such verification. And so, he said, "Written documents can make the truth a lie and a lie the truth in court."[62]

The value of written documents in state courts was well known, but in a different layer of legality, non-state actors had also begun to replicate this process. The *Samāj* in Gonjhé maintained written records of the proceedings of every meeting, and also encouraged written applications from those who had enquiries or wanted the *Samāj* to look into their grievance or dispute (see also Derrett 1978, 78). "Notices are sent usually by hand. Postal notices don't reach on time. We select someone to carry out this job and pay him Rs. 200 for the task. On receiving the notice, the receiver must affix his signature or thumb impression on a copy of such a notice," explained Bhagwan Chogle, the secretary of the *Samāj*. The increasing use of written documentation was attributed to the rising levels of literacy in the Koḷī community. "When we send a notice, it lends a tone of seriousness to our working. It helps in reinforcing our authority in this community," explained P.N. Chogle, a senior member of this body. "Additionally, recording the proceedings of the *Samāj* helps everyone know what happened and transpired

61 See Berti (2011b) for the opposing relationship between depositions of witness in court and their affidavits.

62 Interview with Ravindra Pavshe, Gonjhé (Maharashtra), May 2015. Ravindra's opinion about how written documents worked in state courts was only one aspect of the general perception that people had about dispute processing in the state machinery Other perceptions were not very far from what Derrett observed them to be more than thirty years ago "and no one believes that truth is discovered in the regular courts (in which perjury and forgery figure constantly)" (Derrett 1982, 133).

in the previous meetings, what decisions were taken then, and this reduces the scope for debate about these issues," he continued.[63]

Written documents were also used by *birāderi* or village *pancāyat* in Uttarakhand to record the agreement dispute parties may reach during a *pancāyat*. The *Grām Pradhān* if involved in such *pancāyat* maintained a record of the dispute processing in his register. Explaining the format of written documents used in the *birāderi pancāyats* in Khasi, Mohansingh Meher, the former *Grām Pradhān* said, "We insist that the parties sign on a paper that says: "In the presence of god and the *Grām Pradhān* we have amicably settled the matter and now will not fight again over this issue. By doing so we make sure, the *Gram Panchayat* is not responsible in having compelled any sort of a compromise."[64]

The importance that state forums place on documents has definitely contributed to improving their worth even in negotiations at the societal level. In the villages in the Dharamgarh valley, written documentation was perceived to lend some sort of a finality to transactions; in fact, more than the documents, the process of recording something in writing was seen to indicate the finality of the parties' intent (see also Baxi 1976, 76). Recollecting from his childhood, Bhupalsingh Meher, a retired army man now settled in the big city of Haldwani at the base of the mountains, narrated that earlier the system of *wākdān* – oral promises – was commonplace in Khasi village. "[But today] Nobody is bound anymore by their word. Only when it is recorded in writing can a man be held up to his word," he said.[65] So when Kamla Rawat's husband, Deepak's, ways did not improve despite having been to jail twice after drunken brawls and being abandoned by Kamla and the children thereafter, Kamla got a document signed from him. "Within six months of my departure, my husband came to me. He apologised profusely (*Usné hāth jod ke māfī māngī*). He promised to behave well, give up alcohol and find a job as long I allowed him to live with me. I thought that maybe he was not happy without the children and so when he swore upon the life of his mother and son [*kasam khāi*] to behave well, I allowed him to come back," said Kamla.[66] But then Deepak was unable to stick to his word. One day in a state of complete intoxication, he appeared before the gate of Kamla's workplace – an NGO – and began to abuse her employer. The NGO filed a police complaint against Deepak, but Kamla was sure that a few more days in jail for a man who had been to prison a few times already would not affect him, "now I have got a document signed from him where he promises not to drink, find a job and stop beating the children," said Kamla. A sort of bond of good behaviour, Kamla got this written document from Deepak in the presence of her husband's oldest uncle and her husband's younger brothers (*devar*). "I insisted that they too sign on it and that they would be the "witnesses" [*gavāh*] to this promise," she said. Kamla also got

63 Interview, Gonjhé (Maharashtra), May 22, 2016.

64 Interview, Khasi (Uttarakhand), March 11, 2016.

65 Interview, Khasi (Uttarakhand), February 6, 2016.

66 Notes from conversations with Kamla Rawat, Melatpur (Uttarakhand), May 2015, April 2016, and detailed interview May 15, 2015.

this document notarised. From the experiences of other women who had been in a similar situation, Kamla had learned that such a document could be "executed" and held force as "proof" (*kāgaz dikhā sakte hain̐*) in a police station or in front of government officials, if the need ever arose. She had also consulted one of her brothers-in-law working in the Indian army about this. Kamla felt that this document remained with her as proof of his commitment to better behaviour, and she could hold him up to it, in the manner that Bhupalsingh had articulated.

Non-state actors, such as *Grām Pradhān*s and *Samāj* members, explained that recording the outcomes of dispute processing had a two-fold benefit. First, it secured the position of these actors in any further proceedings – if at all they arose – as having played the role of mere mediators at the instance of the party's request, and who had in no way pressurised the parties into the negotiation. And second, that their intent was recorded in writing deterred people from proceeding into further layers of legality for dispute processing. When I asked Mohansingh, the *Grām Pradhān*, if the documents concerning dispute processing made during *birāderi* meetings were preserved, he stated that this depended on the *shiyāné* who processed the dispute. For himself, he said, "I retained them only to scare people."[67]

Written documentation seemed to be most commonly used in transactions that were out of ordinary practice within the community, and for transactions that were likely to be verified by a party from outside the community. With regard to the first case, an example would be the document that was required to be created if parents decided to give their daughter a share in the family's immoveable property. Even though daughters are entitled to equal inheritance rights along with their male siblings in joint family property under the Hindu Succession (Amendment) Act, 2005, in practice this was still uncommon in the villages in Dharamgarh valley. In some of these villages, custom had it that a daughter who returned to her natal home because she was unable to settle down in her matrimonial home may have received a share in the joint family property, which she could cultivate and earn from in her lifetime. This piece of land, though, was never "owned" by her, it constituted a life interest familiar from post-colonial succession law in India. A document had to be created in the instance the parents decided to bequeath to their daughter a share of such land, which resulted in her becoming the full "owner" of such a piece of land. Shardadevi's daughter Laxmi faced a lot of domestic violence in her matrimonial home and fled to her natal village in Gangapur often. At the time of fieldwork, she lived with an aunt in Delhi and was trying to earn a livelihood there. Shardadevi wanted to give her a part of their land so that she could till it and live off it. But her sons and husband were against this idea. "It doesn't happen this way", they said to her. The house Shardadevi and her family resided in was built by Shardadevi's father, and hence she felt that she had the right to give her daughter a share. "Who will look after her after we are gone?" said Shardadevi, who knew that there were three or four other families in their village who had given their daughters a share in the family property. "A bond

67 Interview, Khasi (Uttarakhand), March 11, 2016.

will have to be made to this effect and signed by the *Grām Pradhān* and other witnesses. The *Tehsildār* makes a copy of this document and accordingly makes changes in the mutation register," explained Shardadevi, when I asked her how such arrangements are carried out to ensure that the daughter can retain her piece of land forever.[68]

The second instance, as a result of which written documentation began to gain significance, was the shift in attitudes that occurred as private services became a more common source of earning income. In the Dharamgarh valley, for instance, the popularity of government jobs introduced people to several types of documentation exercises, ranging from filling forms and contracts to providing proof of their birth, residence, and other aspects of their life. As a result of this, people began to consciously maintain documentary proof of the events in their life. For instance, the celebration of marriages, which were earlier only a social occasion, and a customary function, began to be recorded as an entry in the village register. More crucial though were divorce proceedings, which witnessed an insistence by parties to be recorded in a written format. This was specially to ensure that retirement and other benefits ensuing from such jobs fell into the right hands (and bank accounts!). Explaining this further, Dalbahadursingh Bafila, a local lawyer, said, "There is a customary form of divorce called "*Laduā*", which literally translates as "divorce by mutual consent". Earlier it was very common and still is, particularly among communities where both parties are still dependent on agriculture or other traditional forms of occupation. But with service-*wāllās*, it is a problem, because establishing the proof of customary divorces is quite difficult." By way of example, he then narrated the following experience. "An army officer did not get along with his wife and had divorced her by way of *Laduā*. Eventually he married again. But the name of the first wife remained in the records of his army appointment papers. When he died, the pension cheque was issued in the name of his first wife and this created some trouble as now this first wife was already married to someone else and lived far away. The second wife's claim to this money was then [to be] established by way of court proceeding." Dalbahadursingh had appeared in court for the second wife and recollected to have successfully established the validity of this customary practice, although with some predicament and difficulty.[69]

68 Interview, Gangapur (Uttarakhand), March 2, 2016. It would be useful to mention here that Bailey's (1957, 263) observation with respect to land transactions within communities in Orissa was to some extent also true with regard to the perceptions of the communities in the Dharamgarh valley because as Bailey highlights "systems of transfer of land were initiated by and maintained by the Administration." It cannot be ruled out that to some extent, the emphasis on documentation with regard to practices like the one Sharadadevi wanted to pursue can in part be attributed to the fact that it was a "land transaction", a practice perceived to have originated in the state and therefore could be validly substantiated only with the help of a state-recognised procedure – that of written documentation.

69 Interview, Chilbasa (Uttarakhand), March 26, 2016.

An interaction with the state and the consequent exposure to the value of written documentation has grown to hold such power on the imagination of people that not even processes within the outermost layer of legality, those involving the spirits and deities, have been able to escape its impact. Despite being a mechanism that worked only on faith and belief systems particular to this mountainous district of Uttarakhand, the system involving the intervention of Kokiladevi was also extremely formalised and organised, sharing stark resemblances in its structure (or at least people's understanding of it) to the state judicial system. A separation of powers and duties (see page 89), with the goddess being the decision maker and a staff of deities ("*devike āṇ-bāṇ*") implementing her decisions is one marker of similarity. The other was the intensive employment of written documentation in the worship of the goddess. Several people chose to make an appeal to the goddess in writing, some even going to the extent of using a stamp paper (bearing a pre-printed revenue stamp) for such petitions. On enquiring about the preference for written appeals, a common response was that the written document was considered more private and out of the public eye as compared to an oral appeal to the goddess. "Some people don't like to speak out their wishes. They then just write down what they want from the goddess and leave it at her feet in the temple. This is fairly inconspicuous," explained Prema Joshi from the Brahmin neighbourhood in Pankhu near the main temple of this Goddess.[70]

The procedure that followed conciliatory agreements between disputing parties was also fairly formalised, though not entirely uniform across locations. This included the execution of a "settlement deed" of sorts recording the intentions of the parties and the terms on which they had considered the dispute as "settled". Speaking from his own experience of having carried out several such *pūjās* at the Bhagwati temple in Melatpur, *pundit* Upadhyay explained the form of the "settlement deeds" as follows: "The disputing parties or their heirs record in writing the settlement of their differences and the fact that they have jointly conducted the necessary *pūjā* to thank the goddess for helping them settle the dispute and restore relations. The parties also record in this document how the party (if any) that was treated unfairly at the time of the dispute was compensated, clarifying further that there remained nothing more to be given and taken (*len-den*) between the parties. The paper also contains a statement that both parties do not bear any doubt towards one another. The agreement is made usually on a Rs. 8 or 10 stamp paper. It is signed by the parties, sometimes by the *Grām Pradhān* and other *shiyāné* of the village and also by me. Signatures of the disputing parties remain most imminent. Such a paper is usually drafted in the evening prior to the *pūjā* in order to ensure that no doubts of the disputing parties' intention to settle amicably remain in anybody's mind."[71]

Written documentation, as is evident from the above case studies, was observed to lend a legitimacy that increased the credibility of processes adopted by non-

70 Interview with Prema Joshi in the Bhagwati temple premises in Pankhu (Uttarakhand), March 30, 2016.

71 Interview with Rajendra Upadhyay, Melatpur (Uttarakhand) March 27, 2016.

state actors, thus making them somewhat competent with state actors engaged in dispute processing, who gained their own legitimacy from state legislations.[72] This was believed to have increased the appeal of non-state actors such as the *birāderi* or *Samāj* as "reliable" forums in the sphere of dispute processing. Galanter had earlier remarked in his paper on displacement of traditional law, that "local law can survive only by taking on the character of modern law" (Galanter 1968, 82). While local law, of course, has moved very little in the direction he observed, local actors involved in dispute processing, as we see from the evidence discussed above, definitely have.

Similarity in procedures between the various layers of legality was also claimed to dissuade parties processing their dispute in a legal layer involving the *Samāj* or *birāderi* from simultaneously pursuing their disputes in a state forum. The more similar the procedures, the less aspirational a disputant was perhaps likely to feel about different outcomes from a different forum.

4.6 In transition: Perceptions, notions, and customs

Beyond structural adaptation, the processes of changing perceptions, notions and customs came forth as another manner of engagement between non-state and state actors. Like structural adaptations, transformations in notions, customs and approaches were also meant to increase the appeal of non-state forums in comparison to their state-based counterparts.

4.6.1 Changing local practices

Newer practices at the individual and family levels and evolving perceptions about social circumstances were another approach to limit the processing of disputes to the layers involving non-state actors from within the community. In the village communities of the Dharamgarh valley, the insistence on women to initiate the divorce, and in writing, was one expression of customs being modified to accommodate changing circumstances brought about by penetration of state law.[73] Govindidevi from Nalkhet village, whose experience with the separation of her son from his wife was described in the introductory chapter (see Chapter 1, page 1), articulated this development accurately. Govindidevi's son, Lalit Kumar, she claimed was a little "slow-minded" (*kam dimāg*) and could not manage entirely on his own. Lalit was married to Suman from Chaudmuniyal. Suman was educated up to the fifth grade. "Lalit used to be a bright boy. He even completed his 12th grade examination. But then we don't know what happened. He slowly began losing his mind and this only increased after his marriage. He used to have

72 And this hold that written documentation has over the imagination of people is not just limited to the working of community based non-state actors, but also NGO run forums for dispute processing as well (Vatuk 2013, 89).

73 Similar evidence is brought in also from the north-east of India where customary laws of tribal communities have shown considerable resilience in meeting the challenges of the "modern world" (Pereira and Athparia 2018, 145).

fits of rage and sometimes beat his wife in a fit of madness. Suman started going back more and more to her natal home. Now she lives with her parents most of the time and visits us once in a while. She doesn't tell us if she wants to stay here or not. All she says is that she will continue visiting," said Govindidevi,[74] describing that this had been the situation for four years before the time of this fieldwork. Suman and Lalit also have a son, who at the time of the fieldwork resided with his mother. "She brings him when she visits her matrimonial home. But she always reminds us that he is *her* son and that we have no right over him whatsoever," related Govindidevi. On speaking to Suman, I learned that she had no intentions of returning to her matrimonial home. She confirmed Govindidevi's account of the domestic violence that Lalit inflicted on her but added that she had also to counter sexual advances by her father-in-law. The dynamics of the situation being delicate, I could never discuss this with Govindidevi, who, however, during all her conversations with me stated that she had actively intervened to stop the men from harassing her daughter-in-law. Govindidevi, not knowing how this situation will end, was concerned about her son who she claimed surely could manage on his own. "He needs someone to take care of him," she shared. Govindidevi felt that the most appropriate step would be for Suman to give in writing that "she does not wish to cohabit (*nahi rehenā chāhati haiṅ*) with Lalit and that she has decided to leave him." That the woman would give in writing her intention not to continue cohabitation with her husband was the local practice, Govindidevi had stated and was also evident in several other divorce and separation cases I witnessed during fieldwork. The *shiyāné* in Govindidevi's village cautioned her that women could go to the state courts if the husband or his family acted unfavourably towards them. Govindidevi made very clear that her son would give nothing in writing that would amount to a divorce or separation. "The law is in favour of women (*āj kal aurat ka kānūn haiṅ*). What if she decides to go to court? She is always welcome to come back here. She should look after her husband and she has a right over all the property here," said Govindidevi, who claimed that this was her family's stance. Very different from two decades ago, as the communities recollected, when a man from these communities whose wife remained out of touch and in her natal home for more than six to eight months would consider the marriage had ended and proceed to remarry. Today, men remain unmarried for years until the wife or her family was convinced to give them a letter of separation in writing. Consequently, this modification in custom, which kept marital situations in a state of limbo. restrained many women from being able to go to state forums for dispute processing.[75]

74 Notes from interviews and conversations with Govindidevi Ram and Suman Arya, Nalkhet (Uttarakhand), April 2015. Govindidevi and Suman belonged to the Scheduled Caste communities of Ram and Arya.

75 Interviews with Santosh Ram, Melatpur (Uttarakhand), April 18, 2015, and Deepa Meher, Gangapur (Uttarakhand), January 31, 2016.

4.6.2 Transforming approaches and ideas

The efforts by *pancāyats*, whether in Gonjhé or in the villages of the Dharamgarh valley, to maintain social order, were always underscored by the knowledge of the need for continued coexistence.[76] This enabled the non-state forums to give prominence to different values in different disputes. This meant that an emphasis on postulational values of state law was in some instances carefully adopted. Highlighting the postulational values identified with the state or the "other" was viewed in the communities as an expression of "modernity" in thought, which to some extent secured non-state actors from being labelled as "outdated" or "traditional", in turn improving their credibility and strengthening their authority in the sphere of dispute processing. As a *puḍhārī* from Gonjhé, Pandu Gondivale, said, "Every time a dispute is processed, it is processed according to the context in which it arises, according to the situation of the community at that time. Even if the same dispute arises before the *Samāj* for the second time, over time (*kālāntarane*), the circumstances of the dispute have changed and therefore the dispute has to be processed differently."[77] Such an approach towards dispute processing naturally made scope for varying emphasis on different values at different times, community solidarity being the ultimate goal at all times. What did therefore happen on some occasions was that the aid of postulational values perceived to be advanced by state law was taken to reinforce the postulational values of community law! This is elaborated below with the help of two case studies.

Commenting on married girls returning to their natal home because they were unable to tolerate the abusive behaviour of their husbands, Khastidevi Rathore, a female *shiyānī* from Gangapur village said: "It is alright. These girls are educated now, there are so many job opportunities as well. They will earn and eat their own bread. Why should they suffer at the hands of their husbands, then?" Troubled and scared by the workload and loss of comfort in their matrimonial home, daughters-in-law fled back to their natal homes even a decade ago. However, then it was relatively more unacceptable for a girl to flee from her marital home because such behaviour reflected badly upon the social reputation of the girl's family in her village and of her husband and his family in theirs. It was considered a matter of *beizzati*. But Khastidevi's articulation now reveals that notions of *izzat* in the Thakur community in Gangapur were slowly changing, possibly to accommodate the postulational values of state law, perhaps even including human rights? Partly of course, this "modern" opinion that Khashtidevi communicated was part of the make-up to remain an attractive option for dispute processing. But in terms of actually carrying out her role as *shiyānī*, we know from an earlier section (see page 97), that her efforts, like other non-state actors, were centred around retaining dispute processing within community control. However, what resulted from this as well was the fact that when a daughter knew that she could return to more accommodating circumstances in her natal home, it was less likely that she felt

76 Various interviews in Gonjhé (Maharashtra), and Khasi (Uttarakhand), January 2015 to June 2016.

77 Interview in Gonjhé (Maharashtra), May 22, 2016.

alienated, so as to be compelled to seek the processing of her grievances in avenues outside her community – namely the state courts and police stations. These had become a popular recourse (for threat if not in actuality) among women who felt threatened in their matrimonial homes. The end result of course was a reduction in probability of any woman putting the *izzat* of her community at stake.

Another case study in this context is from Gonjhé where the complex use of, and emphasis on, different postulational values by non-state actors – the *Samāj* in this case – made dispute processing an experiment on the boundaries of tradition, growing rights awareness and global expectations. In this case study, which describes the processing of a dispute concerning a broken engagement, one found in the articulation of the decision by the *Samāj*, awareness about concepts such as "individual freedoms" and "individual choice", which apparently the *Samāj* felt it was necessary to recognise in order to preserve caste rules and the *izzat* of the community, and to reduce incidences that were likely to cause disharmony. In the said case, the *Samāj* in Gonjhé had been requested to intervene in a dispute that arose from a broken engagement between a girl from Gonjhé and a boy from the neighbouring village of Pimpaḷgāv. Both parties belonged to the Koḷī caste community. The girl's side was represented by her parents and on the boy's side, his father along with some men from his village, including a prominent village *puḍhārī* from Pimpaḷgāv, were present at the meeting of the *Samāj*. Neither the girl nor the boy was present at this meeting. While all the men sat in a continuous circle with the *Samāj* in the temple premises, the mother of the girl – the only woman present – sat to one side away from the circle of men, yet within hearing distance of the *Samāj*'s discussion.

The present dispute processing before the *Samāj* had been preceded with dispute processing within the layer involving the families. The *māmā* (mother's brother) of the girl, and an uncle of the boy who had proposed the match, and taken a lead in arranging meetings between the parties, had been at the forefront of this attempt of settlement along with a *puḍhārī* from their respective *Manḍaḷs*.[78] An implosion of successful negotiations at this level had resulted in the boy's family insisting on the intervention of the *Samāj* in Gonjhé. The issue at stake, as explained by the *puḍhārī* from Gonjhé who had been involved in the family level negotiations, was the amount of compensation the girl's family owed to the boy's family. After the initial customary rituals, the wedding preparations had begun; during which the girl had eloped with another boy, who was from Gonjhé itself. When this was discovered, the boy's side demanded from the girl's family compensation for the financial loss they had incurred for the preparations. The boy's side claimed that they had already printed the wedding invitations and paid advance amounts to the music band, the decoration company, and the food organisers for the wedding celebration. They had initially estimated a financial loss

78 The mother's brother is called *māmā* in Marathi. In Gonjhé, however, *māmā* equates with an uncle who the child knows through his mother's family and may not necessarily be the mother's real brother. He could be a distant cousin or a male relative from the extended kinship network.

of Rs. 150,000 (approximately $2,100) as compensation, which claim amount they had been convinced to reduce to Rs. 75,000 (approximately $1,050) during the dispute processing intervention at the family level. However, the girl's parents claimed that they were financially unable to meet such a large monetary compensation. In countering this claim for compensation, the girl's parents also stated that they did not feel they could be blamed entirely for their daughter's elopement, as they too had been as shocked and surprised at the incident as the boy and his family. At the time that the issue was first brought before the *Samāj*, it had been more than two months to the incidence of the girl eloping with the boy from Gonjhé and the disputes between the families that followed. While negotiations regarding the compensation were still underway, the boy's family had proceeded to find another match for their son, who was – by the time of this second meeting before the *Samāj* – already married.

What the *Samāj* therefore had before it was a situation which concerned expenses undertaken for preparatory arrangements of a marriage between parties who were now married and settled with different partners. The *Samāj* was placed with the task of gauging the intensity of a situation retrospectively, very similar to what the state courts did fairly regularly. But the manner in which this private dispute would be settled had implications not just for the individual parties but would also determine the relationship between the Koḷī community in Gonjhé and that in Pimpaḷgāv, constituting a crucial link in the extension of kinship networks.

Since members of the *Samāj* were also members of the community, news about incidences like the one that gave rise to this dispute were public knowledge for several weeks before the dispute actually began to be processed in the layers involving the family and beyond. That a girl from Gonjhé had eloped a few days before her wedding with another boy from their village had fallen upon everyone's ears. Possibly some of the *puḍhārīs* in the *Samāj* even had a fairly good idea of the negotiations that had begun at the level of the families. However, the *Samāj* agreed to intervene only after it had received a formal application to this effect. Notices had thereafter been sent to the applicants fixing the date on which they would have to present their case. Beginning afresh, therefore, was a part of the *Samāj's* protocol – part of the formalisation of procedures to reinstate their authority (see page 100).

During the discussion before the *Samāj*, it was publicly discussed that the boy who the girl had eloped with also belonged to the Koḷī community. The fact that the girl knew the boy she eloped with since before the arrangement of her marriage, and that she had disclosed to her parents her interest in marrying that particular boy, received much attention in the *Samāj*. "She had said that the house of the boy her marriage was being arranged with was very small," someone from the crowd had interjected, as the facts of a suspected "affair" came to the fore. Gossip and discussion took centre stage, while the presiding members discussed the issue among themselves. Finally, when the secretary of the *Samāj* announced maintenance of decorum, Anand Patil, the chairman on the *Samāj*, stood up to put forth his opinion (*vichār māndāylā*). Though coined as an "opinion", what the chairman was about to say was to be the conclusion of the *Samāj* on the issue before them. I will now quote the chairman's entire speech and proceed to analyse how different postulational values were identified with at different points in this decision, ultimately to restore the harmonious relations within the Koḷī community from these two villages. Beginning very formally, Anand said:

> We have gathered here today to settle this dispute. The matter has been brought before the *Samāj* and it is the responsibility of the *Samāj* to do justice to both parties. It is the first time such a matter has been brought before us. We know that the boy has got married again and is now settled. The girl too is married and thankfully to a member of our own caste. Now, even though both parties are actually settled, after hearing the facts, I feel that the girl's family should pay a sum of Rs. 5,000 to the boy's family and close the matter. This amount should be paid as a fine. This fine will act as a deterrent to families from creating such situations again. In these times when love-*jihad* and other such activities are rampant, it is important that parents are more careful with their children in matters of marriage. We must remember that such situations create ill feelings between our communities which are now spread far and wide. The news of this fine that is now being enforced will surely reach our communities in all the villages and they will be more careful in matters of marriage hence-forth.

While the fact that a fine must be paid was agreed upon by all members of the *Samāj*, the amount of the fine, in light of the expenses incurred, seemed fairly small, and therefore after some discussion was increased to Rs. 10,000 (approximately $150). The girl's mother who sat to the side intervened persistently, although discreetly. Nodding her head in disagreement, she kept signalling to her husband and the *puḍhārīs* she knew that they would not be able to pay anything more than Rs. 5,000 (approximately $75). However, the tone of the meeting which was heading towards wrapping up, indicated that there was little scope for further negotiation. The secretary of the *Samāj* began to record the decision of the *Samāj* in the proceedings register, a further indication that the processing had come to an end. It was exactly at this point that the *puḍhārī* from the boy's village stood up to announce that the boy's family wanted to renounce the entire penalty in favour of the village temple in Gonjhé. "We would like to say that we do not want anything. We would request that the fine of Rs. 10,000 be reduced to Rs. 5,000 and that this amount be held as donation from us to the Ram Mandir, here where we have gathered today. We wanted justice (*nyāy*) and we have now got it," said the *puḍhārī*. A murmur went up in the crowd. Visibly some people were impressed, while some others were not. The chairman of the *Samāj*, who seemed slightly annoyed, remarked, "This reduction and renunciation of the penalty is not a reflection of generosity, but an expression of disrespect to the decision of the *Samāj*. The *Samāj* took up this matter and announced this fine because it wants to protect relations and ensure the well-being of the Koḷī community. But since you insist, what we will do is to show in our records a note that "a fine Rs. 10,000 had been levied upon the girl's family in settlement of this dispute. However, at the insistence of the party meant to receive this fine, the amount was reduced [to Rs. 5,000] and donated to the temple." But what must be remembered for future settlements of disputes of such a nature is that the fine levied by the *Samāj* [in such instances] was Rs. 10,000." It was on this note that the matter was closed.

The processing of this dispute reflected a number of postulational values at work. "*Izzat*" that of the Koḷī community as a whole, and of the boy and his family at the level of "self", received much priority. The entire processing of this dispute before the *Samāj* was an effort by the boy's family (possibly in line with the popularly expected code of behaviour), towards restoration of their own *izzat*, which had clearly been disturbed by the elopement of the girl with another boy.

At the same time, this incident had also put the *izzat* of the Koḷī community in Gonjhé at stake. The issue of *izzat* was as much tied up with the self as it was with the community at large. "Sometimes incidences of broken engagements can lead the community in one village to decide not to arrange marriages with parties from another village," said Mayuresh Pavshe, a young lad from Gonjhé. Therefore, a matter that might cause *beizzati* to one individual in a community may also imply *beizzati* for the entire community, especially if the issue at stake involves social relations. The girl belonged to Gonjhé and there was concern that her behaviour could have had consequences for future matrimonial arrangements between Koḷī communities in these two villages. Therefore, the manner in which this case was dealt with was also going to determine the relationship of the Koḷī communities in Pimpaḷgāv and Gonjhé. The imposition of the penalty by the *Samāj* and its insistence to mention in the written proceedings the renunciation of this compensation by the party from Pimpaḷgāv, despite the dissuasion by the *Samāj*, had a two-fold consequence. Firstly, the *Samāj*, by this act, established having given a fair hearing to the dispute, and second, it confirmed (for the public) taking cognisance of the defaulting member from their own village.

The renunciation of the fine by the boy's family in favour of the village temple, as I was to learn later, complemented this effort of the *Samāj* in restoring relations between the Koḷī communities in both villages. Derrett (1968, 65) explains that among Hindus, "gifts to a deity strengthen the communion whose deity it is, and symbolise social identification within that communion." Such renunciations, as Mayuresh Pavshe narrated, were common in incidences of dispute processing by the *Samāj*. Mayuresh being the son of a *puḍhārī* was very aware of the power dynamics that drove these negotiations. "It is a small amount. And their pride/self-respect (*abhimān*) interferes. It would not look good to claim the penalty amount for themselves. Plus, such acts help keep the relations between the community in both villages peaceful. The conduct during inter-village dispute settlements can hamper future relations," he said. The party from Pimpaḷgāv had received a fair hearing, and as Mayuresh explained, it would only be correct that they responded to this with humility and self-respect, further confirming Derrett's (1968, 65) observation that "liberality … gains merit and social esteem at the same time." This imposition of a fine and its renunciation, could also be perceived to constitute a "wealth exchange" in the terms of Strathern (1985), which as she highlights must not be seen only as a non-violent solution, but rather also as "an instrument for specifically political interactions … it helps define relations between such entities as a matter or reciprocity" (1985, 129), as was certainly the case in context of the nature of relationships between the Koḷī community in Gonjhé and that in Pimpaḷgāv.

During this entire discourse of the *Samāj*, prominence was also given to the concept of individual choice and the caste rules of the Koḷī community, the former being emphasised to strengthen the latter. As I mentioned earlier (see Chapter 2, page 43) the *Samāj* is the highest authority of decision-making in Gonjhé, and for certain matters in the Koḷī community of the entire region. Either, after having exhausted attempts of dispute processing at the lower levels, a dispute was heard by the *Samāj*, or if the processing of the dispute had crucial implications for the village or caste community, the matter would be heard by the *Samāj* directly. The above case was a combination of both. By imposing a fine on the family of the girl, the *Samāj*, as Anand Patil highlighted, wanted to curtail families from forcing their children into marriages against their will. Here we find that the *Samāj* was sensitive to the increasing importance of "individual choice" at the level of the self within the youth in the community, and at no point during the meetings accused or blamed the girl for her act. The *Samāj* possibly did not blame the girl too much because, despite having exercised individual choice in resistance to her parents, she had eloped with a boy from the same caste and religion, which the community as a whole seemed fairly relieved about. The value of caste rules being preserved was thus evident. By referring to "growing incidences of love-*jihad*" the chairman's speech was in fact a signal to the parents to ensure that their children do not engage in an activity merely in a fit of rage or rebellion.[79] The girl in question seemed to have also indicated to her parents her preference for marrying the boy she eloped with. So here was a case of forced marriage that the *Samāj* realised needed to be addressed as a social phenomenon in changing circumstances of postulational values. And therefore, allowing eligible youngsters to have a say in choice of partner was important. This thought process falls much in line with the objectives of the final judgment in *Shakti Vahini v Union of India and Ors* (see page 13), which has come only much later in 2018. In the wider context, it can also be drawn from this reference to "love-*jihad*" that the *Samāj* in Gonjhé would have been less tolerant of an incidence of an inter-religious and possibly inter-caste marriage as against the fact of a love marriage, elopement or broken engagement between members of the Koḷī caste.

These processes, whereby the values of state law were incorporated to suit local logic, reflect a form of translation that state law underwent in the process of the engagement with non-state forums. But as Merry (2009) also notes in the case of her study on translations of human rights, in the village communities of Gonjhé and the Dharamgarh valley too, translations of state laws, the postulational values,

79 "Love Jihad," Gupta explains, is a construct of the Hindu right. It is "supposed to have been launched by Muslim fundamentalists and youthful Muslim men to convert Hindu and Christian women to Islam through trickery and expressions of false love" (Gupta 2009, 13). See also Mander et al. (2016, 39–40) and Larouche (2017).

which were perceived as a serious threat to community solidarity, when carried out by non-state actors, were only limited transformations aimed at ultimately keeping state actors at bay.

4.7 Barefoot lawyers

While the female shiyāné and many puḍhārīs acted primarily at the non-state level structuring the course of dispute processing largely within the community itself, a more specialised set of non-state actors – the barefoot lawyers – acted as buffers at the boundaries, dealing with disputants willing to experiment with the state machinery – see Figure 4.1.

The emergence of these actors reveals yet another facet of engagement of non-state forums with their state-based counterparts through the creation of a layer of legality where state laws and community laws were both used, with the postulational values of state laws and community laws often holding equal prominence.

The awareness of state law has witnessed a prominent increase through mediums such as the television, newspapers and hearsay experiences of other community members.[80] Even communities like those in Gonjhé and the Dharamgarh valley responded to this impact, one form of which was the increasing willingness of disputants to explore the value of their bargaining position (Mnookin and Kornhauser 1979) and as to how their dispute would be located within the framework of state law and state forums (Galanter 1981, 6–7). But complexity of legal language, and the time, cost, and perseverance that a court case demands still ensures that people remain cautious while treading into the territory of the state machinery. Barefoot lawyers, I argue, emerged as a response to exactly this situation, operating as niche actors not only advising but also representing parties, and taking a lead in the realm of settlements that are the fate of many court cases in India (Krishnan et al. 2014).These actors are referred to as "barefoot lawyers" because in the roles they performed, they are akin to lawyers (see Kidder 1974b for an overview of lawyers' practices). They, however, do not have any degrees, certificates or formal training to this effect and the term "barefoot" in that sense is meant to indicate this.

80 The television has reached even the remote corners of India today. Soap operas and the news were watched most popularly in Gonjhé and in Uttarakhand. While the news is understandably a source of information about the law; even soap operas touch upon themes of women's rights, succession, crime, and environmental issues. For example, in *Julun Yeti Reshim Gathi*, a Marathi family drama that was watched by my host family in Gonjhé every evening, a senior couple was shown to be considering divorce. There were episodes where each of the characters met with lawyers and learned about how the court would respond to their case; they also attempted counselling and mediation, which in the end was successful, and the couple decided to live together again. While the message (delivered from how the incident ended) was one part of it, these episodes were definitely contributing to raising the general awareness about what one can expect from lawyers and state courts in instances of divorce and the facilities of mediation, conciliation, and counselling that the state machinery encourages and offers.

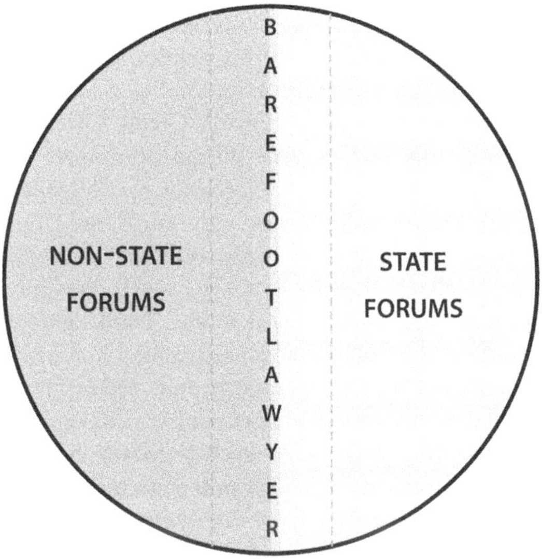

Figure 4.1 Barefoot lawyers functioned on the boundaries of state and non-state law

The state legal system has always been simultaneously a mode of control and a place of resistance. Merry (2004, 576) highlights the necessity to study the new kinds of spaces and cultural categories of persons and duties this creates. The layer of legality where barefoot lawyers act as key players is one such space. The services of barefoot lawyers were almost always used by disputants who intended to pursue or had to respond to the pursuit of a dispute in the state machinery. Barefoot lawyers operated entirely "outside" the state machinery and their appeal lay in their knowledge and familiarity with the state machinery,[81] even as they remained embedded in and therefore appreciative of community values, reciprocities and the power dynamics therein.[82] Barefoot lawyers, as Figure 4.1 indicates, were constantly operating on the borders of state and non-state law, revealing how it is on the limits of these laws that creative settlements actually had the potential to occur (Foblets et. al 2016).

Ravindra Pavshe was one such barefoot lawyer in Gonjhé. Originally from one of the wealthier families in Gonjhé, political factionalism within the family saw Ravindra leaving his house with his wife and setting out to make a life for himself. He moved from selling fish independently to working in the loading department of a fishing company, and at some point, drove a shared tempo traveller that plied

81 The term "outside" here is meant to explain that barefoot lawyers almost never appeared as witnesses in a case they might have helped institute in court, nor were they ever seen interacting directly with a judge on any ground.

82 There is some point of similarity between the individuals that Cohn (1965, 106) and Khare (1972, 86–90) describe as "sea lawyers", and who I refer to as "barefoot lawyers." The category of "sea lawyers", though, I find, is much wider than that of "barefoot lawyers", even though in some respects the functions of both coincide. In fact, I would say that barefoot lawyers fall within the category of sea lawyers.

villagers between Gonjhé and the neighbouring *talukā*. Along with all this he contested more than two court cases that his political opponents had filed in the local *talukā* court, continued to engage in politics as a Shiv Sena campaigner,[83] got elected as chairman of the local Fisherman's Credit Society for two years, and also acted as president of the Dispute Free Village Committee (*Tanṭā Mukti Gāv Samiti*) for a year thereafter. Ravindra's experience as a litigant in court, and his continuous engagement with politics, not only familiarised him with the state machinery of dispute processing but also with court staff, local police officials, and lawyers. Ravindra was well-versed with state law as well. Pursuing his own case in court taught him about the Indian Penal Code, 1860, and his more recently acquired interest in brokering land deals had acquainted him with the Maharashtra land laws, and the Indian Transfer of Property Act, 1882. The village-based dispute processing machinery of Gonjhé was never new to Ravindra, and having been president of the state-supported *Tanṭā Mukti Gāv Samiti*, he learned to recognise the advantages and limits of both state and non-state mechanisms, and how they could be manoeuvred to benefit individual disputants, and at the same time limit dispute processing, if required, to boundaries within community control. Being politically active, and a *puḍhārī* in the community, Ravindra, of course, used his position on occasions of dispute processing to manipulate power relations within the community. Ravindra was a popular focal point for people who sought advice as they negotiated a dispute in the state and non-state arena. He acted as advisor, mediator, and attorney, depending on in which capacity the disputant approached him. The following case study elaborates Ravindra's role as "attorney" and "mediator" in the processing of a dispute. The sole objective of the party who sought Ravindra's services, as we shall see, was to use Ravindra's help to convince the other party to negotiate their differences within layers involving village-based actors.

A dispute between Iqbal Patel and Faizal, from the Muslim community in Gonjhé, had reached the police station in the *talukā* town. When Faizal received a call from the police station in this regard, Azad – Faizal's friend – and Mubeen – the Muslim *puḍhārī* in Gonjhé – first stopped at Ravindra Pavshe's home before proceeding to help Faizal at the police station.[84] "Where is the matter? Still at the Mānjai police station or now in Gorāi?" enquired Ravindra, when Azad suddenly turned up at his doorstep in the early afternoon one day. Mānjai was where the local police station outpost for village Gonjhé was located, and Gorāi was the *talukā* headquarters where the main police station was located.[85] "Still in Mānjai.

83 The Shiv Sena is perceived as a right-wing party in Maharashtra. For more details about the Shiv Sena see Julia Eckert (2003).

84 Notes from fieldwork and observation of attempt towards settlement, Gonjhé, January 12, 2015. Parts of this section have been included earlier in Foblets et al. (2016, 270–275).

85 Hema Pavshe, a fisherwoman, once related: "If a party to the dispute has taken the dispute to Mānjai police station, the opposite party will dance (*nāctil*) because the matter can still be controlled from further processing. If such party has taken the dispute to Gorāi police station for processing, the opposite party will cry and will sweat with fear as the dispute would now have to be processed involving state actors. And if

Come on now," urged Azad, telling Ravindra to hurry up with his tea and join them in the car. We packed ourselves into a Maruti 800 car and Ravindra took the wheel. "So where are we going? Mānjai police station, right?" asked Ravindra. "No, no … we must head to Gorāi. The matter has reached the *Tehsildār's* office there," said Mubeen, the Muslim *puḍhārī*. Mubeen was physically disabled but honing his skills to become a powerful *puḍhārī* in the Muslim community in Gonjhé. He also helped Ravindra with his land brokering business. "How can I come dressed like this? I have a reputation to maintain in the *Tehsildār* office and other places in Gorāi. I must go and change," announced Ravindra, who claimed to have had a certain "professional" reputation in the *tālukā* court and police station. But there was no time for that. Mubeen's phone was ringing continuously; Faizal's mother was calling to check where they had reached. It was important for Mubeen's reputation as an effective *puḍhārī* to be retained, that they reached the *Tehsildār's* office quickly, and so a hurried back and forth of casual comments led Ravindra to be convinced that "he looked just fine, very presentable," and we headed towards Gorāi.

Ravindra was briefed about the dispute by Mubeen and Azad in the car. Faizal, the boy on whose behalf Ravindra was to initiate some settlement, had got into an argument with Iqbal Patel's son, which had ended in some physical fighting. Iqbal had filed a complaint in the Gorāi police station, and Faizal had received a call, on the morning of our trip to Gorāi police station, to appear before the *Tehsildār*, the head of revenue department in a *tālukā*. A *Tehsildār* also holds some magistrate powers. Faizal's father worked in Dubai. He lived in Gonjhé with his siblings and mother. Whether it was to make a point to me, or for his own benefit, Ravindra checked with Mubeen whether the families were all right with Ravindra, a Hindu man, intervening to mediate a dispute between two Muslim families. "Our religion matters only inside our homes. Outside, we are all equal and everyone is the same. There is no Hindu and no Muslim," clarified Mubeen. In the course of the conversation between Mubeen and Ravindra, I learned that Ravindra knew Iqbal Patel, also another Muslim *puḍhārī*, very well, and therefore Mubeen's selection of Ravindra to represent Faizal may have been very strategic.

Outside the *Tehsildār's* office, which doubled up as a court when the *Tehsildār* heard chapter cases, a thin boy barely 18 years old was introduced to Ravindra as "Faizal". "Let us see what we can do, don't worry," Ravindra reassured Faizal. While Mubeen was left chatting with Faizal and his family, Ravindra walked around the *Tehsildār* office, greeting, shaking hands, clapping shoulders, laughing and joking with many people, most of whom I recognised as clerks, deed writers, security guards, and second line court officials. Ravindra was clearly a well-known man in this office. After completing some of his own personal tasks at the *Tehsildār's* office, Ravindra learned over a phone call that Iqbal was having lunch at a

such party has taken the dispute to [the police station in] Ratnagiri (district head quarter), then don't ask. The opposite party is likely to collapse with a heart attack!". Notes from conversations with Hema Pavshe, Gonjhé (Maharashtra), May 2016.

nearby restaurant and would meet him there. On reaching the restaurant, Ravindra realised that Iqbal and his son had proceeded to the police station.

At the police station, leaving Azad and Mubeen in the car, Ravindra went to meet Iqbal. Soon they were joined by Iqbal's son, Ajmal, as well. Ajmal was the man who Faizal had got into the fight with. Ravindra spoke with the ease of an experienced mediator. "Mubeen told me that you were involved in the matter. I have known you for so many years. You are a patient and peaceful man. I wondered what got you to the police station. It was only because I knew you were here that I agreed to come," said Ravindra to Iqbal. "Yes, yes, I am a peaceful man. But look, this is the third time this boy [Faizal] has created trouble. First time, he and his friends clad in masks scared my daughter-in-law in the evening. Another time he squabbled with my other son, held him by the collar and so forth. And now this is the third time. His cricket ball hit the windshield of one of the cars in our garage. My son [Ajmal] confiscated the ball after warning him over and over again. He has beaten my son and even damaged a customer's motorbike with his cricket bat. Worst of all he abused my deceased wife. It is okay to fight, but it is not okay if he abuses my deceased wife. There was no need [for abusing my deceased wife] and so please stay out of this matter, Ravindra. I am going to teach him a lesson and follow this matter right up to the criminal court," said Iqbal, who remained calm but visibly annoyed. That his deceased wife had been abused had troubled Iqbal's "*izzat*" and this was quickly acknowledged by Ravindra, who empathised with him. He agreed with Iqbal and said that his anger was justified. "I will personally sound out this boy, Faizal. But why go to the court. It is unnecessary trouble for you as well." Ravindra kept trying to convince Iqbal. As Ravindra and Iqbal continued to speak, the policeman, with whom the complaint had been registered appeared on his motorbike. Both Iqbal and Ravindra seemed to know him. "Did you send the papers to the *Tehsildār* office already? Is it already numbered?" asked Ravindra. Iqbal seemed to go with the flow. He clearly knew what Ravindra was trying to find out. If the papers were still with the policeman, or had not yet been numbered in the court, there was scope to withdraw the complaint without going before the court. "Yes, I just did that. Now we cannot take back the complaint. There will be at least one date in the case," said Mohite, the policeman. Ravindra turned towards Iqbal. "Let us see whether we can settle this in front of the *Tehsildār*. You are agreeable, right?" Ravindra asked Iqbal. "No, no, Ravindra. I respect your word and I would have agreed to any of your requests. But not this one time. He has abused my wife," repeated Iqbal. Ajmal, who was in no mood to settle, hurried him. When we got into the car, Ravindra told Mubeen and Azad that this situation was going to be hard to negotiate. That the complaint was numbered and in court already was one part of the problem. "This Faizal has created trouble for the third time. He even abused Iqbal's dead wife. How can we resolve this? Anyway, let us try one more time at the *Tehsildār* office. I have an idea. What I might do is to call Faizal and sound him out before Iqbal. I might even slap him once. You please explain to Faizal beforehand that this is part of the strategy, and that he shouldn't feel bad. Explain this to any of his relatives who have come along as well. Otherwise, they might get insulted and get after me without understanding the context," joked Ravindra, obviously speaking from some experience of this kind.

At the *Tehsildār* office, Ravindra tried to speak to Iqbal once again. This time Iqbal's son, Ajmal, and his wife also got involved in the discussion, actively deterring Iqbal's inclination – if any – to settle the matter, "It was my good luck that the bat this Faizal swung hit the beam over my husband's head. What if it had hit his head? He could have been injured and even died. Then who would have looked after me? Faizal's family would have given me some money, but how long would that have lasted me and my two children?" said Iqbal's daughter-in-law. "If I punish the boy, it will be a precedent for everyone in the *mohallā*," said Iqbal. Turning towards me, he continued, "*Bibi*, I am a respected man in Gonjhé. Everyone in the Hindu community respects my word. It is in my own community, unfortunately, that they do not take me seriously. This case will set all misunderstandings and doubts right." In order to deter Ravindra from following this settlement any further, the delicate nature of relations between the Hindu and Muslim community in Gonjhé were also drawn into the discussion and were used by Ajmal and his wife to further justify their determination to pursue the dispute in court. Emphasising the need to be careful that matters between the two communities do not get out of hand, Ajmal and his wife reminded Ravindra that most of the customers at their garage were Hindu Koḷī. "Had any customer been hit amidst this fight, there could have been chances of a communal riot, don't you agree?" said Ajmal's wife to Ravindra.

As more people from among those who had accompanied Iqbal and his family to court, joined the discussion, Ravindra realised a settlement was not to be. He conceded to Iqbal and stated finally that it was Iqbal's decision, and everyone would do as he deemed correct. "Please don't misunderstand me, Ravindra. I know that you have always respected my word and I will always do the same, but please allow me to be proceed this one time," said Iqbal. "Yes. Yes, Iqbal *bhāi*. I understand. Do as you have decided. You understand best. I was requested to try speaking to you and I have done my bit. But I understand that you are hurt and therefore I will not push this any further." With this statement Ravindra bid Iqbal and his family goodbye. As we exited the *Tehsildār's* office, a group of women approached Ravindra, trying to find out what happened. They were related to Faizal. "I tell you, Iqbal would have agreed. He was almost ready. But this other Muslim *puḍhārī* interfered. I will not tell you his name now. But he provoked Iqbal and kept brainwashing him to proceed. Now how could Iqbal not listen to the advice of a man who he himself had decided to consult," said Ravindra to them. The women tried to guess the name of the man. But Ravindra kept this information to himself. It seemed to give him an edge in his interactions with them, a behavioural protocol, as I later learned, that was incidental to his position as a *puḍhārī*. At the same time, by indicating that another person closer to Iqbal had influenced him against a settlement, Ravindra established that the failure to settle was more circumstantial. Thus, shifting the focus of the audience away from his capabilities as a mediator.

Back in the car, Ravindra disclosed to Mubeen and Azad that he was sure this settlement did not go through because of Rauf, another Muslim *puḍhārī* who had been helping Iqbal with filing this case in court. "He brings politics into everything. It is alright to play politics 20 per cent of the time, but at least sometimes you should use your power for social work," stated Ravindra adamantly. By now the news of the unsuccessful attempt for settlement had reached Faizal who had remained out of sight the entire time. Nevertheless, he approached the car to thank Ravindra and Mubeen for their efforts. "Don't worry, my boy. We will pull you out of this. Who is going to give you bail? Or should I stand as guarantor. I will introduce you to the lawyers. This will not go on for more than six months," Ravindra reassured Faizal, who of course was visibly shaken at the thought of having to stand up in court, and possibly spend some days in jail.

This case study illustrates the crucial role a barefoot lawyer played in dispute processing that stood on the border of the state and non-state jurisdictions. In the said case for instance, Faizal and his family wanted the case to be processed at the level of their community, possibly in their Muslim *jamāt* (see Chapter 3, page 59). They did not expect the case to go into the layers involving state actors. However, Iqbal, in order to restore his own *izzat* – a postulational value he as a part of the community identified with – felt that pursuit of the case in court was necessary. That one must act actively in order to restore one's *izzat* was a popularly expected code of behaviour in Gonjhé as is evident from earlier case studies as well (see page 112). Similar to what Paine (1967, 281) observes about the Sarakatsani community, also in the village communities that I observed, failure to avenge an insult brought a person "near to the edge of social obloquy". Culturally in both Gonjhé and the Dharamgarh valley, insulting or abusing a deceased person was treated as a matter of tremendous *beizzati* for the family members of such a person, and Iqbal possibly perceived that he would not have remained well-respected unless he proved to have made enough effort in reprimanding the individual who caused him such *beizzati*. His remark regarding "people in his own community not respecting him" (on page 119) is a hint in this direction. "When egos are hurt, in a moment of anger, people stretch the issue (*vishay tānatat*); taking it to court is a part of this. When their anger calms down, they will stop pursuing the dispute automatically," said Ravindra, one day while conversing with me about dispute processing (see also Khare 1972, 78).[86] Extremely familiar with the sentiments that people in Gonjhé were sensitive to, Ravindra had been in a position to gauge at a fairly early stage that convincing Iqbal would be difficult, as pursuing the court case was part of Iqbal's effort to restore his *izzat* and consequently his credibility within his community. That the involvement of a barefoot lawyer in negotiations will lead to a successful settlement was not guaranteed, but all parties in this case study were evidently aware of this reality.

As we saw earlier (on page 70), when dispute processing involved state actors, its processing was perceived as "having gone beyond the control of the community." This is why, as was also discernible from this case study, much thought was

86 Notes from conversations with Ravindra Pavshe, Gonjhé (Maharashtra), May 2015.

given to the selection of the barefoot lawyer who would lead the negotiations. Felstiner (1974, 74) observes:

> Since successful mediation requires an outcome acceptable to the parties, the mediator cannot rely primarily on rules but must construct an outcome in the light of the social and cultural context of the dispute, the full scope of the relations between the disputants and the perspectives from their view of the dispute. Mediation, then, flourishes where mediators share the social and cultural experience of the disputants they serve, and where they bring to the processing of disputes an intimate and detailed knowledge of the perspectives of the disputants.

In the above case, Ravindra was selected in order to play a role similar to that of an attorney on behalf of Faizal; the main goal of his involvement, made clear from the beginning, was to convince Iqbal to withdraw his complaint in the police station and to accept to negotiate their differences at the level of the community.[87] Mubeen obviously knew that Ravindra and Iqbal shared a history of good relations, friendship and mutual obligations and this factor definitely played a role in seeking Ravindra's assistance. Ravindra, of course, understood this sentiment and statements like: "It was only because I knew you were here that I agreed to come" and "Ravindra, I respect your word and I would have agreed to any of your requests" (see page 118), exchanged between Ravindra and Iqbal, show that Ravindra too banked upon the reciprocities in his relationship with Iqbal in order to help Faizal. Ravindra had probably hoped to pressurise Iqbal into withdrawing his police complaint, by emphasising the connection of this act with the "cooperation and interdependence in their relationship" that both Ravindra and Iqbal always intended to continue. According to Gulliver (1973, 671) "there are a number of strategems that can be used to bring pressure to bear on a recalcitrant party, depending on cultural possibilities and the nature of the relationship, if any, between the parties." In the said case, Ravindra could employ the strategy he chose for the negotiation primarily because of the complex connection between mutual obligations and power dynamics that set the context for relationships between *puḍhārīs* and in this case between him and Iqbal Patel.[88] However, in this case we saw that a shared community value was the cause of conflict, which resulted in a failure of Ravindra's efforts in limiting the dispute from being processed in a state forum. Withdrawing the case would have meant *beizzati* for Iqbal Patel and it being processed in a state forum with Faizal possibly facing the threat of imprisonment (even if for a few days), which spelled *beizzati* for Faizal and his family.

87 In this case since both the parties were Muslim, the non-state dispute processing would have mostly occurred in the *jamāt.*

88 I should clarify here that while all *puḍhārīs* were not barefoot lawyers in Gonjhé, all barefoot lawyers were always considered *puḍhārīs* as well.

While Ravindra's intervention did not have the impact Mubeen, Faizal, and his family had intended, all was not lost. Seeking the cooperation of a barefoot lawyer often helped disputants overcome, in part, some of the challenges faced in pursuing litigations as well: namely, the complexity of legal language and the expenditure of time and money involved in learning about and engaging in court procedures. In the said case, even though the out-of-court settlement did not go through, Faizal had easily secured a good criminal lawyer at a reasonable cost, because Ravindra agreed to put in a word using his connections. Ravindra also spent some time in explaining to Faizal how his appearance in court would proceed, possibly reducing to a certain extent the very intimidating nature of court procedures. As Galanter (1981, 3) highlights elsewhere, the court in this case was "a site of ceremonial changes in status and 'warfare' (the threatening, overpowering and disabling of opponents)." However, Ravindra also knew from experience that litigation pursued in an attempt to restore lost honour, lost pace once the steam died out and the ego calmed (see page 120).[89] And it was this foresight of a barefoot lawyer that often tended to provide much reassurance to the disputing parties. And lastly, but most importantly, investing in a barefoot lawyer required no finances, but a willingness to be part of the games of reciprocity and power that his engagement may entail. Ravindra expected nothing in cash or kind for his involvement. However, his efforts added one more obligation to the web of reciprocities that he was constantly building and fulfilling.

Barefoot lawyers like Ravindra were active in several village communities. In Uttarakhand, Mahesh Pant, a deed writer and local Bharatiya Janata Party (BJP) campaigner based himself in an "office" in the local market in Chilbasa, the *tehsil* headquarters. Mahesh Pant had not held any elected posts at the local level, but his practice as a deed writer had made him popular for this familiarity with the state institutions. A deed writer essentially drafted affidavits and notices and helped people make applications to different government departments. In addition to these tasks, people approached Mahesh Pant for advice if they needed to find a lawyer or in order to know how they could respond to a notice that they might have received from a lawyer, police station or government department. His knowledge of state laws and court procedures sometimes entailed his strategic engagement with dispute processing at the village level. Since Mahesh Pant was located in a market centre, he was approached by people from different villages, unlike Ravindra who operated in a comparatively informal manner, meeting people mostly in his house. He was therefore largely referred to only by people from Gonjhé and the neighbouring villages, who knew of him by word of mouth.

It is important that we do not confuse barefoot lawyers with touts. Even though there was a fair amount of overlap in the role of both, barefoot lawyers usually had – in addition to their experience in dabbling with the state machinery – a powerful position within the community – sometimes both politically and

89 Keebet von Benda Beckmann (1981, 143) highlights similarly that "it is not always in the parties' interest to have their dispute settled quickly. Some parties profit from long procedure".

socially. The processing of disputes was often used by barefoot lawyers to pursue such social and political interests, and improve their leverage within these dynamics (K. von Benda-Beckmann 1981, 117). They were crucial players within the power networks of a community, which made their function in dispute processing a part of their web of reciprocities. At the same time, barefoot lawyers also played a key role in instrumentalising the postulational values of state law and state actors to carry out effective non-state dispute processing.

4.8 Dispute processing and the dynamics of self-preservation

We saw in this chapter that dispute processing in the rural areas of Gonjhé and the villages in the Dharamgarh valley could involve a wide variety of state and non-state actors and mechanisms. Dispute processing, as was evident from the diagrams (see Figures 3.1 and 3.2, page 69 and 70), could follow a path perceived as appropriate by the communities, that is, one that proceeded from the self to the community, and thereafter to the state and then the religious sphere. However, as the case studies revealed, this was not a rigid rule, thereby making space for flexible movement of disputes, with their processing oscillating between all the different legal layers of legality.

My fieldwork in both Gonjhé and the Dharamgarh valley revealed to me that dispute processing depended among other things on the networks of the parties to a dispute and what they wanted to achieve in that time and context. Underscoring all of this, however, was the fundamental instinct of self-preservation that continuously regulated intentions and ambitions. Self-preservation in this context must be understood to include all actions that are necessary for the mental and physical well-being of a person in economic, political, social, and religious spaces. The concept of self-preservation, we must not forget, was at all times linked to the notion of interconnectedness that the communities and individuals within them experienced as part of their religious and socio-cultural backgrounds (see Chapter 3, page 62) and this becomes evident from the community's narrative of the self.

Self-preservation was important as much at the level of the individual as it was at the level of the entire community. Within the social normative of the community, preservation of the self was not perceived to be disconnected from preservation of the community and vice-versa. A common explanation that was prevalent in both communities about this intangible idea that bound individuals to their communities may provide some clarification to this extent. It was explained that a community, be it based on caste, kinship or territory, was to be imagined like the hand. The hand needed the fingers and the fingers needed the hand to be useful. Similarly, the individuals needed the community and the community too was meaningless without the individuals. Like all fingers of the hand were different, there existed different kinds of people in the community. Everyone was not the same. But a single finger on its own was of little or no use, it needed the other fingers of the hand to become functional. In the same way, the communities believed that an individual community member on his own could not survive for very long. Every member of the community needed the support and cooperation of others to move ahead in life. And together all the fingers made a fist, which was perceived to be much stronger than the fingers on their own. Likewise, the community believed that "as one" it was a far stronger unit, which of course they claimed was beneficial for every member as well.[90] This explanation shed light on how the self was perceived to be best preserved as part of the community, or within its circle of solidarity, rather than outside or away from it. This idea resonated as much with individual members of the community, as it did with the community as a whole, and therefore remained well-reflected in the mechanisms of dispute processing that the community-based actors adopted.

Indeed, the rhetoric of interconnectedness between the self and the community could and was at times exploited by those in power. But what cannot be overlooked is that this instinct for self-preservation, at the level of the self and community, possibly arose in the context of cosmic interlinkedness, in that each person's action was perceived to have potentially wide-reaching consequences for oneself as well as others. If this was true, then the interconnectedness in itself acted as a check against the arbitrary use of power by *Bhāvkīs*, *Mandaḷs*, *biraderis*, *Samāj* and other non-state actors engaged in dispute processing. This view then takes the instinct for self-preservation to a realm beyond practical interdependence where preservation of the self is perceived to depend on preservation of cosmic order. Describing the *rta/dharma* complex, the concept from which this idea of "cosmic interlinkedness" derives, Derrett said it was some sort of a "social cement":

> that ties permanently communities with nothing else in common but their domicile in the sub-continent and their millennia-old committal to living together in competitive coexistence in a multi-cultural super-society. (Derrett 1970, 2)

In this background, it becomes clear why all methods of dispute processing by non-state actors, therefore, were directed towards reconciliation between the disputing parties. Non-state actors took particular pride in emphasising this difference between the working of state courts and community-based forums. "We give justice (*nyāy*), the court gives decisions," said Ravindra, while explaining why he perceived the *Samāj* as a body that was higher than the courts.[91] Sen's (2009, 20) description of *nyāy* as a "comprehensive concept of realised justice … that is inextricably linked with the world that actually emerges, not just the institutions or rules we happen to have" provides a helpful understanding of this context. Adversarial processes that characterised procedures of state actors demanding "clarity, certainty and definiteness" (Galanter 1968, 72) were therefore looked upon suspiciously as they placed one person against another. This was perceived as leading towards breakdown of harmonious relations (see page 75, see also

90 Various interviews in Gonjhé (Maharashtra) and villages in the Dharamgarh valley (Uttarakhand), January 2015 to June 2016.

91 Interview in Gonjhé (Maharashtra), March 10, 2015.

Ishwaran 1964, 229; Srinivas 1955, 18),[92] which were of utmost importance because even after the dispute, the disputing parties must continue living together. "In any given dispute, both parties are responsible in some way for the dispute. So, punishing only one person makes no sense. When the parties talk and discuss, there is conversation. Asking for forgiveness is a punishment in itself" – this explanation by Mohansingh probably best captured the sentiment underlying the approach in dispute processing among non-state actors.[93] Consequently, all dispute processing carried out by non-state actors aimed at restoring relations between the disputing parties. This was so with the invocation of Kokiladevi where parties for ultimate appeasement of the Goddess had to conduct a joint *pūjā* (see page 93), or with the intervention of the *Samāj* where all parties were convinced to conciliate their differences not just for themselves, but for the benefit of the community at large.[94]

This overview of the working of non-state actors also indicated that this particular understanding of the self may be why people rarely turned to or were limited from turning to the state for dispute processing, which was perceived to proceed on a very different understanding of the "individual". And probably the continuous focus on lack of education, financial resources, proximity from state institutions, and complicated legal procedures being cited as the main reasons for people choosing to process their disputes in forums other than the state (Vatuk 2013, 81; Galanter and Krishnan 2004) has in a way simplified (and thus perhaps drawn attention away from) this magnanimous task of understanding why state systems may (not) be working at an intrinsic level when it comes to issues like the redressal of rights, a favourite agenda of access to justice scholars.

4.9 Safe-guarding values, reinforcing solidarity: Self-preservation at the level of the community

Solidarity within the community was therefore essential for the preservation of the self as much as for the community. Community solidarity as we have seen in the previous chapter (see Chapter 3, page 62) was dependent upon and at the same time reinforced preservation of shared values, which nurtured the community's sense of order. If understood in this light, resistance of the state and the

92 See Galanter (1968, 69–70) about how people took advantage of adversarial procedures for individual gains, very different from settlement of the dispute.

93 Interview, Khasi (Uttarakhand), March 11, 2016.

94 This preference for reconciliation in the village communities in Gonjhe and Dharamgarh valley is not unique to these jurisdictions alone and in fact comes very close to the emphasis on "*ubuntu*" in the South African context. The concept of *ubuntu* is believed to encompass "communality and interdependence of the members of the community … an emphasis on reconciliation rather than confrontation" (Himonga 2011, 45). Himonga explains that the word *ubuntu* was included in the Constitution of South Africa because it was perceived that it would act "as the country's bridge toward the reconciliation of the people … across the whole country" (Himonga 2011, 44–45).

postulational values identified with "others", only became incidental to the effort towards self-preservation and preservation of the community's identity postulate in law.

In Gonjhé, in contrast to the village communities in the Dharamgarh valley, the Koḷī community's identity postulates were far more active in regulation of its engagement with state law than the identity postulates of the village communities in the Dharamgarh valley. I propose that this was because of the manner in which Gonjhé was structured and located. Gonjhé was positioned in close proximity to popular tourist destinations, the large and fairly urbanised *tālukā* town of Gorāi was only twelve kilometres away, where also the various state institutions such as the court and a police station were situated. Many people from Gonjhé travelled regularly to Gorāi for different purposes, as a result of which there were several public and private vehicles plying between the village and the *tālukā* town on a regular basis. The villages in the Dharamgarh valley, on the other hand, were located fairly remotely with rarely any visitors from urban areas. State institutions such as the police station were located as far as 22 kilometres away and the court even further at about 36 kilometres, the distance only seeming much longer because of lack of proper infrastructure. As a result, the perceived "threat" to the shared postulational values that the community identified with and thereby to community solidarity, was felt far more in Gonjhé than in the villages in the Dharamgarh valley.

As I have argued in the chapter, this resulted in the creation of more layers of legality in Gonjhé than in the villages of the Dharamgarh valley. The layers worked as filters, through which processing of a dispute would be expected to pass. The aim, of course, was to limit it from reaching the layers where state actors or religious entities were involved, and to keep it to the greatest extent possible within the control of the community and its values. As a result, in the majority of instances the disputes never got processed entirely by state actors and if they did, it was only a small part of the dispute in such cases.

Simultaneously, though not necessarily intentionally, postulational values originating in the state or for that reason even in the religious sphere would also have to pass through these several layers in order to reach the self or the individual. As a result, becoming thinner (see page 81) in the process. Therefore in Gonjhé, as compared to the villages of the Dharamgarh valley, it was noticeable that the postulational values of state law, including human rights as well as that of *dharma* (to the extent it originated in the layer involving religious elements) held far less prominence.[95] In comparison, the postulational value of *izzat*, through an increased emphasis on adherence to caste rules and maintenance of power relations, held the same amount of importance in Gonjhé as in the villages of

95 The concept of *dharma* can be divided into different sub-categories (*svadharma*, *stridharma*, etc.). Every such sub-category has different contexts. Therefore, an individual's *dharma* in the context of his religious practice is different (but nevertheless interlinked) to his/her *dharma* in the context of his/her role as a spouse, a child and so forth. In Gonjhé, as compared to the village communities in Dharamgarh valley, the emphasis on *dharma* in the context of the community's religious obligations was less.

Dharamgarh valley. This latter claim I make purely on the basis of my field experience, where I found far more people in the remote villages of the Dharamgarh valley engaging in discussions and debates over the impacts, goals and agendas of state law than in Gonjhé (but see Baxi 1976, 94). These discussions, though, were largely limited to those state laws that were perceived to regulate social structures. So, for instance in Khasi, on many evenings over cups of tea and *hukkā*, men would discuss the state's aim to bring about gender equality through granting sons and daughters equal inheritance rights in family property or allowing women entry as soldiers into the army. There were also discussions about an individual's absolute right over his/her property or the state granting awards to couples who had an inter-caste marriage. In Gonjhé on the other hand, there was little or no reference to state laws or the values they embodied in casual conversations. Here, an example about the people's knowledge and familiarity with a locally selected state-supported forum for dispute processing in Gonjhé further substantiates this point. The Dispute Free Village Committee (DFVC) is a locally selected body set up under a scheme of the Government of Maharashtra and regulated by the local police station to settle petty disputes in the village. A brief survey that I conducted in 100 homes in Gonjhé, to assess the reach of the Dispute Free Village Committee, revealed that only 26 of these households knew about this Committee. Despite the DFVC existing within the village (just like the *Samāj*), of these 26 households, members from only three had ever visited a meeting of the Committee and not necessarily to have their dispute processed by it. This shows that there was a low level of awareness and moreover slight familiarity with state institutions, state laws and the values they embody. This, I propose, is a result of the many layers of legality that existed for dispute processing in Gonjhé.

Of course, it would be naïve to believe that the interconnection between the self and community, as proposed through the example of the hand and its fingers is flawless. In fact, it is this very social normative pattern that on the one end is exploited by those in power but at the other end causes people to engage in skilful navigation when preservation of the self is not in perfect consonance with that of the community.

In the next chapter, we shall see how individuals in the Dharamgarh valley who identify with certain postulational values embodied in state law and human rights work towards emphasising them by engaging with a diverse set of actors and mechanisms.

5 Subtly but surely: Embracing the values of state law

The previous chapter described and analysed the various types of non-state actors that are working in the sphere of dispute processing. Laws encompassing the postulational values that enable the community to preserve its identity in law find prominence in the processing of disputes at the level of the community, incidental to which are mechanisms that result in resistance to state law, its systems and values. Despite this, however, as the diagrams produced earlier made clear (see Chapter 3, Figure 3.1 page 69 and Figure 3.2 page 70), the values of state law are not and do not become completely absent in the layers of legality dominated by non-state actors, including the self. I argued that in locations such as Gonjhé, where there were several layers of legality, the values of state law became very thin as they travelled inwards to the individuals. However, in the village communities of Dharamgarh valley, the lesser number of layers allowed the values of state law to travel in a fairly uncondensed form to the self. This was rather evident from the many and diverse ways in which individuals "made themselves heard" (Basu 2015, 60) through interacting actively with state law. They were producing several translations of state law through the embracement of its values. Of course, individual behaviour that emphasised the postulational values of state law was often perceived as a challenge to the postulational values that the community cherished, demonstrating a typical situation of conflict in law (Chiba 1998). This placed individuals making such choices in a fairly precarious position. The case studies in the next section reveal how people became rather innovative in emphasising the postulational values of state law that they as individuals may have identified with, without disturbing the postulational values of community laws to the greatest extent possible.

In each of the case studies below, I present the experiences of two individuals faced with a similar disputing situation and compare the mechanisms they adopted, in order to emphasise the same set of values. These case studies should not be understood as absolutely representative of the manner in which the values of state law were embraced by individuals in the villages of the Dharamgarh valley. Nevertheless, they are chosen as discursive illustrations of the modalities of the crucial role of individual agency in dispute processing, which often tends to get undermined in the debates concerning the implementation of state law.

5.1 Case study 1: Protection of natural resources

This case study compares dispute processing mechanisms adopted by two village leaders who aimed to achieve efficient protection of resources in their respective village forests. Forest conservation has remained important to the village communities in the Dharamgarh valley because of their extensive dependence on forest resources for everyday life. The forests were used for grazing of cattle, collection of firewood, medicinal plants, berries, and fruits. The forest was also the focal point of several customary rituals within the local village communities in the Dharamgarh Valley.[1] At the same time, forest protection also came to be identified as a value of state law as formation of *Van Pancāyats* was carried out under the Indian Forest Act, 1927. The objective of *Van Pancāyats*, to protect and develop forests, and distribute their produce among stakeholders in an equitable manner, received much attention during the debates and discussions around increasing acquisition of forest lands by corporations and in the context of debates about climate change. As a result, government stakeholders in these debates, as observed by the village communities, had become more active about forest conservation in the recent past (Negi, Chauhan, and Todaria 2012; Bandi 2016; Chaudhury 2016). Therefore, protection of forests was a postulational value that was identified with the state, but also shared by many in the community. To understand how the sharing of values, such as forest protection, between local communities and the Indian state played out in times of conflict, this section elaborates the different dispute processing mechanisms adopted by local leaders.

Hayatsingh Bhandari, was an aspiring local leader when a dispute involving some "delinquents" from his village, who engaged in tree-cutting from the village forests in breach of the village rules, occurred.[2] Hayatsingh belonged to a fairly prosperous family in village Panchwari. He was himself an aspiring *Grām Pradhān*, and the said dispute, a matter that he took a lead in, occurred while he was still completing his graduation. My stay in Panchwari revealed to me that Hayatsingh was also known to be a very religious man. It was said that his work for society, willingness to help people, and steady worship of the local deities, caused him to be especially blessed. That he could be possessed, and deities would communicate with the audience through him at the time of religious rituals, was perceived by the local community as a sign of such blessings. At the time of our conversation, Hayatsingh had already completed his term as *Grām Pradhān* and now only enjoyed a socially and politically prominent position in his village community. "I was still young then. A fight broke out between the village headmen [*mukhiyās*] and their disagreement led to them giving up protection of the forest [*jangal ko choḍ diyā*]. The forest had a temple. We used to use the forest to cut grass and graze our sheep. As kids we played in that forest,

1 For example, village communities believed that the wind of the forest could possess individuals, and rituals to free persons from the hold of wind were all carried out within the precincts of the forest.

2 The word delinquents is placed in quotes because this was Hayatsingh's perception of the people he proceeded to describe later.

too," narrated Hayatsingh.[3] When the village headmen stopped protecting the surrounding forest, there was a downpour of hailstones in Panchwari, which led to the destruction of many fields. The hailstorm was seen as an indication of the local deity's displeasure with the forest being ignored. A village meeting was therefore called and, with Hayatsingh in the lead, it was decided that the forest, being the villagers' common ancestral "wealth",[4] would be protected by everyone together. "Everyone would cut grass and wood together and it would be equally distributed between the households in the village. It was decided that whoever cut grass stealthily in the forest would be fined five to ten rupees," explained Hayatsingh. However, not everyone had equal integrity and soon Hayatsingh, who had by then proceeded to become chairman of the *Van Panchāyat*,[5] received a complaint regarding some villagers who had been cutting wood in violation of the rules. "At the time we allowed people to cut dry trees and charged them about twenty rupees. These people had been cutting trees stealthily. A police complaint was made, which was then pursued and led to a court case. The court gave us [Hayatsingh's party] an order to protect the forest until the matter was decided," he explained. While Hayatsingh did not articulate it so, my understanding was that unsuccessful negotiation at the village level led to a court case being filed by the *Van Pancāyat* against the defaulters. At the stage of evidence, the court asked Hayatsingh to bring to court the tree that had been felled. "This tree was 45 feet long and 4 feet in diameter. We told the judge that we are neither Hanuman nor Bheem to transport such a large tree to the court,"[6] said Hayatsingh, according to whom, the opposite party that cut the tree had bribed the judge in order for him to make such an incredulous demand for evidence. "But I did not give in. If the judge wanted to see the tree, I said that the court would have to arrange to send an officer on their behalf, or arrange for the [village] road to be widened so that a trolley could pass, and the tree could be brought in. The judge became irritated and started muttering something. Chaos broke out in the court, amidst which one of the *shiyāné* from our village said that the judge had abused him. So, I threatened police action against the judge for his behaviour," narrated Hayatsingh from his experience in court. Soon, however, things were brought under control with the judge apologising to Hayatsingh and the other petitioners. Hayatsingh and the others on his side, that is the *Van Pancāyat,* eventually won the case.

3 All the quotes in this case study are based on several conversations with Hayatsingh Bhandari and one detailed interview in Panchwari (Uttarakhand) on April 2, 2016.
4 The forest was perceived as "wealth" by the villagers, and this was different from just perceiving it as a piece of land or natural resource.
5 A *Van Panchāyat* is a locally selected body that regulates the use of the forest surrounding the village for natural resources. The main responsibility of the *Van Panchāyat* is to ensure that forest resources are not excessively exploited. *Van Panchāyats* have been set up under Section 27 of the Indian Forest Act, 1927.
6 Hanuman and Bheem are both characters from the Indian epics Ramayan and Mahabharat. In the epics, each of the two were described to have immense physical strength, their primary source of power.

That village rules regarding forest protection are breached was not uncommon. However, going to court, like Hayatsingh did, was an exception. More often, in order to deal with such "delinquents", the village heads, or *Van Pancāyats*, in agreement with the rest of the village community, dedicated the village forest to Kokiladevi for a fixed period of time. In a similar dispute that occurred in another village near Didihat, the village head, also the head of the *Van Pancāyat* in that village, initially filed a case in court, but soon grew tired of following it up because of procedural and financial hurdles. Frustrated with the hassles of a court case, he along with the rest of the village had dedicated the forest to Kokiladevi to tackle the offenders. In many parts of the Dharamgarh valley, entire village forests or parts of these were dedicated to Kokiladevi. Dedicating the forest to the goddess involved extended ritualistic practices. Once the forest was so dedicated, no one was allowed (by the goddess) to cut trees or grass or even pick flowers and fruits from the forest. It was believed that misfortune would befall the person or the family of the person who did so. As Hayatsingh said from experiences in his village, "If anyone dares, a leopard will come into their *verānḍāh* the same evening."

The above examples reveal that while both leaders were not hesitant to embrace the postulational value of forest protection, they both chose to process their disputes and emphasise it in fairly different ways. While Hayatsingh went forth to successfully emphasise the values of the state laws pertaining to forest protection, by processing his dispute in a layer involving state actors; other village headmen, like the one in Didihat, preferred to emphasise the very same postulational values by dispute processing in the outermost layer of legality by invoking the intervention of Kokiladevi. Why did Hayatsingh choose to process the dispute in a manner so different from common practice? Hayatsingh himself reasoned that pursuing the case for forest protection vigorously in court was more fruitful than dedicating the forest to the goddess for its protection. "If we dedicate the forest to the *Mātā* we must continue to do *pūjā* in the forest. We cannot use the forest for any purpose. But in court, we have to fight the case *once* – for six months or one year. If we are successful, we are free to use the jungle and protect it in the way we like. But people do not want to go to court. The matters remain pending for many years. Village headmen these days are elected and do not want to depose against anyone for fear that they will lose votes. So, these days the forests are threatened." Despite a rather arduous experience in court, Hayatsingh held the view that pursuing a case for forest conservation in court had more practical consequences than the practice of dedicating the forest to Kokiladevi, and therefore this strategy was more beneficial.

Experiences from the Dharamgarh valley, however, brought forth that the system invoking the intervention of spirits and deities was no less gruelling than pursuing a case in a state institution. Respondents having taken recourse to dispute processing involving Kokiladevi admitted that they could not be sure whether they will find the injustice done to them counterbalanced speedily, or even during their lifetimes, making their situation little different from court cases that were known to be stuck in a whirlwind of delays. In relation to expenditure (see Chapter 4, page 92), an aggrieved person could incur expenditure anywhere from twenty rupees to several thousand rupees in appeasing the goddess and her assistants. Dispute processing in either of the two layers, therefore, was equally challenging, and as the above examples bring forth, also resulted in the same outcome. In one instance, people feared the wrath of the goddess, and in the other, the success of this case in court acted as a threat to prospective offenders. However, despite the likely success of such cases in state courts – not only because their objective is the emphasis of a value that state law itself embodies, but also increasing pressure for forest conservation from external forces, such as NGOs and international bodies on state courts – a large number of forests remain dedicated to Kokiladevi for their protection. Thus, revealing that there were still very few individuals like Hayatsingh who were inclined to, and capable of, exercising agency in the manner he did and would aggressively pursue a case for forest protection in layers involving state actors. Hayatsingh was empathetic to the cause of people who preferred non-state mechanisms of dispute processing and explained that pursuing a court case was not simple. First, he pointed out, it required money. Then, he highlighted, it required the petitioners to convince people to stand as witnesses, particularly the security guards (*chauwkidār*). The fear that violation of the local rules for forest protection would result in a court case apparently deterred many people from becoming *chauwkidārs*, he explained. "They have to go to court to stand as witnesses and also listen to the bad temper of the opposite party," said Hayatsingh, and he continued, "And after all this they [the people] don't get justice (*nyāy*). So, many villagers decide to dedicate the forest to the *Mātā*. Here there is neither the fear of not getting justice nor the trouble of appointing *chauwkidārs*." However, lest we forget, what Hayatsingh's statement also brings forth is that there are factors active at the level of the individual disputant, at the level of the self, enabling such an exercise of agency that is required to pursue a dispute involving the intervention of state actors. For one, Hayatsingh was from a prosperous family in Panchwari. His family had seen several members as *Grām Pradhāns*. As Hayatsingh once narrated from his memories of his grandfather, "Local political campaigners, school teachers and other visitors to the village never left without visiting my grandfather." At the time of the dispute, Hayatsingh was also an aspiring *Grām Pradhān*. A "litigant's goals", in this case Hayatsingh's, as Comaroff and Roberts (1981, 115) have shown, "significantly influence … both its procedural and political career." *Grām Pradhāns* being selected through a process of elections, it was important that Hayatsingh built up a reputation of being an efficient service-provider and a person who could be trusted if brought into power. Having been a religious individual who respected caste-rules and worked according to "*dharma maryada*" (see Chapter 4, page 76), he could already be trusted in the social sphere. The willingness to pursue the dispute in a state forum probably gave Hayatsingh the edge that he needed over his opponents. His secure financial background and education (though limited) enabled him to pursue the case rigorously in court. As is evident from the case study, Hayatsingh did not get deterred from this pursuit, even though the judge tried to make the case procedurally challenging. Playing a prominent part in a protracted litigation before the larger public gave Hayatsingh the opportunity "to demonstrate his political acumen and the strength of his support or [and] enabled him to test and reaffirm relationships with both followers and opponents" (Comaroff and Roberts 1981, 115). Clearly, therefore, there were many factors for Hayatsingh at the level of the self that helped him engage in emphasising postulational values of state law in a layer involving the state. But this, not without reason, once again connected to stressing those values that were important to him at the level of self as part of the community – *izzat* and possibly even *dharma*, as he himself articulated as a motivation.

In the above case, Hayatsingh and many others chose to embrace a postulational value of state law that held shared importance even within the community. In fact, one might even go as far as saying that state law "in practice became an 'extension' of redressing wrongs *mala in se*", that is, wrongs in themselves (Khare 1972, 84). But what happens when individuals decide to emphasise those postulational values of state law that are perceived to challenge the postulational values the communities hold close for self-preservation?

5.2 Case study 2: Ensuring maintenance and freedom from violence

While some postulational values, like forest protection, hold a similar level of prominence in state and community legal orders, there are others, like domestic violence, where its form of eminence in the state legal order differs from that in the community legal order. The right to maintenance, in order to avoid destitution of women, and the right to be free from domestic violence, have been the focus of state agendas, laws, and schemes in India for many years now. While there were community-based mechanisms in the agrarian villages of Dharamgarh valley to ensure these rights for women, securing them was admitted to be a challenge in the context of the biases arising from a patriarchal structure and the resulting skewed power balances between men and women (see Shardadevi's case on page 103, for example). As a result, women seeking maintenance from violent and abusive husbands often considered turning to the layer involving state actors for dispute processing, in the hope of a more effective guarantee of these rights. Dispute processing involving state actors, however, was always deterred by the community and the self, as part of the community, (see Chapter 3, page 75). Moreover, as the experiences below will clarify, dispute processing in the state machinery sometimes also had limited benefits. Despite some common ground, emphasising the values of state law along with those of the community, also becomes fairly challenging. The exercise of individuals' agency became crucial to manoeuvre such limitations and create a situation to best preserve the selves.

In this case study, the first experience is that of Miradevi Arya who was married to her husband Kailash Arya at the age of fifteen. At the time of the interview, Miradevi had been married for close to fifteen or sixteen years and had four children, three daughters, and a son. Miradevi's husband had a government job and was employed with a unit of the Agricultural Department. Miradevi and Kailash, their children, and Kailash's mother resided together in the market area of Chilbasa, a big *tehsil* town. Miradevi had faced a lot of domestic violence and abusive behaviour at the hands of her husband. "What else, it is the same. He drinks and then beats me," she said, knowing fully well that this was a common story in many households in the hills. But, besides being an alcoholic, Miradevi suspected that Kailash suffered from some kind of mental illness. "He undresses publicly, sometimes on the terrace and many times in front of the children. It is very shameful. He says things like (referring to Miradevi) "this woman does not sleep with me" in front of his office staff and neighbours. It is very embarrassing," said Miradevi, who had grown tired of his antics and had begun to fear the impact of Kailash's behaviour on their children, who were now growing teenagers. "My neighbours often tell me that they would have never let us remain in the neighbourhood if they had young children. They keep telling me to convince him to improve his behaviour," she continued. "But what can I do? He has always been like this and his mother never seems to object. In fact, she laughs and smiles when he beats me!"[7]

Kailash's job involved location transfers, as a result of which the family had to shift homes many times, sometimes living in big district towns and at other times in remote *tālukā* locations. It was when they were all living in Bageshwar, a large district headquarter, that Miradevi lodged the first police complaint against her husband. "He had beaten me black and blue and I had fainted out of the pain. We lived in a good neighbourhood. There were well educated people living around us. When the women there saw my condition, they remarked that I had been suffering too long and should have considered going to the police station by now. 'One night in jail will set this man right' they told me. And so that was the day I decided to go to the police station," recollected Miradevi. This was only four years ago, almost 12 years after her marriage, and possibly also since the first incident of domestic violence. Miradevi remembered being scared about going to the police station. The fact that it would bring shame (*beizzati*) upon her family was one part of it, but also that she was unsure about whether she would have been able to comprehend the procedures and conduct of a police station. It is important to understand the social context that Miradevi was culturally conditioned in, to be able to grasp why going to a police station may have seemed so daunting to her. As a result of the social structure of the villages in most parts of Uttarakhand, women did not engage frequently in activities outside their village (see Chapter 2, page 47).[8] The opportunities to do so were also few because women were primarily responsible for household and agriculture-related activities. Additionally, the lack of infrastructure, such as motorable roads and public transport in a landscape marked with thick forest areas, steep slopes, and unpredictable weather conditions, made it quite difficult for many women to go alone even to the market areas, let alone a police station. "But when I went to the city, I learned a lot," said

7 Case study based on interview with Miradevi, Nalkhet (Uttarakhand), April 19, 2015.

8 The women who engaged in income earning and other activities outside their villages as a requirement of their caste-based occupation are an exception. For example, Bhotiā women who were traditional weavers have in more recent years joined their men in the business of trading these items in the market areas.

Miradevi, who after being advised by the women in her neighbourhood in Bageshwar, approached the police station on two occasions before being advised by the police to file a case against her husband. "He would come to the police station every time and promise not to harass me. But each time things would go back to square one after a few days. The police probably grew tired of my complaints and told me that I would be better off without him. If I went to court, they told me, I could claim money to maintain myself and the children and then I could live peacefully."

When Miradevi decided to file a case for maintenance in court, her natal family was not very pleased with her decision. But probably because her suffering was so evident, her father nevertheless supported her, in that he helped her to find a lawyer and accompanied her to the court on every session. At the time of the case, which took one year to be decided, Miradevi and her children lived in her natal home with her parents. When I asked Miradevi how she arranged the funds to pursue the case, she said, "I did not spend a single penny besides what it cost for me to commute. I told everyone from the clerk to the lawyer that I had no money and they recovered everything from my husband." However, Miradevi's case ended soon because she decided that she would go back to reside with her husband.

"There was another lady in our *birāderi* who had also filed a case for maintenance. Her case ended only recently, after seven years. At that point (when Miradevi's case was disposed), it had been three to four years that her case was pending in court and she had not received any money till then. Everyone advised me to settle the matter because I would only end up spending time and money pursuing a court case. Therefore, when I told the court that I had decided to go back (to my husband), the judge said that he would in any case order my husband to pay me Rs. 5,000 per month. I could use it if I chose to return to my natal home again because of the harassment. But what would I do with Rs. 5,000? My parents have only two daughters. They don't even have much land. I did not want to burden them any further. I have four children and I wanted to educate them well. They should have a better life than I did. Therefore, I just came back. The situation is no different now than it was before. He still misbehaves, speaks vulgarly and beats me – although less than before. But my children are being educated, are well fed and that is what is important," said Miradevi.

Since Kailash's behaviour had not improved drastically and there were still incidences of physical violence, Miradevi did sometimes end up going to the local police station in the vicinity of where they were living at the time of the interview. This was, as she described, more for her own mental peace than in the hope of any actual reparation. The police, Miradevi claimed, did nothing really. They told her to try and resolve things with Kailash and if this was impossible, they advised her to leave the man. "I would be very happy to leave him, but then how do I feed myself and my children? Do they have a solution for that?" she asked. At one point when she got frustrated with the police's inactivity, Miradevi even wrote a letter to the District Magistrate in Bageshwar. In response to this, the local revenue collector (*patwāri*) visited their house to sound

Kailash out.[9] "In front of the authorities he acts so well that they are bound to be convinced that his behaviour will improve. He will swear not to misbehave and even falls at their [the authorities'] feet, but then again this pretence wears off soon after they are gone," she said.

However, by the time Miradevi returned to live with her husband again after the court case, Kailash's conduct with his wife had become well-known in Kailash's workplace. Not only had this fact brought much *beizzati* (shame) to his family, but on Miradevi's return, Kailash's employer suggested that he would transfer Kailash's salary to a joint account held by Kailash and Miradevi together, rather than to the one that only Kailash operated. Miradevi shared that since then she operated the account, withdrawing whatever she needed to meet the household expenses. She then gave the rest to Kailash "Otherwise, he would just spend all the money on alcohol, like he did earlier," she said.

Confronting her circumstances in the manner that she did, clearly, had made Miradevi very bold. Miradevi's decision to return to reside with her husband was taken in light of certain long-term considerations. While pendency of cases in state courts was one part of it, the other was the possibility of inheriting her husband's job after his retirement or death.[10] The position that Kailash held with the unit of the agricultural department had been inherited by him when his father passed away, and Miradevi knew that her application for this post after Kailash retired was entitled to a preference. Meanwhile, the financial arrangement that Kailash's employer had created, had secured her children's education as well as her own. In preparation for a job, along with her children, Miradevi too had re-started her education and was giving her twelfth-grade examination at the time of my fieldwork. She managed to do a course in typing and even learned to ride a motorbike. A few months after my interaction with Miradevi, I also learned that she, Kailash, and the children had begun to live separately from her mother-in-law. Now being the sole senior woman in the house, Miradevi had full charge of managing her household in the manner that she deemed correct, thereby giving her more leverage in the power relationship she shared with her husband as well.[11]

The second experience belongs to Draupadi Panchpal, also married at the age of about fifteen. Draupadi's marriage to Bhimsingh Panchpal was her second marriage. Her first one had been arranged when she was only nine years old, after which she had been widowed because of the sudden death of her first husband. Draupadi's natal home was located in a village located beyond Munsiyāri, a town

9 The *patwāri* is responsible for registering land records, physically measuring lands for entry into his records, and for evaluating the quality of land (A. Gupta 1995, 379). His authority is usually to be invoked in land-related disputes, but also, as we see from these case studies, is possible in other types of disputes as well.

10 This seemed to be an informal practice where clerical jobs were often "inherited" by eligible family members of deceased employees.

11 See Derrett (1978b), who highlights how in a conventional family "the subordination of the wife is … primarily to her parents-in-law, who run the household" (1978b, 103). Whereas in the nuclear household "daughters-in-law … are queens almost from the first" (1978b, 105).

that in more recent years became popular as a trekking hotspot. At the time when Draupadi was young, though, Munsiyāri was difficult to access because of being located very remotely with little road access. "It is actually, a long walk ahead from Munsiyāri," said Kamla, Draupadi's daughter-in-law.[12] After Draupadi's marriage to Bhimsingh she moved to Jamkuda village in the Dharamgarh valley. Bhimsingh had a job in Delhi and he earned very well. Draupadi however was unable to describe what sort of a job this was, all she knew was that he did a lot of driving. Bhimsingh spent most of his time in Delhi and returned annually to the village. "Whatever was needed for the house came from his income," said Kamla, who claimed to have never seen a sane version of her father-in-law. After several years of a peaceful marriage, Bhimsingh started to become very violent towards Draupadi, who felt that something had caused him to lose his mind ("*Unka dimāg kharab ho gaya tha.*") Thereafter, Draupadi would apprehend every visit that Bhimsingh made to the village, which had by then become more frequent. On many occasions, the violence would escalate to such levels that Draupadi's sons recollected hiding their mother in the homes of other people in the *birāderi*. "We would tell him that she has gone somewhere they didn't know," said Naveen, Draupadi's older son. But on one such occasion, Bhimsingh discovered Draupadi and became so violent towards her that she fled out of fear for her life to her natal village. "She must have lived there for a few months, when she had a dream. In that dream, a woman told her to return to her marital home. The woman assured Draupadi that her life would regain shape, she would find a source of income, and all the people who did not speak to her or treat her properly would come to her door on their own," said Kamla, on the basis of a story Draupadi often recollected. Draupadi believed that this woman was an *avatar* of their family deity (*ishṭ devtā*).

After this dream, Draupadi said that she returned to her marital home. "On the very next morning, I found some people waiting to meet me. They said that they had heard that I could help them with their grievances," said Draupadi, who is today a well-established *puchiāri*. People from different parts of the district visited her for advice and her interpretation of the cause of their disputes. From 8 a.m. to well past noon, Draupadi's living room was filled with people as she made her way through sachets of rice that people brought from their homes to tell them whether their misfortunes were the consequence of the intervention of a deity or spirit. She also prescribed herbal medicines for those who were ill, listening to their pulse in the manner an Ayurvedic doctor would. As a *puchiāri*, she was believed to be bestowed with special knowledge and powers, a blessing of her *ishṭ devtā* (deity of

12 Most parts of this case study are based on information collected over a period of time between January 2016 and May 2016 in Jamkuda village. Some parts about Draupadi's life history were related by her daughter-in-law, whereas many others of her own experience about how she processed her dispute were narrated by Draupadi herself. I had to follow this method of fieldwork since Draupadi spoke a dialect of Kumaoni that was difficult to follow. Quotes from her are based on my own conversations with her, whereas other parts of her story are narrated by her daughters-in-law and sons who spoke a more popular form of Kumaoni and Hindi as well.

one's choice). She was also known to become possessed by the deity on certain occasions. People who sought her advice brought donations in cash and kind as a token of their gratitude, which at the time of this fieldwork were the main source of income for Draupadi and her family.

According to Draupadi's narrative, Bhimsingh's behaviour towards her did not cease to be violent after she returned from her natal village. However, the growing crowd of people that trusted Draupadi's instincts and respected her for the advice was perceived to have had an intimidating effect on him, slowly deterring his inclination for violence towards her. A few years ago, Draupadi's son received a call from Bhimsingh's employer that he had taken very ill and had been admitted to the hospital in Delhi several weeks before. Consequent to his illness, Bhimsingh had a paralysis stroke. "So, he (Naveen) went and got him back. He was bedridden for long and now he is slightly better. Walking around a little. But even now, he becomes a little crazy and starts shouting at her (Draupadi) and the grandchildren. Then we all intervene and stop him," said Kamla. My observations revealed that nobody in the family paid much attention to Bhimsingh anymore. He was seen around walking like a shadow in the house, which was evidently headed by Draupadi. He silently sat in their courtyard watching a steady flow of people visiting the house to seek Draupadi's advice. Her income from being a *puchiāri* was the main source of livelihood for the family, and with Bhimsingh unable to physically manage on his own, Draupadi took the lead along with her sons in managing many activities beyond the household as well. "It is all a result of his *karma* (*karam ke phal bhugat rahe hain*)," Draupadi said to me once, when I asked her about how she felt about her life's experiences and Bhimsingh.

Miradevi and Draupadi's stories are remarkably similar in several respects; right from the age at which these women got married, to their experiences of a violent and abusive married life and their continued residence in their marital homes with their husbands despite this. Violence and maintenance were a complex connected reality for many women in the village communities in this region of Uttarakhand.[13] In many cases, the violence was a result of alcoholism, but in some, it was also a result of mental illness. Many women, for lack of alternative arrangements, chose to remain in their marital homes to secure their maintenance, which concept should be broadly interpreted to include not just financial security, but also safeguarding themselves from the social predicaments of living as a single woman. In full consonance with this reality, the Indian legislature brought into force the lauded Domestic Violence Act, in 2005, which makes a provision for women who have been victims of domestic violence to enforce a right to residence in their matrimonial homes if they choose. The court, in such a situation, may pass a protection order to ensure that such a woman can continue to reside in her matrimonial home safely (Government of India 2005, vol. 43, sections 17–19). However, the Domestic Violence Act remains only a tool in the hands of lawyers,

13 During preliminary fieldwork in November to December 2014, I interacted with several women in different villages of Pitthoragarh and Bageshwar districts of Uttarakhand who narrated similar experiences of domestic violence.

claimed by them to facilitate primarily the speedy disposal of maintenance petitions in the lower courts of India. For a majority of women in the villages of the Dharamgarh valley, the stories of Miradevi, and even more so of Draupadi, were far more familiar, where dispute processing to protect the self was dependent on the skilful exercise of agency, instrumentalising social structures to one's advantage.

Customary practice based on patrilineal norms, among all castes in the Dharamgarh valley and beyond, had it that, what was perceived to be a girl's right in her natal family property was given to her in the form of gold, money, and other gifts at the time of her marriage by her family.[14] Once this happened, a daughter could not claim any further rights in her parent's property. However, upon marriage her right in the family property of her husband's family also devolved upon her. Marriage was socially perceived to entitle a woman with a rightful share in properties and decision-making in her matrimonial family, which she could choose to legitimately enforce whenever and in whatever manner she willed. That upon marriage, a girl transforms into a woman and her opinions begin to count and are more respected,[15] was observed to lend some confidence to women's character.[16] Additionally, the status of being married within this community in many senses was perceived to be far more liberating than being an unmarried girl in the same society, as the latter were individuals who enjoyed very little mobility.[17] Married women often capitalised on this position, interacting more easily with people outside their home, laughing and joking more freely, unlike the unmarried girls who had to always be cautious of their conduct for fear of being labelled as "of loose character". At the same time, for a married woman to return to the natal family because of her inability to settle down in the matrimonial home could create a tricky situation in her natal home. In case of women, like Draupadi, who had married brothers, the return of a married sister to her natal home was apprehended to lead to unpleasant circumstances, as this was often perceived by the brother's wife as an unfair (and unexpected) sharing of – sometimes quite

14 Part of these gifts comprised dowry and part of them constituted her *strīdhan*. Dowry generally indicates the entire assets transferred from the bride's family to the groom's family at the time of the marriage (Menski 1998). *Strīdhan* is the gifts that a bride receives from her family before, at the time of, or after her marriage. It is the woman's property and the husband cannot alienate this property against her will (see Solanki 2011, 140). Under the Hindu Marriage Act, a woman has absolute right over her *strī dhan*. It is however usually difficult to distinguish (and particularly at the time of marriage) between what constitutes dowry, and which properties constitute a woman's *strī dhan*.

15 It was often said that upon marriage a lady no more remained a girl, but became a woman ("*ladki se mahila ho jāti hai*"). Colloquially, the terms *ladki* and *mahila* are used synonymously with "unmarried woman" and "married woman" respectively.

16 See the conclusion of Lemons' PhD dissertation on how marriage is space, which may provide "women with room for manoeuvre rather than simply robbing them of freedoms of movement." (Lemons 2010, 172).

17 The mobility of unmarried girls is limited as a measure to control their "sexuality" (E. Moore 1993, 526).

limited – resources. The right explained above (see page 139), that Draupadi held in her in-laws' home, is what her brother's wife was entitled to in Draupadi's parent's home.

In light of all these circumstances, both Draupadi and Miradevi probably felt more secure in continuing to reside in their matrimonial homes, despite the violence. However, they both realised, and for which purpose they adopted entirely different mechanisms, that it was crucial for their self-preservation that the issue of their violence be made "public".[18] In order to understand, the gravity of making an issue – such as the one that Miradevi or Draupadi faced – public, it is important to spend a little time on understanding the notions of "public" and "private" in the communities in the Dharamgarh valley.

As in the state legal order, so also in the social sense of a community, there lies an understanding of "public" and "private" domains.

Generally, in the broadest sense, both in Gonjhé and in the villages of the Dharamgarh valley, the boundaries of the "private" sphere end with the territorial limits of the village. All interactions and transactions with individuals or institutions from outside the village were considered to comprise the "public" sphere. In Figure 5.1 (see page 141) this sphere is indicated by the darker shades of grey (to the extreme left). So long as knowledge of a dispute and its processing remained within the layers involving non-state actors from within the village or caste community, it was considered a "private matter" and would remain within the knowledge of the residents of that village only. The area to the right, indicated by the lighter shades of grey constitutes this private sphere. But the moment a dispute was pursued in a layer involving state actors, to the extent of even being discussed with a lawyer, who was not a part of the community, the issue was seen to have become a matter of public knowledge.

In the villages in Dharamgarh valley, I noticed that the divisions between the public and private became even more intricate at a level within the community. Therefore, as the figure reflects, there was a further division between what constituted "public" and "private" knowledge at an intra-community level, with the shade of grey becoming lighter to indicate the private sphere within the community. Domestic violence, if it occurred between the husband and wife, was one such issue that fell within the periphery of the innermost column (indicated by the lightest shade of grey) in the figure and constituted what was deemed as "private", even within the community. As a result, that domestic violence occurred was a matter of common knowledge,[19] but whether and how such incidents occurred in a particular home constituted the sphere of "private" knowledge of the couple and its immediate family. On the subject of attitudes towards incidence of domestic violence, I learnt from Geetadevi Meher, a former *Grām Prādhan* of Khasi, that

18 See also Iyengar (2007) on her observation about how "nari adalats" (women's courts) used the public square to put the perpetrator under public scrutiny, which is believed to put in him a strong motivation to change his behaviour.

19 Ishwaran's (1964, 235) description about common knowledge is fairly accurate: "Though much secrecy is attached to the nature of the dispute and the procedure in handling it, everybody in the village knows something about it."

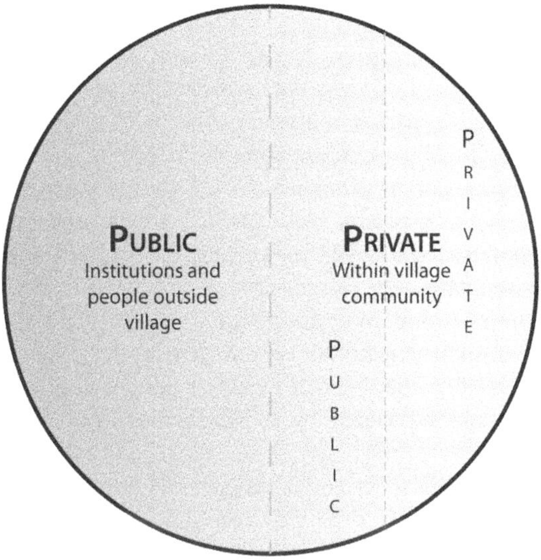

Figure 5.1 Notions of "public" and "private" in the communities of Dharamgarh valley

men in her community did not like any outsider intervening in spousal disputes. "They get very angered and will abuse anyone who interferes. So as a result of this fear no one even bothers interfering," said Geetadevi and she clarified further that whatever had to be done in this regard, then, was to be decided by the wife and her husband only.[20] Such disputes being considered "very private" (Ishwaran 1964, 235), members outside the immediate family (those living in the same household, that is) were not expected to interfere in them. Consequently, discussions about actual incidences of domestic violence, even between community members, were absent. But, take the subject of property division between brothers because of arguments between their respective wives – this fell within the understanding of "public" knowledge at the community level. This was therefore openly discussed with the family concerned as well as within the community members generally. How the village communities decided which matters fell within the innermost private sphere (the column to the extreme right in Figure 5.1) at an intra-community level remained unclear. Ishwaran's (1964) observation based on his fieldwork in Shivapur, near Dharwad provides some direction. "They do make a distinction between private and public delict, and this is made taking into account the nature and magnitude of the offence, the persons involved in the dispute, their status and position in the community, etc. … People say such disputes should not be discussed in public and should be settled within the precinct of the family." This, as we have seen, was clearly the attitude towards disputes between husbands and wives, one of the subjects that fell within the private sphere. At the level of "public" and "private" within the community, the

20 Interview in Khasi (Uttarakhand), February 4, 2016.

boundaries between what constituted "public" and "private" knowledge, I observed, were constantly changing. In the diagram, the subtle change of colours indicates that the "public" and "private" spheres, though different, were nevertheless always perceived as part of a unitary whole with boundaries that remained fuzzy at the edges. The shifting boundaries were dependent to some extent on how disputing parties chose to process a dispute that was perceived to fall within the most private sphere. A person may choose to make the cause of his or her dispute, which is popularly perceived as "private", a "public" one, and thus transgress such social boundaries. Or, like property matters, which by the very nature of their processing often became immediately more public, also responses to disputes between husbands and wives, could become visible to others in the forms of bruising and other visible injuries as a result of domestic violence or odd behaviour, or some kind of "exposure" by a disturbed individual such as Miradevi's husband.

Going back to what Miradevi and Draupadi did, the manner in which these women chose to process their situations resulted in bringing the incidences of domestic violence into the public sphere at different levels. While Miradevi involved state actors to process her dispute, Draupadi made people from her *birāderi* a part of her dispute processing at the level of the self. That domestic violence existed as a clearly defined issue for the communities in the Dharamgarh valley was evident from the specific manner in which it is located in the social context of this society. Thus, the manner in which it was dealt with was inevitably bound to be tied up with notions of *izzat, dharma* and power. The fact that these women chose to process a dispute from within the most private sphere involving agents of the public, indicated (both for their husbands and the communities) that their tolerance level with respect to the violence had reached its peak indicating a "crisis" (E. Moore 1993, 535) situation,[21] which in a way legitimated their bold exercise of agencies, crossing a boundary, so as to bring these issues out of their homes and into the public sphere. It is exactly by such exercise of agency that they embraced the newly gendered postulational values that state laws such as the Domestic Violence Act of 2005 seek to emphasise through legislating about intra-family relationships.

Rai (1996) points out in the context of India how a considerable emphasis is placed on "power (or lack of power) of the state to formulate, legislate, and enforce laws" (1996, 11) to bring about equality between men and women. Miradevi's experience, however, showed us that state actors can enable dispute processing in the sphere of matrimonial disputes only to a limited extent. While repeated visits to the police station truncated the violence in her home – it was only for brief periods. The court order directing her husband to pay her maintenance was a successful display of the state's efforts in this regard, but again with

21 Moore (1993, 535) observes similarly in a Rajasthani village that "fights between husbands and wives, fathers and sons, or mothers and daughters-in-law are not taken to a panchayat until they reach a crisis", in that, a situation of 'crisis' legitimated invocation of public intervention.

limited consequences. Miradevi's statement (see page 135) with regard to her anticipated difficulty in managing the education, health, and household necessities of her family, as well as finding a place to live (because she could not remain dependent on her parents), were a clear indication of this. However, the court order remained a valuable bargaining tool for Miradevi with her husband. "The document is with my parents, because my husband gets very angry when he sees it," said Miradevi, when I asked if I could see the court order. Even though Miradevi did not proceed to have this order executed, she knew that she could do so if the need arose, and until then admitted to only use it to remind her husband of the rights it granted her, thus improving her bargaining ground in the power equation between the two.

Draupadi, unlike Miradevi, never seemed to have processed her dispute in any layer beyond her own self. Agency, as is drawn from the experiences of women who confront violence, was observed to be demonstrated "in terms of one's judgments of what one can do with whatever skills she has. It refers to one's capacity and motivation to define her own life choices and pursue her goals, despite the opposition that she faces" (Magar 2003 citing; Kabeer 1999 and; Bandura 1995). By taking to practising as a *puchiāri*, regardless of it being the consequence of a spiritual revelation as she claimed, Draupadi put to work her skills as a fantastic orator. She used the existing social situation, and its close association with religious and customary beliefs, to create a public space within her domestic sphere that simultaneously worked to shield her from the violence inflicted by her husband. In a highly patriarchal set-up, like in the agrarian communities in the Dharamgarh valley, the power that female *puchiāris* wielded was astonishing and it stood out. This "public" position enabled such women to take a wide variety of risks in their personal space, which remained buffered by their role as *puchiaris*; a role that placed them in perfect parity with the postulational values of the community. The agency exhibited by the politically active Shiv-Sena women in Mumbai while disbursing "justice and advice to their neighbours while sitting by their stoves" (Bedi 2010, 47) is not too far from the what was exhibited by Draupadi sitting in the remote corner at the other end of the same country. Both the roles of the Shiv-Sena women and of those of the likes of Draupadi, result in the private space of the home "becoming an increasingly fluid category." And "while [these roles] did not de-centre the gendered division of labour or place of a female figure in the home … [they] did unsettle the individual practices of feminine conventionality" (Bedi 2010, 46–47). Consequentially, Draupadi could boldly assert herself in retaliation to her husband's behaviour without being too worried about posing a challenge to community values by virtue of doing so.

Miradevi managed to engage the layer involving state actors in the processing of her dispute because of the exposure and support she received from the women in her neighbourhood on moving to the big district headquarter. Draupadi, who had never lived outside her village, first her natal one and then her matrimonial one, managed, however, to achieve for herself the same end as Miradevi by processing her dispute entirely on her own with the support, though without the involvement, of non-state actors from other layers. Here again, we see how contexts and processes, rather than the end situation become crucial factors towards understanding and assessing whether and how the postulational values of state law are actually being embraced.

5.3 Case study 3: Inter-caste marriages and value of individual choice

The previous two sections discussed postulational values that were understood by the community and the state legal orders in the same way, but shared by them in different ways. Case study 3 is based on experiences with disputes arising from inter-caste marriages. Inter-caste marriages are perceived to be based on postulational values that challenged the values on which community legal orders in the Dharamagarh valley were understood to be based. Inter-caste marriages were a social taboo (Derrett 1978b, 2–5) in the villages in the Dharamgarh valley. In the Dharamgarh valley, customarily, inter-caste marriage between individuals who belonged to different villages, though not encouraged, may still have been allowed by the families and eventually accepted by the community. However, an inter-caste marriage between individuals belonging to the same village, though not unheard of, was strongly disapproved by the village community, with the couple often being ostracised from the village of the partner belonging to the higher caste. On many occasions, the family of such a partner, and other people, also faced social boycott if they chose to remain associated with the couple. Speaking about a recent incident of an inter-caste marriage in her village where a higher caste girl eloped with a lower caste boy, Gangadevi, a *shiyānī* in Gangapur village said: "Right now we don't know where the couple is. But if she returns, we will disassociate with her and her family. If her parents refuse her entry into the home, they will continue to remain part of the community, but otherwise the family will be expelled from the community," she said. When I asked her why inter-caste marriages were such a grave social taboo, she said, "If we don't do this, anyone will marry anyone. How will that work?" (see also Cohn 1959, 81).

Derrett (1978b, 102) observed that the secure way of life and source of income, the range of relations, friends, and associates through marriage and birth, and the mutual support of a "tightly coherent unit" would be lost if every individual went his or her own way. Therefore, according to him, inter-caste marriages – which were likely to jeopardise such a situation – were probably forbidden by the *dharmaśāstra*. Indeed, Derrett's point holds ground in light of the ways of life of people in the villages of the Dharamgarh valley. But what also cannot be overlooked is that strict adherence to caste rules and maintenance of this hierarchical structure was part of the mechanisms to reinforce power structures, and maintain social order and solidarities, based on caste networks in the particular village. This became further clear by the fact that enforcement of caste rules was territorially limited, in that, couples belonging to different castes, but the same village, faced greater discrimination than couples in an inter-caste marriage, where the partner from the lower caste belonged to a different state, district or region. People in the village communities of the Dharamgarh valley observed what has been conceptually termed as a "spatial version of legal pluralism" (Merry 2015, 72), in that, they perceived that different laws existed in different physical spaces. Therefore, people did not feel compelled to adhere to caste rules when they were outside the village, and more so in urban areas. Mohansingh Meher, another former *Grām Pradhān* of Khasi, who was also a former army officer, explained: "We follow one law when we are in the army and another law when we are in the village. There is no Hindu, Muslim or Christian in the army (*fauj*). Being a soldier (*fauji*) is our only duty (*dharma*). Then we eat with the Muslims and drink with the Christians." This behaviour, however neither surprised nor troubled the sentiments of his family or co-villagers.[22] But here, in his village, things were different. Mohansingh would not eat the food cooked by a lower caste person; nor would he allow an individual belonging to a lower caste community to enter his kitchen. It was thus evident that these rules and their postulational values were village (and therefore context) specific, and were required to be emphasised and followed for community solidarity, and social and self-ordering for peaceful coexistence in the village.

In this context, I proceed to explain and analyse the following two case studies. The first experience is that of Dhana Panchpal and Amar Rathod who married inter-caste.[23] While Amar belonged to the Thakur caste, Dhana belonged to the Scheduled Tribe, Bhotiā – a caste that is looked upon as inferior to themselves by the Thakurs. Not only had Dhana and Amar married inter-caste, but by virtue of living in the same village of Gangapur, they had also married intra-village, a fact that further increased the social unacceptability of their decision to come together. Dhana and Amar had studied together until high school. Thereafter Dhana joined an NGO active in creating livelihood opportunities in the area. Her role at the NGO required her to expand the reach of the NGO and encourage more and more people to join in the various income-earning programmes offered by the NGO. As a result, Dhana's skills of interacting with different types of people in different villages came to be honed. By the time Dhana and Amar decided to get married, Dhana had completed many years of working at the NGO, which she described made her more confident and outgoing than other women in her village. At the same time her extended interactions inside and outside the village gave her a lot of exposure and experience, and helped her build a powerful network of mentors and friends, which went beyond her kinship networks, something quite uncommon among women her age in the Dharamgarh valley. Amar, after completing his high school had moved away to the capital city of Delhi, like his brothers, to find a job. He worked in Delhi for several years and as a result, like many other men from his village, was well informed about social, technological, and other developments in the urban areas of the country. While Dhana and Amar did not share any history of having dated one another, Dhana claimed that there was always something "special" between the two of them. And therefore, when Amar defied his family and asked her to marry him, she was not surprised. Since Dhana belonged to a lower caste, and was marrying

22 Interview in Khasi (Uttarakhand), January 27, 2016.

23 This case study is based on one detailed interview, Melatpur (Uttarakhand), April 19, 2015 and several other interactions between May 2015 and June 2016.

into an upper-caste, her family did not see any reason to object. Additionally, Dhana had no brothers and was the main income-earner of her family that consisted of her mother and one of her older sisters who continued to live, even after marriage, in her natal home with her two children. For the courage she had shown in taking on this responsibility of her family, she was well respected in the Bhotiā caste community in Gangapur. The objection to Dhana and Amar's marriage, as was expected by them, came from Amar's family and the Thakur caste community in Gangapur. Amar, by deciding to marry a girl from a lower caste was accused of having brought shame, dishonour, and ill reputation (*beizzati*) upon his entire *birāderi*. An inter-caste marriage also meant a challenge to established power structures within the village that were reinforced by the maintenance of such caste hierarchies. At the level of the self (for Dhana and Amar) it was also perceived as not fulfilling one's *dharma*, because adherence to caste rules was perceived as part of one's duty towards the abode of the Gods (*dev bhoomi*), i.e. the mountains – the geographical location that this community perceived they were blessed to be living in. Therefore, Dhana and Amar were perceived to have acted in defiance of community laws in the form of the popularly expected behaviour, in line with perceived notions of *izzat* and *dharma* (see Chapter 4, page 75).

At the insistence of Amar's older brother's wife (*bhābhi*), a *birāderi* meeting was called prior to the marriage. "She arranged for some *shiyāné* from the village to gather. She wanted them to oppose the marriage since it would bring *beizzati* to their family. And she requested them to make a decision to the effect that Amar would not have a share in the family property if he married me," said Dhana, according to whom Amar's sister-in-law had her own personal reasons for opposing the marriage. But since her personal biases would not have been a legitimate ground for opposing the marriage, as many others in Amar's family had consented to the marriage; she called a *pancāyat*. "Once the *pancāyat* decides to oppose something, no one, including those who supported us is able to act according to their will and go against the decision of the *birāderi*," continued Dhana. The *pancāyat*, however, did not go as far as ousting Amar from his right in the family property. According to Dhana and Amar, they knew that the *pancāyat* could not prevent Amar from enforcing his legal right (under state law) in the family property. "And therefore, they probably saw no point in making an order that could not be implemented," added Amar. The *shiyāné*, however, decided that Amar and Dhana would be ostracised from the Thakur community in Gangapur, if they continued with their decision to be married. Being ostracised meant that they would not be invited to any celebrations or mourning in the community, that they would receive no help or support of any nature during or after their marriage from the community, and that anyone from the Thakur community who chose to associate with them would also face the same treatment.

Dhana and Amar, nevertheless, decided to get married and in doing so exercised their understanding of the postulational values of "individual choice" and "absolute equality". It was well known within the rural communities in the Dharamgarh valley that these values were actually promoted through several state-sponsored schemes to encourage inter-caste marriages.[24] Nobody from Amar's family or *birādari* attended the wedding, which, however, remained fully supported by Dhana's family, caste network, employers at the NGO and other friends. "In our community inter-caste marriages are very common. So, my uncles were alright with the match. But they were concerned about my wellbeing in the Thakur community. The Thakur community is not known for very successful marriages. Many Thakur girls return to their natal homes after marriage because they are unable to settle down with their in-laws and husband. Sometimes it is the nature of the girl, but many times it is also because she is not treated well in her marital home. In the *Bhotiā* community it is very different. The girl will never return to her natal home; whatever the circumstances in her marital home, she will make things work. I do not remember any aunt or cousin in my immediate or extended family who has returned to live with her parents for good after her marriage," said Dhana.

After marriage, Amar and Dhana lived in Delhi, where Amar had a job, for a short period. However, soon afterwards Amar had a paralysis attack, which caused him to be bedridden for two years. Lack of financial resources, then, compelled the couple to return to Uttarakhand, where Dhana restarted her job with the NGO to support now her own as well as her natal family. At the time of the interviews, Amar had recovered to a great extent. He could walk, eat, and bathe on his own, but did not feel confident enough to take up a job. Dhana and Amar had been married for five years at the time, of which for six months they lived in Delhi. For the rest of the time they lived in a market area not too far away from their village, Gangapur. Dhana often met people from Amar's *birādari* in the market place. "They will discreetly ask about him. His brothers have even offered us some money to help with his medical treatment. But this is all informal and quiet. Why can they not convince the *birādari* to accept us back into the community? After all, we were not the first couple to have an inter-caste marriage in Gangapur," said Dhana. At the time of the last interviews, Dhana was pregnant with their first child. "Amar's sister-in-law knows that many in the *birādari* and even her own husband – Amar's older brother – visit and interact with us quietly. Since her effort to have us ostracised by the *pancāyat* has not been completely successful, I learned from a *puchiāri* that she invoked the intervention of Kokiladevi. My husband being suddenly paralysed is a result of the goddess's wrath is what I have learned. But I want all this sorted out before the baby arrives," related Dhana, who felt that in order to be able to conduct any joint *pūjā* before the goddess, their being reaccepted into the caste network was important. Dhana and Amar believed that only upon pressure from the community would Amar's sister-in-law probably relent and agree to negotiating their differences, and conducting a joint *pūjā* to appease the goddess, which would among other things – as Dhana

24 State governments in India offer allowances in the form of social welfare schemes for couples who marry inter-caste or inter-religion. In the state of Uttarakhand, a couple marrying inter-caste or inter-religion is entitled to an award of Rs. 10,000 from the State Government (Government of Uttarakhand 2017).

shared – also improve Amar's health. In our last conversations about the issue, Dhana shared that she had decided to call a *birāderi* meeting of the Thakur caste in Gangapur and ask the *shiyāné* to reconsider their previous decision. "This is the only way his sister-in-law will be forced to put aside her personal prejudices and become ready to conduct a joint *pūjā* and restore relations," said Dhana, who also knew that broken caste relations and an ostracised status could be persistent impediments in the child's future, which were probably what she and Amar were still not ready for.

The second experience comes from a village close to the Dharamgarh valley, in the Chaudmuniya area. Hansa, a Thakur girl, had married Deepak Berma, from the Sonār caste. Here, unlike in Dhana and Amar's case, it was a girl from the higher caste of Thakurs marrying into the Sonār caste, which was perceived to be lower than the Thakurs in the social set-up. Hansa and her husband lived in the Dharamgarh market area, which is where I met them.

Hansa returned with her family – consisting of her parents, a younger sister, and a younger brother – to live in their village after several years of residing in Mumbai, where her father had a job. Hansa, the oldest of the three siblings, completed her high-school education in the metropolitan city of Mumbai. Since she had a better education than her younger siblings, who completed their school in the village after they returned, Hansa's father arranged for Hansa to complete her graduation and post-graduation in the district headquarter of Pitthoragarh. At the insistence of her family, Hansa, who held a Masters in Arts (MA) degree, also tried to live in Bangalore, with her cousin's brother and his wife, to find a job there. "It was such a big city. All roads looked the same. And the one time when I sat in a rickshaw all by myself I could not find my way back home. I just shut my eyes and prayed that the driver would take me the correct way back home," she said, stating how she only knew the name of the road and nothing else. "I stayed there for six months and all the while I cried because I wanted to go back home. Ultimately my cousin's brother and his wife who had hoped I would settle down in Bangalore gave up and sent me back. But now I wish I had remained there. I would have married someone there only. I would have learned something new and done better for myself," said Hansa, half-jokingly in a conversation with me one day.[25] At the time of the interviews, Hansa, along with her sister – Poonam, ran a beauty parlour-cum-cosmetics and tailoring shop in the small market of Dharamgarh. Her husband, who pursued the traditional occupation of members of his caste, ran a small jewellery shop where he made and sold gold and silver jewellery.

Hansa was already 23 years old when she received a formal marriage proposal from Deepak. By standards of the village community in most parts of Uttarakhand, Hansa was already "too old" to receive any noteworthy marriage offers. Therefore, when she received a proposal from Deepak – despite his being from a different caste – she accepted it almost immediately (though not without thought,

25 Interview with Hansa and her sister Poonam, Dharamgarh market (Uttarakhand), February 20, 2016.

as we shall see later). "It was hardly a love marriage. I didn't even know him. We got married within 12 days of the proposal," narrated Hansa. "His family made the proposal and I said 'yes'," recollected Hansa.[26] Having grown up in big towns, Hansa admitted to have had no practice with farm-related work. Moreover, being twenty-three years old, Hansa felt that age was not on her side in order for her to wait any longer in hope of an exceptional match. "In Thakur families there is a lot of farming work. Lot of hard work. And I knew I was not capable of any of that. My husband is a Sonār. This community has little land and their source of livelihood is largely business based. Also, I was already 23, so I accepted the proposal right away," said Hansa, who as we learn had weighed out the factors in her favour, if she accepted the proposal. "But I became very scared as the date of the marriage neared. An inter-caste marriage and that too within the same village was socially unacceptable, and people from our *birāderi* had begun to trouble my father, taunting him for permitting the match. I was worried for my father and my sister, who would continue to live in the village and so on the day of the marriage I told my husband that I did not want to get married," recollected Hansa.[27] But Hansa's own sister and Deepak's sister were very supportive of the wedding and said that they would ensure that the ceremony went through peacefully. Hansa and Deepak's marriage ceremony was attended by only half her *birāderi*.

After the marriage, there was a *birāderi* meeting in Hansa's caste community who decided what would follow. "The *Grām Pradhān* and other elders from the *birāderi* sat together and told my father that they would accept him as part of the *birāderi* only if he broke all ties with me. But my father refused to do so and so they ostracised my family," remembered Hansa. Following the *birāderi's* decision, Hansa's father and sister were not invited to community weddings. They were constantly taunted for the *beizzati* their daughter had brought upon the caste.

Hansa, of course, was not disconnected from all this. Even though Hansa did not articulate it so, similar to what Grover (2009) observed in a *basti* (slum) in Delhi, for a woman to seek refuge in her natal home in times of crisis in the marital home was a common practice also in the villages of and around the Dharamgarh valley. Consequently, women ensured to maintain very warm and cordial relations with the *birāderi* in their natal villages, not just in response to an emotional need, but also on instinct of preparation for unpleasant eventualities. Therefore, despite being in her matrimonial home, Hansa remembered being very

26 It deserves to be mentioned here that inter-caste marriage proposals are usually preceded by an interest that the individuals may have shown in one another. Therefore, most inter-caste marriages are popular for being "love marriages". Hansa's case was slightly unusual in this respect. As she said, she did not even know Deepak before the proposal came. Deepak, who as I learned from Hansa, had been involved with a girl from his own caste for many years, who had however cheated him. Deepak had thereafter resolved that he would not marry a girl from his own caste. Deepak also already much beyond the traditional marriage age, used the opportunity, to formally propose a girl of his own choice anyway. Like Dhana's case, Deepak's family had little objection since Hansa belonged to a higher caste than them.

27 Interview, Dharamgarh market (Uttarakhand), February 23, 2016.

affected by the hardships her family was being made to face, making her resolve to somehow change things even stronger. Hansa was well aware that "objecting to an inter-caste marriage" was not acceptable under state law. "The state even awards couples in inter-caste marriages Rs. 50,000. But for that we would have had to be married in court. I didn't want that. I had a *proper* marriage (*Merī śādī toh achhī tarah se huī*)," she shared (emphasis mine).[28] And therefore Hansa knew that she could call upon the state machinery for help, if she decided. Seeing their father so distraught, Hansa and her sister finally decided to write to the District Magistrate (DM) of their district. "This is when my sister drafted a letter to the DM. The DM had come to Kamēḍī [the *tālukā* headquarter] for some work and was entertaining applications [from local residents]. My sister also handed in this letter, where she had stated how our *birāderi* had ostracised our father because he had consented to the inter-caste marriage of his older daughter. Very soon thereafter, possibly within a week, the *paṭwāri* [local revenue collector] arrived. He held a meeting in the village temple in our village. He asked those who had an objection to our marriage, to sign to that effect on a document he had created. Their behaviour towards our family was wrong and they would have all been arrested. That is when they got scared and apologised. Now they treat us all with respect. My father is no more, but I am invited to weddings and celebrations in my natal village (*māika*)," revealed Hansa, who at the time of the interview had been married to Deepak for over ten years. They had a son, and Hansa's sister – Poonam – who had still not got married was also living with them in Dharamgarh.

Hansa and Dhana were both women who entered into inter-caste marriages of their own free will, in a society that forbade such unions. Both women were educated and well informed through a range of interactions with people and events outside their community that their respective life experiences had enabled. These experiences were also in part the genesis of why each one may have wanted to emphasise the value of "individual choice" (see also Derrett 1978b, 83), which as I have stated in an earlier part of this case study, was perceived to be embodied in state law and state schemes and therefore was a value belonging to "others" (see Chapter 3, page 77). Both women faced ostracism from their villages, Dhana from her in-laws village and Hansa from her natal one. However, both these women, as the case study reveals, chose extremely different paths to tackle the conduct their respective villages had adopted towards them. While Hansa chose to invoke the intervention of state actors to process her dispute, Dhana wanted to depend on the layers of legality involving the *birāderi* and religious and supernatural elements to help her process the dispute and negotiate differences with her sister-in-law.

In both cases, the caste communities of the partner who belonged to the higher caste, perceived that their respective decisions of marriage brought *beizzati* upon

28 And by 'proper', Hansa had meant a marriage complete with all religious ceremonies and customary practices. A court marriage, unlike this, only involves the formal exchange of garlands and signatures of the couple and their witnesses on the registration document.

the community and at the same time resulted in each of these individuals not fulfilling their *dharma*. Marrying within one's own caste was considered to be part of every local community member's *dharma* in the Dharamgarh Valley. Addressing me, 40-year-old Govindi Rathod, a farmer lady in Gangapur said: "We don't know how it happens in your side. But this is the abode of the gods (*yeh dev bhūmi hai*) and when someone breaks the caste rules, it upsets the gods," when I asked her about why the community was so strict about marriages being conducted only within the caste.[29] However, in neither of the cases did the women decide to break all ties with the community and move out their community's circle of solidarity. Despite having boldly embraced postulational values that challenged the established rules of social order (and thereby the values embodied therein), all efforts made by Dhana and Hansa were, in fact in order to be reincorporated within this circle of solidarity.

But then, Dhana and Hansa chose two very diverse mechanisms to achieve this, in that they exercised their agency very differently. That she could seek the intervention of state actors was probably known to Hansa, because she had lived in urban areas long enough to know that inter-caste marriages (and love marriages) were not only common but perfectly permissible and in fact encouraged by the state. However, in practicality, was it really as simple as it had been for Hansa and her sister, to access the DM – the highest judicial authority in the district – and get him to act to promptly on their issue? "Well, it is easy for anyone who has the right connections/networks (*jiski pahunch hai*). My husband's older brother-in-law (*jijāji*) is the chairman (*Zillā Adhyakṣa*) in the *Zilla Pancāyat* and it was because of him that our application was processed quickly," said Hansa. But had she not been deterred by the slack working of state systems and the corruption that was rampant in it? "It is at the lower levels that there is so much corruption and dilly-dallying. If we had gone to the police or even the *patwāri* directly, he would have made us run back and forth several times demanding different sums of money. But because we went straight to the DM, things got sorted out pretty quickly and efficiently," clarified Hansa, who had come to learn from the experiences of others that it was important to be networked with the upper level of bureaucrats in order for any aspect of state law (and thus state values) to be set in motion. In this aspect, Hansa's circumstances clearly differed from that of Dhana's who had no such networks that she could actualise for effective processing of her dispute in the layers involving state actors. And Dhana was not new to this, either. She had previously helped a girl from her village, Kamla Rathod, to recover maintenance from her husband through a case filed in court. Dhana's experiences of the delays, the bribes, and the mental stress that those processes brought to Kamla and her family remained with her and taught her to know better than to get involved in the vicious circle of lawyers, police

29 Interview in Gangapur (Uttarakhand), February 18, 2016. The locals in the Kumaon region of the Himalayas believe that most of the gods (*dévtās*) lived on this earth and specifically in the Kumaon mountains (Fanger 1990, 185).

officials, and courtrooms on her own accord.[30] Hansa's own statements, in this regard, only confirm this situation.

Besides the difference in connections, there were also social circumstances that caused the two women to exercise their agency so differently. The processing of disputes, as I realised during fieldwork, was not just related to the present but was also complexly connected to the future. This meant that several aspects that may have mattered in the long run impacted on the processing of a dispute in the present. In this context, what Dhana could have expected from the future differed greatly from Hansa. At the time of interviews, Dhana's husband, Amar, was still recovering from his paralysis attack. She had been the sole earning member of her household ever since she got married – not a very common situation in the rural societies of the Dharamgarh valley where Dhana had grown up. In addition to her own family, she was also supporting (as she had always done) her natal family. The birth of a child meant not only additional expenses, but also additional chores and work, which probably Dhana felt she would not be able to cope with alone and for which she would need to seek out the support of family and community members. If Dhana continued to depend on her natal family for such support – despite her conditions for this being different – it would have nevertheless placed her in the same position as a married girl who returned to her natal family because she was unable to adjust into life in her matrimonial home. This, as is evident from Dhana's own statements (see page 147) would probably have been fairly unpleasant for those in her natal family.

In addition to this, the future of the child was also something Dhana needed to think about. In this respect, Dhana's situation was very different from Hansa's, who being of a higher caste had married into a lower caste. I learned about these dynamics when I asked Hansa whether her decision to have an inter-caste marriage would impact on her son's future in any way, "Had I married a man from the higher caste, maybe it would have interfered at the time Priyanshu [her son] is to find a bride. But now we are all Sonār. And when they ask for the caste of the mother, I am Thakur, which is higher than the Sonār, so it should be no problem," Hansa had explained. During traditionally arranged marriages in the Dharamgarh valley, the children of mixed-caste couples were known to have some difficulty in finding a partner, more so if the mother belonged to a lower caste. Custom across most parts of India has it that the girl moves into the family and the village of her husband; along with this she also adopts the caste and surname of her husband. Nevertheless, if the mother of the prospective bride or groom belonged to a lower caste – like in the case of Dhana – and this was revealed due to disharmony between the couple and their *birāderi*, it could go a long way in hampering their child's smooth settlement into the social structure. While this might, at first thought, seem a very distant occasion to think about, it is clear from the way Dhana decided to process her dispute that these factors played an active

30 Kamla Rathod worked with Dhana at the NGO. Known for being bold and outgoing, Kamla had sought Dhana's help in helping her process her matrimonial dispute, which had ultimately resulted in a case being filed in the state court that Kamla admitted having successfully pursued only because Dhana was by her side. Interview in Ganagapur (Uttarakhand), May 2015.

role in the manner she exercised agency. Dhana chose, unlike Hansa, to keep her dispute processing limited to layers involving community actors because invoking the intervention of state actors would have only resulted in further widening the rift between the *birāderi* and herself (see Chandrasingh Rathore's statement in Chapter 4, page 75).

In all these respects just described, Hansa's situation was slightly easier. She did not have to worry a lot about the rift that may have occurred between her and her *birāderi* because she involved state actors in the processing of her dispute, as she had already moved *out* of her village and *into* that of her husband's. In the normal course of things Hansa reasonably expected (and would be expected) to be largely dependent on her husband and his family for financial and other support. And in her case, Hansa's relationship with her in-laws and her husband's *birāderi* was not disturbed by this marriage. As for the situation of her father, brother, and sister – who continued to remain in the village after the processing of their dispute – formally at least, state actors had been involved in the dispute processing at the insistence and initiative of Hansa and her husband. Therefore, there was little reason for the *birāderi* to continue blaming her father for this act.

As for long term factors, with respect to the future of her son, Hansa's position was more secure than that of Dhana for reasons she articulated (see page 152). But another factor that seemed to have been a consequence of Hansa's inter-caste union was Poonam's (Hansa's sister's) inability to find a match for marriage. In all likelihood, it may have become challenging for Hansa's family to arrange Poonam's marriage through traditional processes because of Hansa's inter-caste marriage and the family's decision to remain associated with her despite this. At the time of the fieldwork, as noted, Poonam resided with Hansa and her husband. Hansa's parents and brother had by this time passed away and in the rural areas of Uttarakhand it was very unconventional (and therefore possibly unsafe) for a young woman to be unmarried and living on her own (see also Basu 2015). That Poonam's residence with Hansa and her husband was well accepted by her in-laws was a hint that this situation had probably been predicted, previously thought out, discussed, and arranged.

As mentioned earlier, inter-caste marriages were a social taboo for several reasons and therefore people feared being associated with this practice in any form for reasons of their own self-preservation. Not only that the type of marriage into which a woman entered crucially affected her access to post-marital support (Grover 2009, 5), as in the case of Dhana.[31] It also impacted on the course of life of those closely related to the woman, as in the instance of Hansa. Arrangement of marriage with a daughter from a family that stood by the inter-caste union of another in their immediate family, was almost like acquiescing to the practice of

31 See also the case of Laxmi (see Chapter 4, page 103) and the sort of support Shardadevi extended to her in a situation where her matrimonial relations have broken down. This type of help from Shardadevi might have been inconceivable, had Laxmi not been in a marriage that fits community norms.

inter-caste marriages yourself and thereby also endorsing the values that the community shunned.[32]

Since caste solidarities bound its members in such a complex manner, the inter-caste marriage of one member in one family could have repercussions in diverse ways on other members of the family; thus linking the self and community in an inseparable manner. Both Dhana's and Hansa's experiences show that the embracement of postulational values that were perceived to threaten the values of the community had almost a sort of rippling effect, impacting on individuals and situations beyond the self, and thus increasing the precariousness of such decisions. The contexts in which Dhana and Hansa made their decisions were very different, which intimately impacted on the manner in which they decided to cope with the consequences of cherishing the postulational values of the "other". Thus, while Hansa's case might quickly come to the fore as a forthright example of identifying boldly with the values of equality and individual choice; experiences of that like Dhana are far more common and no less courageous, especially if understood in the context of the ultimate goal, that of both being able to reincorporate themselves into the circle of community solidarity without having to give up what they hold dear. Dhana and Hansa's experiences exemplify the creation of spaces where values of contrasting laws – in this case the community's and the state's – are seen to reconcile and to that extent reconstitute one another.[33]

5.4 Analysis

Conflict of laws is an inevitable consequence of legal pluralism. And therefore, as Chiba (1998) articulates "what is expected of us living under the law is never to try to simply disregard or hate conflicts, but to manage them wisely in response to their nature and our social needs." At the level of the community, as we saw in Chapter 4 (see page 80), keeping the conflicting values at bay through different mechanisms of resistance was one way of managing this conflict. And at the level of the self, the above set of case studies provides powerful examples of how persons under legal pluralism are not only "passive recipients of legal regulation but also active agents for the law by their choice of an alternative legal rule among the plural" (Chiba 1998).[34]

The experiences of each of these individuals reveals that "legal change may sometimes be a highly effective way of transforming ideology" (Felstiner, Abel, and Sarat 1981, 643). Not only is it evident that postulational values of state law find resonance at the level of the self, but also that these values are equally dependent (and possibly more so) on the layers involving non-state actors, as they are on those involving state actors, for their realisation.

32 See Cohn (1959, 84, 1965, 99) for observations about similar concerns arising in the Chamar and other communities on the consequences of being outcaste.

33 See also (Hertogh 2008) who says that any normative order constantly involves continual creation and re-creation of that order in the face of disagreement.

34 See also Martin Chanock (1998) about similar observations in Malawi and Zambia.

This chapter provides an understanding that choice of mechanism for dispute processing is, among others, prominently influenced by three factors: the dynamics of values, familiarity, and an understanding of the self.

5.4.1 The choice of a mechanism and values

It has been established through many parts of the book up to now, that going to the state courts, among other things, also implies recourse to adversarial procedure, which was not looked upon very favourably in both communities that were studied. However, from the above three case studies, it is evident that some people do seek the intervention of state actors for dispute processing without disturbing (and sometimes to re-establish) community relations. In conclusion, certain indications can be drawn from the three case studies, as regard the embracement of postulational values and recourse to state actors. For instance, in the first case study, the postulational values embraced by Hayatsingh coincided to a great extent with community values. As a result, the choice of forum, whether state or non-state, did not matter so long as the aspirations of the individuals were effectively achieved. The second case study was more complex in that sense. What Draupadi and Miradevi aspired to was not in conflict with community values per se, but the process of achieving freedom from domestic violence did result in a challenge to established power structures (which were the base of other social structures) within the community. Individuals, therefore, had to be strategic in order to fulfil such ends, and the choice of mechanism really depended on the extent to which such individuals could justify the choice. Miradevi's husband caused public embarrassment to the family on several occasions and his antics were slowly becoming a public nuisance as well. Possibly, this enabled Miradevi to have enough reasons to approach state actors without fear of drawing any criticism from her community. In the third and last case study, though, Hansa and Dhana's communities perceived the values that they sought to embrace in total opposition to community values, possibly because of the fear that the latter would collapse on embracement of the former. Here, the process of embracing these values was in itself a challenge, and therefore the choice of mechanism had been made very carefully. We see from Dhana and Hansa's experiences the various factors – both in the immediate future and those pertaining to long term goals – that they had to consider as they worked their way towards bringing about an equitable coexistence of the values that were important to them as individuals and those that they had to adhere to as community members.

The layer that every individual, therefore, chose to process his or her dispute in, depended on how the values of the state law such individual sought to translate were positioned in regard to the community values. In these three cases, the values that were sought at an individual level were embodied in state law particularly, but there could be other values, not necessarily embodied in the state law, perceived as belonging to "the other" from the community's perspective and nevertheless being embraced by individuals. Khare (1972, 84) speaks in terms of goals and says that "lawyer's law" can serve as an extension of the laws of a community "only so long as the aims do not conflict." I would extend this understanding to the postulates that underlie these different types of laws and propose that the more the values of state law coincide with community understanding and conscience, the easier it is for the latter to embrace them. Every state legislation subsumes certain values, and in its broader agenda for legislation to become meaningful, and for the state to become more accessible, it is important that there is an engagement with communities at the level of values.

5.4.2 Choice of mechanism and familiarity

The case studies presented here show that a wide variety of mechanisms are brought into play in order to maintain a balance between one's own interests and that of the community. In all the three case studies, we find that dispute processing in the layer involving state actors, as is confirmed by some other studies (Kidder 1973; Chaudhary 1999; Krishnan et al. 2014), was possible because people were informed and aware, but also because they developed the networks and became familiar with the system. Financial resources are indeed an important condition for access to state resources. This is evident from Hayat-singh's example where, despite the case having been prolonged, Hayatsingh could pursue it ferociously because of a strong financial backing. But at the same time, examples like that of Miradevi and Hansa reveal that information and familiarity with the forum, whether through networks or experience, went a long way in reinforcing the "type of confidence" people perceived one to have in approaching state systems.

As it is clear from the narrative up to now, approaching state actors for dispute processing meant risking *izzat* and possibly even *dharma* for having taken up a revengeful attitude towards one's own kin. Unfamiliarity with the processes of the state actors added a degree of unpredictability, making the use of this dispute processing mechanism almost like a "gamble" (Khare 1972, 78). For instance, the image of the police was not very favourable in both communities. Describing the attitude of the Koḷī community towards the police, Narendra Talathi, the local doctor in Gonjhé said: "They are as much in awe as they are fearful of the police. The authority of the police and the powers they (may) have is what the people fear. Therefore, they are always hesitant about appearing before the police or approaching the police for any help."[35] Along with being known for the indiscriminate use of force, the police were reputed as being corrupt in both village communities. "There is no use of police officials. They only threaten and show power. They don't make any settlements," said Mohansingh, the former *Grām Pradhān* of Khasi.[36] His sentiments were echoed by Anandibai Meher, the female *Grām Pradhān* from Bilbār, "The police only want money, they eat money (*paisā khāte haiṅ*). They are good to the person who offers them more money," she said.[37] Consequently, people could never be sure about how the police would respond to a particular dispute and this created a lot of fear and

35 Interview, Gonjhé (Maharashtra), March 25, 2015.
36 Interview Khasi (Uttarakhand), March 11, 2016.
37 Interview, Bilbār (Uttarakhand), March 18, 2016.

uncertainty, which situation, however, automatically changed when there was some familiarity with the forum. As Khare (1972, 77) observed during his fieldwork in Uttar Pradesh, "The ways of the court are regarded as foreign and deceptive at every step, unless there is someone acquainted who can help find the way." Janabai, a fisherwoman from Gonjhé, had been dragged into a dispute between Ravindra Pavshe and Laxman Pavshe, because of which she ended up in the police station responding to complaints and filing cross complaints. This was her first time in a police station, and she admitted to being fairly scared. "Neither me nor my husband have ever come to the police station. Gorāi is too far, but not even in Mānjai have we ever gone to the police station. It is scary. But I do exactly as Ravindra says. It is because he is there that we feel more confident (*dhīr vaṭato*)."[38] Ravindra, as we have seen in Chapter 4 (see page 114), was a barefoot lawyer and was known to be extremely familiar with the state systems of dispute processing. He was also a *puḍhārī* and Janabai was confident that he would in no way act to disadvantage her.

If it is familiarity that gave Miradevi, Hayatsingh, and also Hansa, the confidence to seek the intervention of state actors in their dispute processing, it is familiarity itself that caused Dhana, Draupadi, and the other village *pradhāns* that Hayatsingh mentions, to take recourse to non-state mechanisms of dispute processing. Whether it was invoking goddess Kokiladevi, or seeking the intervention of the *birāderi*, people in the mountains have grown up witnessing such meetings of the elders and the performance of rituals to appease Kokiladevi and other deities. Knowledge about the forums lent a sense of comfort, but also, every case being treated as unique in its own right, allowed scope of manoeuvring. Circumstances and contexts were important, but also time, as Dhana's or Draupadi's case studies revealed, was crucial.

In many respects, dispute processing involving state actors and that involving non-state actors is similar. Both are time consuming (as against what is usually argued in other literature) and both can involve a fair amount of expenditure. The deciding factor, therefore, becomes the goal of the parties involved in such disputes, which as mentioned earlier continued to be regulated by the instinct of self-preservation. Recourse to non-state mechanism remains embedded within the community, unlike seeking out intervention of state actors. At the same time, the former remained more widely used because of familiarity and its conduciveness to an understanding of agency and autonomy that existed within the members of these communities.

5.4.3 Choice of mechanism and an understanding of the self

The need to live together with one's community is undeniable, but as the examples of Dhana, Miradevi, Draupadi, and Hansa reveal, this could be achieved even while ensuring the protection of one's own interest. In cases like those involving Hayatsingh, Draupadi, and Miradevi, where what they desired at the level of the individual was not so far apart from community values, agency was exercised more

38 Interview, Gonjhé, May 20, 2016.

for the strategic use of available resources in order to achieve their maximum impact. Whereas in the case studies of Dhana and Hansa, their individual interests lay in total contrast to the social normative that the community prized and here the exercise of agency was necessarily an effort to bring about a balance between these apparently opposed values.

The processes, by way of which each of the individuals in all three case studies embraced the postulational values of the "other" hold crucial revelations about how individuals in the Dharamgarh valley perceived themselves. Their exercise of agency reflected that they, at all times, remained fully aware of what really mattered to them, who they deeply care about, and what their capacities and limitations were (Meyers 2000, 476).

Be it a consequence of their religious conditioning, or the result of practical necessity, in all the case studies, each individual adopted a process, which was marked with the effort of remaining within the community's circle of solidarity and therefore reflected an awareness of interconnectedness. In the first case study, the efforts of Hayatsingh and those of the chiefs from the other villages resulted in reinforcing community solidarity. In the second case study, Draupadi and Miradevi acted in a manner such that their intra-community relationships were not disturbed. And in the third case study, Hansa and Dhana's efforts were chiefly directed towards re-establishing a bond with their respective communities. The exercise of agency in every case, then was not an acontextual, ahistorical and isolated act, but rather an exercise that was very much alive to the dynamics of interconnectedness that these individual experienced and practised as a part of their identity.

5.5 Conclusion

The above case studies show how the values of state law are successfully embraced by individuals in various situations of conflict. Even if individuals stayed within their own social contexts, they were not unaware of the wider state-based legal and postulational values. Observation of the processes of such embracement witnessed state law and its regulatory systems often being adapted and appropriated. This chapter highlights that every individual in his or her own right, is a skilful navigator and it is only a matter of the right environment and appropriate time before he or she put his or her agency to work to make legislative interventions, that seek to regulate power equations at social and familial levels, more impactful.

6 Concluding thoughts and reflections

The present study of two communities in rural India has shown how dispute processing as a social phenomenon within a particular community is a site for interaction between the values of the different types of laws governing it. The nature of these interactions is determined by the community's sense of order cultivated on the basis of its religious and cultural background and everyday life practices. The influence of state law and its systems, as one such type of law, on communities and their members can be properly assessed only through an analysis of the various translations of state law that occur on account of the processes by way of which a community's sense of order regulates its interaction with state law. Translation of state law and its systems is the process of giving meaning to the structure and essence of state law and its systems in the context of local circumstances (Merry 2009).

State law and non-state law are not separate social and legal fields, they are intricately intertwined and are at all times connected to values. This last chapter of the book will present an analysis of the empirical findings laid out in the previous chapters in the broader context of how non-state dispute processing is a site where state and non-state laws constitute and re-constitute one another, thus establishing that the forums within the state and non-state spheres stand not in opposition to one another but act virtually as wheels of the same process. The book thus confirms Chiba's theorising in a broad way. The chosen field sites illustrate the lived realities of legal pluralism for the people who made this project possible by giving generously of their time and insights. The conclusion also emphasises inter alia the significance of ethnography to the study of law and legal processes as part of the legal discipline.

6.1 A community's sense of order regulates its engagement with state law

Pirie (2013, 186) highlights that simply the "sense of law" is important in its own right, sometimes as a "statement of values" and at other times as "an assertion of difference". This research establishes that the village communities of Gonjhé and the Dharamgarh valley had a sense of order that was cultivated on the basis of their experience of interconnectedness. Chiba's hypothesis that certain postulates within every community help it develop a sense of order that enables it to preserve its cultural identity in law, helped the present project. It allowed me, on the basis of the empirical evidence, to identify *dharma* and *izzat* as two of the identity postulates of the community laws in both these village communities. The community's experience of interconnectedness expressed through an emphasis on these values controlled its interaction with state law, sometimes bridling and sometimes encouraging, thus resulting ultimately in different perceptions and pronunciations of state law.

The two communities studied in the course of fieldwork were predominantly Hindu in terms of their religious and cultural backgrounds. They were located in rural areas and the people depended on their respective traditional occupations as a primary source of their livelihood. Innate to the dispute processing mechanisms within both these village communities was the element of self-preservation and an awareness of interconnectedness. Both concepts have to be understood as experiences at the level of the communities as a whole and at the level of the individuals as members of such communities. These are, then, manifestations of agency, of individuals and groups as social and legal actors, and clearly these spheres are not perceived and operated by people as separate and autonomous entities. The experience of interconnectedness was revealed partly as an expression of the experience of cosmic interlinkedness and partly a consequence of everyday socio-cultural and socio-economic life practices, while always intensely connected to the respective natural environment, which, though very different, was in both cases crucial for day-to-day survival. The nature of daily life practices, whether related to religion, livelihood, or anything else made interdependence inevitable in both communities studied here. People also needed each other, and each other's support, more than they need the state and its – largely remote – support systems.

On this kind of connectedness, we need to be aware that this is not something exclusively present in India or only in Hindu communities, for that matter. Capra and Mattei (2015, 4) state that until the "Middle Ages", cultures around the world observed nature very closely and adapted their ways of life accordingly,

> nature and its laws were seen as emanating from God or some divine power … even law itself was a deeply spiritual concept, based on obligation and on the proper role of an individual within a community and in relation to the life-sustaining earth.

The evidence in Chapter 2 indicates how the communities in both Gonjhé and the villages in the Dharamgarh valley lived in very close interaction with nature, also because their means of livelihood were so extensively dependent on it (see Chapter 2, pages 38–41 and 49–52). Capra and Mattei's observation about this could be extended to explain the experience of interconnectedness within these communities resulting from their ways of life and daily social and economic activities. Their religious conditioning as Hindu only complemented it and gave it a specific cultural, and not necessarily religious, hue or flavour (Menski, 2003).

Within Hindu communities, as described earlier (see Chapter 3, page 62), the experience of interconnectedness arises largely from *the rta/dharma* complex and the element of self-preservation must necessarily be understood within this context. The key point of the *rta/dharma* complex, which lies at the base of the Hindu sense of the imagined order, is the awareness of cosmic interlinkage and any individual's obligation towards the universe, however vaguely perceived. Menski (2003, 98) explains:

> By thus placing everything into a complex network of cosmic interrelationships, the holistic conceptualisation of dharma suggests that any human activity, including inaction, becomes perceived as having potentially wide-reaching consequences.

Without directly prescribing any particular form of action or behaviour as "appropriate" the *rta/dharma* complex circumscribes the fact that whatever one does, inevitably has further consequences. The underlying notion of "*karma*" further strengthens this abstraction with the caution of retribution as a result of action. But it does not restrain individual discretion, rather, it expects individual decisions and thus elicits agency and more or less conscious action.

By virtue of their religious and cultural conditioning as Hindus, for the "actions of individuals within communities to bear fruit" (Lingat 1973, 4), including those for self-preservation, it was necessary that individuals submit themselves to the "laws that govern the universe" (Lingat 1973, 4) and in that context remain sensitive to cosmic interlinkages. This submission is sometimes visible, even today (Doye 2015), but is often a completely invisible phenomenon, a mental state of awareness not translated into direct action, but potentially influencing how individuals act and react to all sorts of life scenarios. This realisation helps to explain the culture-specific experience of interconnectedness.

Since there are no strict guidelines from any superhuman authority on how to act within this experience of interconnectedness towards preservation of the self, I analyse that the basic postulates of *dharma* and *izzat* and the laws encompassing them were used to cultivate and retain a broad a sense of order. Ishwaran (1964, 229) points out that in rural India, law, religion, and morality are not severed but are found closely related forming an organic whole. The present research verifies this basic framework for human action.

It would, of course, be naïve to suggest that the values of *dharma* and *izzat* were foolproof in the sense of deterring people from acting in a manner that challenged the threat of interconnectedness (in the form of *karma*) or its local expression of community solidarity. And at such times, in order to remind individuals of their obligation towards the universe, the state law and it values were appropriated in different ways to complement the mechanisms of the community to retain or reinforce this sense of order.[1] (see Chapter 5, pages 133–153).

1 Menski (2003, 107–120) refers to this as "assisted self-control".

6.2 Resistance and embracement: Engagement with state law

A central finding of this study is that in both Gonjhé and the villages in the Dharamgarh valley both forums and individuals within the respective communities were conscious of the presence of state values along with their community values in the different layers of legality in which disputes were processed. This meant that individuals making decisions constantly encountered this plurality and potential conflicts between these elements. At the same time, the community's sense of order, essentially derived from certain values, determined in many ways the manner in which the communities, as well as individuals within them, would engage with state law. As explained in Chapter 3 (see page 67) and Chapter 4 (see page 75), the postulational values of state law held more eminence in the layers involving state actors, but were present even in those layers in which non-state actors were active. Coexistence naturally brought about engagement, sometimes through embracement and at other times in the form of resistance, in turn accounting for the different mechanisms adopted by non-state forums and actors in the processing of their disputes. This in itself often increased the intensity of the studied conflict scenarios. Fitting with Fitzpatrick's (1984, 128) notion that state law is "constituted in relations of opposition and support with other social forms," this research found that it is through a detailed examination of these mechanisms adopted by non-state forums and individual agents that the processes of centralisation of law that lawyers seem so interested in can actually be understood and evaluated in all their complexity. Therefore, in addition to evaluating the extent of access to state forums (Aditya 2016), gaining an understanding of the manner in which non-state forums work and are used is important to assess the impact of state law and its systems. This, then, makes this project a combination of law and anthropology.

I have argued throughout this book that resistance is also a form of engagement with state law. Mechanisms for resistance of state values in both Gonjhé and the villages in the Dharamgarh valley, as Chapter 4 sets out, were often directed towards inducing people to choose community-based forums and actors over state forums for dispute processing, though not necessarily to completely bypass state law. More often than not these mechanisms resulted in non-state forums adopting and appropriating forms and procedures of their state-based counterparts for dispute processing in order to improve their credibility within this competitive sphere of dispute processing; thus, revealing acute awareness of state law. The local reach of state-based rules and related processes is thus – or can be – very deep, but there may still be notable divergences about the values connected to such rules and processes.

The question of embracement of the values of state law, as described in Chapter 4, was found to be far more complex in some scenarios than in others, in that it depended on the extent to which values of the state and those of the community coincided or competed with one another. The embracement of state law did not occur on fixed understandings of state law, but rather involved multiple processes of translation of it. Retaining an emphasis on the essence of state law at the level of its postulational values, translation occurs through incorporating these values through locally understood frameworks and always endorsing the circumstances of local contexts (Merry 2009, 266–267) and perceived or actual individual needs. In both Gonjhé and the Dharamgarh valley embracement of the values of state law happened largely through non-state forums and mechanisms of dispute processing (as shown in Chapter 5) with their experience of interconnectedness underscoring the individual's and community's actions. Any translation of state law that occurred, therefore, could be appreciated only with an understanding of this. In Gonjhé, the *Samāj*, where possible, made space for recognition of state values in order to retain its credibility (see Chapter 4, page 108), but also to ensure that men and women continued to remain within the community's circle of solidarity. Similarly, in the Dharamgarh valley, customary practices, for instance the one relating to divorce (see Chapter 4, page 106) was modified to accommodate state legislation on the subject, but ultimately sought to ensure that couples did not seek recourse to state actors for dispute processing, where community values were perceived to not retain as much eminence. At the individual level, this meant that there was less negotiation at the level of the self where the state values that individuals in their own right sought to embrace coincided in essence with the community values. The case study of Hayatsingh Bhandari (see page 129) brings this forth clearly. However, individuals were not always at the losing end, even if the state values they embraced were perceived within their communities as being in complete opposition to community values. Here, as the two other case studies in Chapter 5 elucidated (see pages 133–153), it was important to incorporate observation of how individuals exercise agency into evaluating the impact of state law and its systems. Focus on the positive aspects of state law and its systems has kept the attention of legal scholars limited to court rooms and the black letter law. However, when attention is centred on the manner in, and the extent to which, values of state law are embraced by people, we achieve a deeper insight into what form the translations of state law may acquire, thus providing us with a more nuanced and effective understanding of the "impact of state law and its systems".[2]

The dynamics in the processes of embracement of the values of state law in context of the community's sense of order also question the alleged dichotomy between the effective securement of "rights" and mechanisms of reconciliation that is so often adopted or emphasised in non-state mechanisms of dispute processing. "Rights", as is established through the various examples in this book, were not comprehended as an individualistic experience but were rather to be exerted within the context of community reciprocities, kinship, caste, and village ties. The view that made people more agreeable to this reconciliation again originates in their religious and cultural environment, and conditioning, and ultimately again reinforces this experience of interconnectedness. Khare (1972, 76–77) articulated this on the basis of his own fieldwork:

2 The term "impact of state law and its systems" is placed in quotes here because "impact" in this context is often understood within legal discourses as something only positive. This project however differs to this extent and understands even resistance to state law as a form of "impact of state law".

> The 'failure' is immediately rationalized and explained, partly in terms of personal fate and karma, and partly on divine wish 'for our own good', which we do not understand because of our myopic foresight, but which does become apparent to us with time.

Reconciliation did not always trouble the individual, because a compromise or negotiation did not necessarily mean the settlement of a dispute. It was and remained part of an ongoing process of contestation, but also of connectivity that is highly dynamic and volatile in nature.

6.3 Non-state forums and actors: Questions of legitimacy

As outlined in the introduction, this study partly found its roots in a human rights-based debate in India about the decisions by non-state forums that were widely perceived to have violated – and continue to infringe – individual rights and freedoms. Underscoring these debates were questions pertaining to the legitimacy of such forums to exist and be involved in the processing of disputes, particularly those relating to individual freedom and choice. Obviously, this raises important questions about the relationship of state law and non-state law, and of the interaction between law and anthropology, or law and society. This specific question of legitimacy of non-state institutions to process disputes, that has arisen a fair number of times in the Indian state courts (see Chapter 1) over the last ten years, thrives largely on a monist perception of law, which has been strongly identified by Griffiths (1986) as a fiction, a "legocentric" (Frankenberg 1985, 433) aberration that curtails people's agency as responsible individuals, members of groups, and citizens. It often utilises arguments based on "rule of law" ideology (see Redding 2014, 942 for more details on how this ideology is used), within which state law and its systems are viewed to be the only appropriate source of legitimacy for forums and actors seeking to process disputes about issues that state law specifically regulates and has jurisdiction over. This would be especially so, if such regulation touches upon the concern of individual freedoms, "human rights" or "fundamental rights" as they are articulated under the Indian Constitution. Non-state forums, therefore, are not viewed as "legitimate" in this light, as they gain their legitimacy from sources outside of state law.

However, such dominant perceptions and presuppositions run counter to the lived legal reality of common people, who are not just citizens of a state and, by extension in today's world, global citizens with rights anchored in international law and human rights, but remain also members of social groups and, of course, individuals with their own agency. The very existence of non-state forums, their active engagement in the processing of disputes, and their continued appeal in the communities within which they exist, has often been seen by scholars, activists, and the legal fraternity of judges and lawyers as an indicator of the failure of the state judicial machinery.[3] From a state-

3 The situation, in this regard, is not very different from that in the post-colonial African countries. See Woodman (2001) on perspectives of lawyers and human rights activists towards the prevalence of customary law and its systems in this context.

centric perspective, this of course looks like a logical conclusion. But as this book confirms, it runs counter to people's lived experience, certainly of the kinds of people living in Indian villages or the rural contexts that this book explores. The perceived dichotomy between state and non-state forums and actors engaged in dispute processing propelled by monistic notions, adds vigour to the movement to increase intervention of the state systems in dispute processing. Collaterally, this seeks to reduce, to the extent of complete elimination and denial of legitimacy, the involvement of non-state forums and actors in this particular socio-legal sphere. The primary concern evident in these several movements that have used the courts and the media as their platforms for public agitation, thus, is that the involvement of non-state forums in dispute processing is believed to obstruct the efficient dissemination of state law and poses harmful barriers for an effective securement of rights and, therefore, of justice.[4]

Challenging such state-centric presuppositions, the evidence that this study lays out establishes that indeed community based non-state forums and actors are and remain very active in the processing of disputes and the ascertainment of rights and duties, but that they exist in varied forms and not in "parallel", but rather in constant and rather intense multi-dimensional engagement with the state law and its systems. Ethnographic observation revealed that we are not dealing with parallel systems here or a directly adversarial scenario, but find a complex picture of intense hybridity, plurality and interaction.[5] In order to understand the nature and extent to which non-state forums and actors engage with state law, it is first necessary, as indicated and reiterated at the beginning of this chapter, to develop an understanding of the community's sense of order. Based on the empirical evidence from Gonjhé and the villages in the Dharamgarh valley, this research has clearly found and argues that rural communities like those studied nurture certain values, which, among other things, are derived from their religio-cultural backgrounds and social structure. These values cultivate the community's sense of order and are the "identity postulates" (Chiba 1986) of the community's laws, customs and traditions. At the same time, the state as a community also nurtures certain values, and therefore state law, like other types of laws, is of course also founded on certain values. The postulational values of state law, in fact, are its very essence and justify its existence. This study therefore approached "engagement with state law" through an examination of whether and the ways in which values

4 For instance, see the petition in the case *Vishwa Lochan Madan v Union of India (Vishwa Lochan Madan v Union of India and Ors 2014)*. The petitioner based his demands for abolition of Dar-ul-Qazas on two aspects of the Constitution. Redding (2014, 949) describes them as follows: one that the Constitution, "as a foundational source of law in India must hold supremacy in the legal and political life of India" and two "that the Constitution's creation of a state system of courts is fundamentally compromised by the existence of any competitor in the form of non-secular, non-state system of legal governance."

5 Sundar (2009) describes similarly about the Adivasi communities in Jharkhand, highlighting that "Adivasi identity and dignity lie not in 'keeping the state away' … but in drawing the state into an orbit which the adivasis have defined." Sundar's usage of "orbit which the adivasis have defined', comes very close what I describe as "community's sense of order".

of the state and values of the community co-existed and how the two communities researched here tackled this coexistence of competing value systems. Translation of state law through the appropriation of its structures and form and framing of its values to suit local contexts is the main evidence of engagement with state law as well as the extent of its impact, which a narrow state-centric approach all too easily overlooks.

6.4 The Supreme Court's view in light of the empirical evidence

In the introductory chapter (see page 10), I explain that the Supreme Court has been used as a prominent battleground by socio-legal activists and public-spirited citizens alike to oppose the involvement of community based non-state forums in dispute processing. Using procedural delays and legislative (bureaucratic) developments to their advantage, the Supreme Court has strategically managed to steer clear of making any statement on the status of non-state forums and actors vis-à-vis the state law and its systems particularly and dispute processing generally. Judgments in other cases that came after the filing of *Shakti Vahini v Union of India and Ors*, referred to the pendency of this case, at the time, as the ground for their refusal to comment on the subject (see various orders in Re: Indian Woman says gang-raped on orders of Village Court published in Business & Financial News dated 23.01.2014 2014; *Vishwa Lochan Madan v Union of India and Ors. 2014*). The judgment in *Shakti Vahini v Union of India and Ors.* – the very case that could have determined the status of non-state forums vis-à-vis dispute processing – continues to leave things unsettled. Taking a clear stand against the activities of certain types of non-state forums, particularly *pancāyats*, assemblies, and groups of people gathering to object and decide upon the consequences of matrimonial alliances perceived to insult caste honour, the Supreme Court reaffirmed its position in *Vishwa Lochan Madan v Union of India* and expressed zero tolerance for actions resulting in the violation of human rights. But in the same breath (and in this case the same judgment), the Supreme Court also clarified that it was not its intention to quash or thwart such groups or pancāyats "engaging in any constructive work" (Supreme Court of India 2018, vol. 7, para. 49). For scholars, but also for lawyers in courts of law, what is meant by "constructive work" certainly remains relative and open to debate an interpretation. On reading together the judgments in *Vishwa Lochan Mandan v Union of India* and *Shakti Vahini v Union of India*, it would not be going too far to say that whether it be non-state forums and mechanisms within Hindu, Muslim or Adivasi communities, the Supreme Court seems to prefer a stance of non-interference with respect to people's preference to seek recourse to non-state forums for dispute processing. State law keeps a cautious but watchful distance to allow self-controlled ordering.[6]

6 Interestingly, the Supreme Court has even used people's right to privacy as a ground to justify the reduction of state interference and keeping this distance. See *Joseph Shine v Union of India* and *Navtej Singh Johar and Ors. v Union of India* in the context of

Given that non-state forums and actors gain their legitimacy on account of a combination of factors ranging from tangible elements like type of education and occupations to more intangible aspects like values; the rejection of such forums and actors by state law would never result in their complete annihilation. The values of state law and those underlying community laws will continue to compete in every layer of legality and therefore a mechanism enabling the existence of both state and non-state forums and actors synchronously could be the best possible solution (Chiba 1986, 388) for legal systems that do not appear to follow a lego-centric pattern of development. The present research shows that state law and local laws within the communities researched in India, which is not merely, as we read so often, a "common law country" (M.P. Singh and Kumar 2017), "combine to regulate people's behaviour, although some of them may surpass others in individual cases" (Chiba 1989, 150–153). A complete rejection of non-state forums and actors by the state would compel people to make choices, posing the risk of rejection of state law or its systems as many studies have shown.[7] Moreover, "banning" dispute processing activities by non-state forums and actors will not make them disappear because reasons for their existence, as this research shows, go beyond merely the irregularity in proximity to state forums and actors (see page 164). On the contrary, such an action would only push them underground, making it then challenging to understand how and in what manner they engage with state law, if at all. This book would thus strongly argue that the Supreme Court actually perceptively recognises this and therefore tends to respond fairly moderately to the litigation-oriented manifestations of these excessive, almost preposterous, expectations. If anything, the response of the Supreme Court to matters concerning the legitimacy of non-state forums and actors may be a testimonial of the judiciary in India being more in control of – and more in tune with – the lived reality of their populations than they let their audience believe.

One wonders to what extent this attitude of non-interference of the judiciary is a sign of the state's unwillingness (and possibly incapacity) to be the main or only player, also because of the knowledge it possesses about the fact that the state is only one of the many players that people rely upon for self-preservation. Whether it is in matters concerning choice of secular law over personal law (*Shabnam Hashmi v Union of India and Ors. 2014*), preference for state courts over community-based forums (*Vishwa Lochan Madan v Union of India and Ors. 2014*) or letting customary practices take precedence over codified law (Plumber 2015; Lal

discussions about non-criminalisation of adultery and decriminalisation of homosexuality respectively.

7 Examples from other jurisdictions, such as Canada (Virdi 2016) and United Kingdom show how South Asian communities faced with choosing between the state order and non-state legal order for dispute processing usually end up favouring the latter over the former (Menski 2006a, 4–5). An example closer to home comes from experiences with informal mining in the state of Jharkhand, where people engaged in informal mining did not report fatal accidents to the police since their activities were ostensibly illegal (Sundar 2009, 3).

2015; Choudhary 2015),[8] state court judgments in the last decade reflect a trend of acknowledging that state law and state forums are not the only elements regulating and governing the lives of Indian people.[9] From a different disciplinary angle, too, Solanki (2011) concluded on the basis of her research on adjudication of religious family laws in the city of Mumbai, that the Indian state willingly shares adjudicative authority in this sphere with religio-cultural groups and civil society actors in order to "shape family and gender from above while balancing the plural demands of groups" (Solanki 2011, 326).

Chapter 4 shows that individuals are not merely passive recipients of any type of law. The Supreme Court's stance may also be indicative of the fact that the state judiciary is not just aware of, but to some extent even depends on people to act in their best interest by navigating between different types of laws and competing values, hence, revealing the sharp sensitivity of the Indian Supreme Court to individual agency. Thus, a close reading of recent Indian legal developments suggests a judicial trend of reiterating for campaigners and the legal fraternity alike that dispute processing is a matter of competing values that individuals must navigate at a variety of levels. The lengthy discussion by the Supreme Court in cases such as *Shakti Vahini v Union of India and Ors.* and *Joseph Shine v Union of India* on the need to safeguard individual autonomy, especially as an integral aspect of people's dignity and right to privacy, only endorses this further. Of course, this approach of the judiciary is bound to have its own costs. By depending on people's exercise of agency in terms of navigating forums and values, the judiciary may certainly risk exposing some individuals to face, what might sometimes be "harsh" consequences of the manner in which they choose to process their dispute. The incidences cited in the Vishwa Lochan Madan's petition against *dar-ul-qazas* were precisely of such a nature. However, as the evidence laid out here shows, people's exercise of agency depends on their situation-specific experiences, and mistakes or misguided judgments or decision-making occur all the time and in all forums. And therefore, in order to mitigate as far as possible adverse situations, it is important that the state, civil society, schools, and even parents must work towards making individuals more skilled navigators.

At the same time, it would not remain helpful (and would in fact violate the same obligation placed on the judges as individual citizens) if the judiciary desists from establishing a steady dialogue with non-state forums and actors. At present, the Supreme Court judgments reveal that the state judiciary acknowledges the presence of non-state actors and forums in the sphere of dispute processing (and in this manner even expects them to make responsible decisions). However, with the exception of instances in the lower courts (Solanki 2011; but see Berti 2011a), the state courts largely proceed in any given case without taking account of what may have transpired in a non-state forum despite proceedings in the courtroom (in the form of evidence)

8 Here I use the word custom to mean both traditions as well as contemporary practices.

9 Chiba (1989, 49–52) points out that with regard to relevance of the state to law, the "Western state" differs from its "Non-Western counterpart".

alerting the court to pursuit of the dispute in this sphere.[10] Consequently, in such cases the state courts may end up deciding a dispute largely independent of its contexts and factual circumstances. This is, of course, based on the processual assumptions that lower courts are to deal with the facts and the evidence, while the higher courts work with procedural rules and higher principles. Since this again segregates different levels or layers of law, it is evident that basic principles of connectivity are ignored if one uses such simplistic taxonomy. This carries a huge risk of potential harm. For this reason, the facility of state courts as a forum often gets perfectly exploited by disputing parties and the orders of such courts ultimately remain difficult to execute.

In *Shakti Vahini v Union of India and Ors.*, the Supreme Court made its first attempt in establishing a dialogue with non-state forums (Kokal 2013), by inviting the *khāp pancāyats* to submit their say in the petition against them. Unfortunately, though, this dialogue did not result in the development of any sort of discourse on the relationship of the state with non-state forums. Of course, this could be interpreted as informal acknowledgement of a continuing engagement, which cannot lead to a definitive resolution either way. The probably somewhat deliberate silence of decision-making keeps the process going, enabling the different actors involved some scope for manoeuvring and exercising discretion in the light of constantly changing contexts. On one level, of course, this reflects the "living" nature of law itself, which is evident also in other jurisdictions, such as South Africa, where it is being recognised through developments of distinctions between "official customary law" and "living customary law" (Bennett 1991).[11] This observation here, however, is in no manner meant to be a recommendation for institutionalisation of non-state forums, for past attempts in India as well as in other countries in that direction have been researched and found to be unsuccessful (see Meschievitz and Galanter 1982 on Nyay Panchayats; Woodman 2001, 2–3 on institutions of customary law; Ingole 2015 and; Bhattacharya 2016 on the Dispute Free Village Committee). Any sort of institutionalisation or formalisation through legislation of non-state forums can only mean – by way of obligation or expectation – an imposed centralisation of state law. This could lead only toward new forms of fuzziness and not the complete abolition of non-state dispute

10 In matrimonial disputes, especially those concerning divorce and maintenance, state court judges have been observed to be extremely alert to what transpires in the non-state sphere (Solanki 2011). However, the same cannot be said of other types and civil and criminal disputes, which more often than not are spun in a complex web of state and non-state proceedings. The cases of *Meenakshi Kumari v State of Uttar Pradesh and Ors.* (*Meenakshi Kumari v State of Uttar Pradesh and Ors 2015*) and *Abdur Rahman v Secretary to Government* (*Abdur Rahman v The Secretary to Government 2017*) could be taken as examples in this regard. The issues in these cases may have been framed differently if the state courts were to take cognisance of the processing of these disputes in the non-state forums.

11 Bennett (1991, 49–50) describes "official customary law" as the written version of customary law that is contained in the formal legal codes. The "living customary law" contrastingly, as he describes, is the customary law that is lived out by the people and applied in different community based non-state forums.

processing forums and actors. Previous research and the empirical evidence in this study indicates that institutionalisation may end up ultimately drawing people away from such forums and actors and creating yet other focal points of dispute processing. But more subtle efforts by state courts to peruse – in relation to the dispute before them – evidence of proceedings in a non-state forum and bring on board the non-state actors involved for a dialogue about the dispute – in their capacity as adjudicators or mediators (and not as witnesses, as it presently happens) – may be an experiment worth carrying out. For such dialogue to be sustainable and substantial, it is necessary that its establishment should proceed on the footing of mutual recognition by both state and non-state actors as somewhat equal partners and certainly actants with their own voice.

6.5 Thinking together is thinking ahead

"Laws" gain their legitimacy from the "laboratory of real-life experiences", and experiences as we may all agree cannot be imposed, but rather require the creation of spaces where they can be facilitated and sustained. Facilitating and sustaining experiences based on values that the communities do not fully identify with is a challenging task, but one that is not impossible. In the present book, Dhana and Hansa's case studies (see Chapter 5, page 144) depict the struggle individuals might have to undertake if they seek to challenge established social structures, in their case the caste rules determining inter-caste interactions. Miradevi and Draupadi's case studies (see Chapter 5, page 133) were similar, though what they sought to challenge were the power relations between husbands and wives that were reinforced through a gender-based division of labour and life experiences derived from it. In all four situations, each of these women managed to create spaces for the coexistence of these different types of values by working through the framework of the community's sense of order. But a proactive lower level bureaucracy and the opportunity to earn a money income, remained factors that contributed to enabling these women to build on the potential of their own agencies. The case of non-state forums, too, was not very different. The competition to its power that state actors provided, led the *Samāj* in Gonjhé to make space for the value of individual choice, even as it justified the need for this embracement in light of the community's *izzat*.

The language of rights and the values of state law still remain largely unfamiliar for the rural communities in Gonjhé and the Dharamgarh valley. However, the awareness that they exist alongside community values in itself, compels engagement with them, a tension that is as productive as it is provocative. The aggressive imposition of state-centric values of whatever kind that do not coincide with a community's sense of order is an approach that is clearly limited. The Koḷī community in Gonjhé that was most likely to become exposed to such forces of the values of "others" as a result of their proximity to urban centres and state institutions was observed to have countered such forces of imposition with equal aggression, through developing diverse mechanisms of resistance. Galanter (1968) highlighted a long time ago that every legal system is faced with this dilemma of bridging the gap between its elaborate legislations and local practice. Several years later, Fitzpatrick (1984, 128) argued that such gaps are inevitable and "unbridgeable" because state law "depends integrally on what is contrary to it." Chiba (1986) through his theorising of the symbiotic and ambivalent relationship between "official law" and "unofficial law" also makes the same point. In light of such insights, the empirical evidence in this book shows and confirms that allowing the values of state law "simply to be absorbed and accepted gradually through persuasion and example by various groups in society" (Galanter 1968, 82–83) is actually a (and may actually be the only) realistic aspiration for Indian legislators, courts, and activists. This may – and will – take time, but the process itself is already in progress, as the case studies in the book strongly confirm. The state legal order in India, not merely by coincidence or historical accident, but by design, provides for a plurality of laws ranging from state laws to religious laws, and customs to govern and regulate the lives of Indian people (Menski 2001, 2003). As Santos (2002) explains through his concept of "interlegality", in a situation of legal plurality, different legal orders remain "superimposed, interpenetrated and mixed" (Santos 2002, 437) in people's minds as also in their actions and are manifested in the trajectories of their lives. Dispute processing, therefore, will always remain a contested territory, with different options for different types of forums and laws as long as the values cultivating the orders within which they exist compete.[12] In light of this, outlawing non-state forums and actors engaged in dispute processing in the hope that this will prompt the creation of more "just" circumstances for dispute processing will be equivalent to "asking for the moon" (Menski 2006a, 2016), because justice as Sen (2009, 18) points out:

> cannot be indifferent to the lives that people can actually live … That institutions and rules are, of course, very important … but the realised actuality goes well beyond the organisational picture, and includes the lives that people manage – or do not manage – to live.

Just like the plurality of laws, also the plurality of forums that exists in India provides people with a flexibility – and therefore choice and options – to tackle their disputing situations in a manner most suited to their specific circumstances and contexts, sometimes through combining the services of different forums (Solanki 2011) and at other times by playing one against the other (*Abdur Rahman v The Secretary to Government 2017*). Presently, when individuals choose to follow certain practices that are not in cohesion with their respective community values, they may turn to the state courts in order to legitimise (and seek protection of) their actions. Conversely when dispute processing with the involvement of state actors does not satisfy a disputing party or parties, the processing may continue to be

12 "the unconscious conflict between *dharma* (righteousness) and mere law India has struggled, struggles now dramatically, and will struggle" (Derrett 1978b, 49). This prediction by Derrett (1978b) in his work on marriage law is particularly relevant and to a great extent reconfirmed in light of (though not limited to) the evidence presented in this research study.

pursued through the involvement of non-state actors. The manifest plurality of forums and actors in dispute processing, thus prevents the concentration of power in the hands of any one of these types of forums, thereby acting as a useful check on potentially arbitrary actions. In all of this, individual agency remains a crucial ingredient, justifying the methodological foundations of the present research as a study in law and anthropology.

Disputes need to be re-envisioned not (only) as a subject of law and order but (first) as a social process. Forums and actors engaged in dispute processing should be observed as spaces for mobilisation of a productive tension between the values of state law and those underlying a community's sense of order. Tension is after all necessary to question prejudices, vested interests, and unexamined preconceptions; it is the vitamin of law, both in its formal and informal manifestation. This will help ripen the experiences of not just individuals as more informed navigators, but also those of the state and other stakeholders in developing more conducive and productive dialogues of state law.

6.6 Perceiving law as a social process

As the evidence in this and several other studies around the world has exemplified, dispute processing is an extremely complex and dynamic phenomenon (Topidi 2018). State law and its systems are as much part of this as are factors pertaining to religious, cultural, socio-economic circumstances, livelihood practices, and education of the individuals engaged in such processes as well as nowadays, concerns of human rights and international law. Unfortunately, law school education in India prepares students only with respect to one part of these aspects of dispute processing,[13] those related to the official state law and courtroom procedures. Consequently, most law school graduates, as a result of little experience with actual legal practice and only brief exposure to social science subjects that are formally, reluctantly, and somewhat superficially, part of the Indian law school's five-year programme's curriculum, develop a fairly positivist perspective of "law",[14] and thereby a rather reductionist and in many ways restrained worldview of what is to be the very crux of their later daily practice – "disputing" (Menski 2011).

Discourses in anthropology about law, disputing and conflict, however, provide a rather different insight into those same processes of state law, showing and analysing the synthesised ways in which all these systems of lawyers, judges, courts,

13 My own experience relates to India. However, the inter-disciplinary engagement between lawyers and other social scientists reveals that this may be a phenomenon true for law schools in many other countries across the world.

14 Cotterrell (2009, 483) observes that the view of law harboured by "Western" lawyers is "monistic"; "autonomous" as a normative order as well as an object of study, makes the state and its agencies central and assumes that state law has an effect on society that cannot be ignored. This description of the perception of law amongst "Western" lawyers may be extended to the views of state law endorsed in law school education in India as well.

and the police machinery actually work in any given social context. Analysis of empirical research into actual disputing situations, one of the core areas of this discipline, shows the constant interactions and clashes between different legal orders, and illustrates how the elements of power, politics, morality, and behavioural routine interfere with the cogency of diverse legal phenomena (von Rossum and Taekema 2013, 156). Though the objectives of law and anthropology as two independent disciplines are different, there is a lot that students of law can draw from an insight into the ethnographic study of state law and its systems. As June Starr and Mark Goodale in their insightful edited volume titled *Practicing Ethnography in Law: New dialogues, enduring methods* highlight,

> Ethnographic methods are useful tools for accessing the complex ways in which law, decision-making, and legal regulations are embedded in wider social processes. (Starr and Goodale 2002, 2)

The present study, for example, even though at its core it aspires to be a contribution to legal studies, would have remained incomplete without its ethnographic fieldwork element and the critical approach of "unpacking" everything that one observes, a methodology that anthropology as a discipline emphasises and insists on. The process of "unpacking" demands the observation of any action, situation or concept as a phenomenon embedded in a certain context. For the present project, such problematising of the concepts of law and act of dispute processing revealed the many meanings these concepts held for different stakeholders within the dynamics of community life and various ways in which law and dispute processing were pronounced as part of it. For instance, Chapter 3 refers to the concept of "*tamāshā*" (see page 60). The element of *tamāshā* in dispute processing had several implications for the person(s) engaging in it as well as for its audience. In fact, observation of the element of *tamāshā* in dispute processing compels one to consider the many threads of a dispute that cause it to be processed in the manner that it is, which may very well include the use of state courts or the spaces of police stations (Kokal 2018). Despite state courts and state law being critical sites of performance, emotion or life details are met by lawyers, judges, and legal academics with impatience as being inefficient (Basu 2015, 59–85). Approaching the phenomenon of dispute processing through the lens of the legal discipline alone, therefore, would not have been sufficient or may not even have prompted me to observe and appreciate the significance of the element of *tamāshā* that is possibly a central factor in the processing of several types of disputes. An ethnographic observation complemented this study of engagement with state law to reveal how *tamāshās* are also a form in which people interact with state law and its regulatory systems.

In intensely plural societies, India being only one example, where state law contends with several different types of laws and their values, an introduction to anthropological approaches towards the study of law has crucial significance in legal education. As this study evidences, such an approach would not only encourage students to develop a more nuanced approach to the study of state law and legal processes but would also equip them with a more realistic understanding of the manner in which state law functions and is used within the dynamics of dispute processing.

The study of state law as a unitary and state-centred phenomenon sets certain rather rigid bounds for legal scholarship. Since state law and its regulatory systems are tools of power, politics, and speculation, as a result they are forever constituted, co-constituted and re-constituted through their interaction with other forces of social regulation. This is why this book, inevitably, seems to emphasise what may be perceived as "grey zones" for day-to-day regulation. The challenge in the present conditions of India, thus, is to ensure the closest possible compliance of local people with the expectations of justice that the Indian Constitution of 1950, as amended to date, has laid down. Studying this through the pluri-focal lens of law and anthropology, confirms thus the basic theorising of experts such as Sen (2009) and others, in the field of justice, that this is an arduous, never-ending challenge.

Bibliography

Abel, Richard L. 1974. "A Comparative Theory of Dispute Institutions in Society." *Law & Society Review* 8(2): 217–347.

Agarwal, Bina. 1994. *A Field of One's Own: Gender and Land Rights in South Asia*. Cambridge: Cambridge University Press.

Agrawal, C. M. 1992. *Golu Devata. The God of Justice of Kumaun Himalayas*. Almora: Shree Almora Book Depot.

Ahmed, Tufail. 2016. "Madras HC's Order Declaring Sharia Courts Illegal is a Start; Supreme Court Must Follow Suit." *Firstpost*, December 20, 2016. Available at: www.firstpost.com/india/madras-hcs-order-declaring-sharia-courts-illegal-is-a-start-suprem e-court-must-follow-suit-3165480.html.

Aditya, AK. 2016. "Where Does India Rank in Terms of Access to Justice?" *Bar & Bench* (blog). October 13, 2016. Available at: http://barandbench.com/india-rank-terms-a ccess-justice.

Ansari, Mubarak. 2014. "Jaat Panchayat Strikes in City." *Pune Mirror*, December 11, 2014, section Civic. Available at: www.punemirror.in/pune/civic/Jaat-panchayat-strike s-in-city/articleshow/45461417.cms.

Asian News International. 2017. "Minister Gifts 700 Brides Wooden Bats; to Be Used on Husbands If They Turn Alcoholic." *The Indian Express*, April 30, 2017. Available at: http://indianexpress.com/article/trending/bizarre/minister-gifts-700-brides-wooden-bats-to-be-used-on-husbands-if-they-turn-alcoholic-4634468.

Bailey, F. G. 1957. *Caste and the Economic Frontier: A Village in Highland Orissa*. Manchester: Manchester University Press.

Baindur, Meera. 2015. "From Stamp Paper to Brass Bells: Procedures of Petition and Justice in Golu Dev's Territory." In Nonstate legal practices in India. Manipal: Manipal Centre for Philosophy and Humanities, Dec. 5–6, 2015.

Bandi, Madhusudan. 2016. "Is There an Underlying Pattern in Implementation? Forest Rights Act." *Economic and Political Weekly* 51(19). Available at: www.epw.in/journal/2016/19/commentary/forest-rights-act.html.

Bandura, Albert. 1995. *Self-Efficacy in Changing Societies*. Cambridge: Cambridge University Press.

Bandyopadhyay, D. 2005. "Nyaya Panchayats: The Unfinished Task." *Economic and Political Weekly* 40(51): 5372–5375.

Bardhan, Pranab. 1999. *Political Economy of Development in India*. 2nd edition. Oxford, New York: Oxford University Press.

Bardhan, Pranab. 2001. "The Political Economy of Reform in India." *Democracy in India*, edited by Niraja Gopal Jayal. Delhi: Oxford University Press. 397–417.

Bashi, Gopika. 2017. "Baghpat and Caste & Gender Discrimination in India." Amnesty International, September 9, 2017. Available at: www.amnesty.org/en/latest/news/2015/09/baghpat-and-caste-gender-discrimination-in-india/.

Basu, Srimati. 2015. *The Trouble with Marriage: Feminists Confront Law and Violence in India*. Gender and Justice. Oakland, CA: University of California Press.

Baxi, Upendra. 1976. "From Takrar to Karar." *Journal of Constitutional and Parliamentary Studies* 10(1): 52–115.

Baxi, Upendra. 1982. *The Crisis of the Indian Legal System. Alternatives in Development: Law*. New Delhi: Vikas Publishing House.

Beals, Alan R. 1962. *Gopalpur: A South Indian Village*. New York: Holt, Rinehart & Winston.

Bedi, Tarini. 2010. "The (Im?) Possibilities of a Situated Feminist Subject in Shiv Sena: Shiv Sainiks, Governance, and Adjustment in Maharashtra." In *Histories of Intimacy and Situated Ethnography*, edited by Karen Isaksen Leonard, Gayatri Reddy, and Ann Grodzins Gold, 21–82. New Delhi: Manohar.

Bennett, T. W. 1991. *A Sourcebook of African Customary Law for Southern Africa*. Edited by N. S. Peart. 1st edition. Cape Town [u.a.]: Juta.

Berreman, Gerald Duane. 1963. *Hindus of the Himalayas*. Berkeley, CA: University of California Press.

Berti, Daniela. 2011a. "Courts of Law and Legal Practice." In *A Companion to the Anthropology of India*, edited by Isabelle Clark-Decès, 353–370. Malden, MA:Wiley-Blackwell.

Berti, Daniela. 2011b. "Trials, Witnesses, and Local Stakes in a District Court of Himachal Pradesh." In *The Politics of Belonging in the Himalayas: Local Attachments and Boundary Dynamics*, edited by Joanna Pfaff-Czarnecka and Gerard Toffin, 291–313. New Delhi: SAGE.

Berti, Daniela, and Gilles Tarabout. 2012. "Criminal Proceedings in India and the Question of Culture." In *Rechtsanalyse als Kulturforschung*, edited by Werner Gephart, 193–206. Frankfurt am Main: Vittorio Klostermann.

Bhatla, Nandita, and Anuradha Rajan. 2003. "Private Concerns in Public Discourse: Women-Initiated Community Responses to Domestic Violence." *Economic and Political Weekly* 38(17): 1658–1664.

Bhattacharya, Aritre. 2016. "Maharashtra's 'Dispute-Free Villages': Can Justice Be Delivered If Caste Is Denied?" *The News Minute*. May 12, 2016. Available at: www.thenewsminute.com/article/maharashtra-dispute-free-villages-can-justice-be-delivered-if-caste-denied-43122.

Blunt, E. A. H. 1931. *The Caste System of Northern India*. London: Oxford University Press.

Bose, Nirmal Kumar. 1960. "Conflict and Its Resolution in Hindu Civilisation." *Journal of the Department of Letters, University of Calcutta* 3: 1–49.

Boyd, Marion. 2013. "Ontario's 'Shari'a Court': Law and Politics Intertwined." *Islam and English Law: Rights, Responsibilities, and the Place of Shari'a*, 176–186, Cambridge: Cambridge University Press.

Capra, Fritjof, and Ugo Mattei. 2015. *The Ecology of Law: Toward a Legal System in Tune with Nature and Community*. 1st edition. Oakland, CA: Berrett-Koehler.

Chanock, Martin. 1998. *Law, Custom, and Social Order: The Colonial Experience in Malawi and Zambia*. African Studies: History. Portsmouth, NH: Heinemann.

Chatterjee, Partha. 1986. *Nationalist Thought and the Colonial World: A Derivative Discourse.* London: Zed Books.

Chatterjee, Partha. 1997. "Development Planning and the Indian State." In *State and Politics in India*, 271–297. Delhi: Oxford University Press.

Chaudhary, Muhammad Azam. 1999. *Justice in Practice: Legal Ethnography of a Pakistani Punjabi Village.* Oxford, New York: Oxford University Press.

Chaudhury, Chitrangada. 2016. "Making a Hollow in the Forest Rights Act." *The Hindu*, April 7, 2016. Available at: www.thehindu.com/opinion/columns/making-a-hollow-in-the-forest-rights-act/article8442490.ece.

Chiba, Masaji, ed. 1984. *Law and Culture in Sri Lanka: A Research Report on Asian Indigenous Law.* RGAIL Working Paper. Tokyo: Research Group on Asian Indigenous Law, Research Institute of Law, Tokai University.

Chiba, Masaji, ed. 1986. *Asian Indigenous Law: In Interaction with Received Law.* London: KPI.

Chiba, Masaji, ed. 1989. *Legal Pluralism: Toward a General Theory through Japanese Legal Culture.* Tokyo: Tokai University Press.

Chiba, Masaji, ed. 1998. "Other Phases of Legal Pluralism in the Contemporary World." *Ratio Juris* 11(3): 228–245.

Choudhary, Amit Anand. 2015. "Couple Living Together Will Be Presumed Married, Supreme Court Rules." *The Times of India*, April 13, 2015. Available at: https://timesofindia.indiatimes.com/india/Couple-living-together-will-be-presumed-married-Supreme-Court-rules/articleshow/46901198.cms.

Cohn, Bernard S. 1959. "Some Notes on Law and Change in North India." *Economic Development and Cultural Change* 8(1): 79–93.

Cohn, Bernard S. 1965. "Anthropological Notes on Disputes and Law in India." *American Anthropologist* 67(6): 82–122.

Comaroff, John, and Simon Roberts. 1981. *Rules and Processes.* Chicago, IL: University of Chicago Press.

Correspondent. 2015. "जातपंचायत समूहावर कारवाई करा." *Loksatta*, February 9, 2015. Available at: www.loksatta.com/maharashtra-news/jat-panchayat-anis-maharashtra-andhashraddha-nirmulan-samiti-1069712.

Coser, Lewis A. 1956. *The Functions of Social Conflict.* Glencoe, IL: Free Press.

Cotterrell, Roger. 2009. "Spectres of Transnationalism: Changing Terrains of Sociology of Law." *Journal of Law and Society* 36(4): 481–500.

Darian-Smith, Eve. 2012. "Ethnographies of Law." In *Legal Pluralism and Development: Scholars and Practitioners in Dialogue*, edited by Brian Z. Tamanaha, Caroline Sage, and Michael Woolcock, 545–561. Cambridge: Cambridge University Press.

Dasgupta, Kumkum. 2014. "Why People Go to Shariat Courts, Khap Panchayats." *The Hindustan Times*, July 8, 2014. Available at: www.hindustantimes.com/india-news/did-shariat-courts-thrive-on-india-s-overburdened-time-consuming-legal-system/article1-1237953.aspx.

Davis, Donald R. 2007. "Hinduism as a Legal Tradition." *Journal of the American Academy of Religion* 75(2): 241–267.

Deliege, Robert. 1997. *The World of the "Untouchables": Paraiyars of Tamil Nadu.* Translated by David Phillips. Delhi, New York: Oxford University Press.

Derrett, J. D. M. 1961. "The Administration of Hindu Law by the British." *Comparative Studies in Society and History* 4(1): 10–52.

Derrett, J. D. M. 1968. *Religion, Law and the State in India.* New York: Free Press.

Derrett, J. D. M. 1978a. "The Concept of Duty in Ancient Indian Jurisprudence: The Problem of Ascertainment." In *The Concept of Duty in South Asia*, edited by Wendy Doniger and J. Duncan M. Derrett, 18–66. London: Vikas Publishing House.

Derrett, J. D. M. 1978b. *The Death of a Marriage Law: Epitaph for the Rishis*. New Delhi [u.a.]: Vikas Publishing House.

Derrett, J. D. M. 1982. *The Judicial Panchayat: The Future of an Ancient Indian Rural Institution*. Paris: Dessain et Tolra.

Dhar, Rajib Lochan. 2014. "Job Search Processes for Tribal People from Jharkhand and West Bengal." *South Asia Research* 34(3): 191–208.

Dhawan, Rajeev. 2014. "Supreme Court's Ruling on Fatwas Is Faulty." *Mail Online*. July 13, 2014. Available at: www.dailymail.co.uk/indiahome/indianews/article-2690781/Supreme-Courts-ruling-fatwas-faulty.html.

Doye, Eli. 2015. "Indigenous Beliefs and Practices among the Galos of Arunachal Pradesh." *South Asia Research* 35(3): 334–348.

Drewes, Edeltraud. 1982. "Three Fishing Villages in Tamil Nadu – A Socio-Economic Study with Special Reference to The Role and Status of Women." Working Paper No. BOBP/WP/14. Madras: Food and Agriculture Organization of the United Nations. Available at: www.fao.org/3/ad954e/ad954e00.htm.

Dube, S. C. 1955. *Indian Village*. Ithaca, NY: Cornell University Press.

Eckert, Julia Maria. 2003. *The Charisma of Direct Action: Power, Politics, and the Shiv Sena*. New Delhi: Oxford University Press.

Ehrlich, Eugen. 2002 [1936]. *Fundamental Principles of the Sociology of Law*. New Brunswick, NJ; London: Transaction Publishers.

Epstein, Arnold L., ed. 1974. *Contention and Dispute: Aspects of Law and Social Control in Melanesia*. Canberra: Australian National University Press.

Epstein, Scarlett. 1974. "A Sociological Analysis of Which Beliefs in a Mysore Village." In *Tribe Caste and Peasantry*, edited by B. C. Agrawal and K. S. Mathur, 361–374. Lucknow: Ethnographic and Folk Culture, U.P.

Express News Service. 2016a. "Maharashtra Passes Law against Social Boycott." *The Indian Express*, April 14, 2016. Available at: http://indianexpress.com/article/india/india-news-india/maharashtra-passes-law-against-social-boycott/.

Express News Service. 2016b. "PIL in Madras High Court to Ban Illegal Shariats." *The New Indian Express*, September 22, 2016. Available at: www.newindianexpress.com/cities/chennai/2016/sep/21/PIL-in-Madras-High-Court-to-ban-illegal-shariats-1522151.html.

Fanger, Allen C. 1990. "The Jāgar: Spirit Possession Séance among the Rajputs and Silpakars of Kumaon." In *Himalaya: Past and Present*, edited by M. P. Joshi, Allen C. Fanger, and C. W. Brown, 173–191. Almora: Sri Almora Book Depot.

Felstiner, William L. F. 1974. "Influences of Social Organization on Dispute Processing." *Law & Society Review* 9(1): 63–94.

Felstiner, William L. F., Richard L. Abel, and Austin Sarat. 1981. "The Emergence and Transformation of Disputes: Naming, Blaming, Claiming." *Law & Society Review* 15(3/4): 631–654.

Fitzpatrick, Peter. 1984. "Law and Societies." *Osgoode Hall Law Journal* 22(1): 115–138.

Fitzpatrick, Peter. 2001. *Modernism and the Grounds of Law*. Cambridge Studies in Law and Society. Cambridge: Cambridge University Press.

Foblets, Marie-Claire, Katayoun Alidadi, Jonathan Bernaerts, Petra Burai, Kalindi Kokal, Mareike Riedel, and Elizabeth Steyn. (2016). "Which Law for Which Religion?:

Ethnographic Enquiries into the Limits of State Law Vis-à-Vis Lived Religion." *Rechtsphilosophie: Zeitschrift für Grundlagen des Rechts* 3: 237–282.

Foucault, Michel. 1979. *Discipline and Punish: The Birth of the Prison*. New York: Vintage Books.

FP Politics. 2014. "Not Just Shariat Courts: Supreme Court Order Also Includes Khap Panchayats." *Firstpost*. July 8, 2014. Available at: www.firstpost.com/india/not-just-shariat-courts-supreme-court-order-also-includes-khap-panchayats-1608069.html.

Frankenberg, Günther. 1985. "Critical Comparisons: Rethinking Comparative Law." *Harvard International Law Journal* 26(2): 411–456.

Freed, R. S. 1995. "The Legal Process in a Village in North India: The Case of Maya." In *Folk Law*, edited by Alison Dundes Renteln and Alan Dundes, vol. 2, 671–688. Madison, WI: University of Wisconsin Press.

Galanter, Marc. 1968. "The Displacement of Traditional Law in Modern India." *Journal of Social Issues* 24(4): 65–90.

Galanter, Marc. 1972. "The Aborted Restoration of 'Indigenous' Law in India." *Comparative Studies in Society and History* 14(01): 53–70.

Galanter, Marc. 1981. "Justice in Many Rooms: Courts, Private Ordering, and Indigenous Law." *The Journal of Legal Pluralism and Unofficial Law* 13(19): 1–47.

Galanter, Marc. 1989. "Panchayat Justice: An Indian Experiment in Legal Access." In *Law and Society in Modern India*, edited by Rajeev Dhavan, 54–91. New Delhi: Oxford University Press.

Galanter, Marc, and Jayanth K. Krishnan. 2003. "Debased Informalism: Lok Adalats and Legal Rights in Modem India." In *Beyond Common Knowledge: Empirical Approaches to the Rule of Law*, edited by Erik Jensen and Thomas Heller, 96–141. Stanford, CA: Stanford University Press.

Galanter, Marc, and Jayanth K. Krishnan. 2004. "Bread for the Poor: Access to Justice and the Rights of the Needy in India." *Hastings Law Journal* 55: 789.

Galligan, Denis J. 2007. *Law in Modern Society*. Clarendon Law Series. Oxford: Oxford University Press.

Geertz, Clifford. 2000. *Local Knowledge: Further Essays in Interpretive Anthropology*. New York: Basic Books.

Ghosh, Deepshikha. 2014. "Shariat Courts Have No Legal Sanction: Supreme Court." *NDTV*. July 7, 2014. Available at: www.ndtv.com/article/india/shariat-courts-have-no-legal-sanction-supreme-court-554180.

Ghurye, G. S. 1957. *The Mahadev Kolis*. Bombay: Popular Book Depot.

Gill, Aisha. 2009. "'Honour' Killings and the Quest for Justice in Black and Minority Ethnic Communities in the UK." *Criminal Justice Policy Review* 20(4): 475–494.

Gluckman, Max. 1963. "Papers in Honor of Melville J. Herskovits: Gossip and Scandal." *Current Anthropology* 4(3): 307–316.

Gluckman, Max. 1972. *The Ideas in Barotse Jurisprudence*. Manchester: Manchester University Press.

Gough, Kathleen E. 1960. "Castes in a Tajore Village." In *Aspects of Caste in South India, Ceylon and North-West Pakistan*, edited by E. R. Leach, 11–60. Cambridge: Cambridge University Press

Griffiths, John. 1986. "What Is Legal Pluralism." *Journal of Legal Pluralism and Unofficial Law* 18(24): 1–55.

Griffiths, John. 2006. "The Idea of Sociology of Law and Its Relation to Law and To Sociology." In *Law and Sociology*, edited by Michael Freeman. Current Legal Issues. Oxford, New York: Oxford University Press.

Grillo, Ralph D. 2015. *Muslim Families, Politics and the Law: A Legal Industry in Multicultural Britain*. Cultural Diversity and Law. Farnham, Surrey: Ashgate.

Grover, Shalini. 2009. "Lived Experiences Marriage, Notions of Love, and Kinship Support amongst Poor Women in Delhi." *Contributions to Indian Sociology* 43(1): 1–33.

Gulliver, Philip H. 1963. *Social Control in an African Society. A Study of the Arusha: Agricultural Masai of Northern Tanganyika*. 1st edition. International Library of Sociology and Social Reconstruction. London: Routledge.

Gulliver, Philip H. 1973. "Negotiations as a Mode of Dispute Settlement: Towards a General Model." *Law & Society Review* 7(4): 667–691.

Gulliver, Philip H. 1997. "Dispute Settlement without Courts: The Ndendeuli of Southern Tanzania." In *Law in Culture and Society*, edited by Laura Nader, 24–68. Berkley, CA: University of California Press.

Gupta, Akhil. 1995. "Blurred Boundaries: The Discourse of Corruption, the Culture of Politics, and the Imagined State." *American Ethnologist* 22(2): 375–402.

Gupta, Charu. 2009. "Hindu Women, Muslim Men: Love Jihad and Conversions." *Economic and Political Weekly* 44(51): 13–15.

Gurjar, Kaumudi. 2014. "Not Legally-Binding, but Not Banned Either." *Pune Mirror*, July 9, 2014, Pune edition. Available at: www.punemirror.in/pune/others/Not-legally-binding-but-not-banned-either/articleshow/38029417.cms.

Gurung, Shobha Hamal. 2004. "Women Weavers in Nepal: Between Global Market and Local Production." In *The Power of Women's Informal Networks: Lessons in Social Change from South Asia to West Africa*, edited by Bandana Purkayastha and Mangala Subramaniam, 89–104.

Guruswamy, Menaka, and Aditya Singh. 2010. "Accessing Injustice: The Gram Nyayalayas Act, 2008." *Economic and Political Weekly* 45(43): 16–19.

Hansen, Thomas Blom. 2001. "Governance and Myths of State in Mumbai." In *The Everyday State and Society in Modern India*, edited by C. J. Fuller and Veronique Benei, 31–67. New Delhi: Social Science Press.

Hapke, Holly M. 2001. "Petty Traders, Gender, and Development in a South Indian Fishery." *Economic Geography* 77(3): 225–249.

Harper, Edward B. 1957. "Hoylu: A Belief Relating Justice and the Supernatural." *American Anthropologist* 59(5): 801–816.

Hayden, Robert M. 1984. "A Note on Caste Panchayats and Government Courts in India." *Journal of Legal Pluralism and Unofficial Law* 22: 43–53.

Hayden, Robert M. 1999. *Disputes and Arguments Amongst Nomads: A Caste Council of India*. New Delhi: Oxford University Press.

Headley, Zoé E. 2015. "'The Devil's Court!'" In *Regimes of Legality: Ethnography of Criminal Cases in South Asia*, edited by Daniela Berti and Devika Bordia, 227–257. New Dehli: Oxford University Press.

Helfand, Michael A., ed. 2015. *Negotiating State and Non-State Law: The Challenge of Global and Local Legal Pluralism*. ASIL Studies in International Legal Theory. New York: Cambridge University Press.

Hertogh, Marc. 2007. "What Is Non-State Law? Mapping the Other Hemisphere of the Legal World." SSRN Scholarly Paper ID 1008451. Rochester, NY: Social Science Research Network.

Hertogh, Marc. 2008. *Living Law: Reconsidering Eugen Ehrlich*. Portland, OR: Bloomsbury Publishing.

Himonga, Chuma. 2011. "The Future of Living Customary Law in African Legal Systems in the Twenty-First Century and beyond with Special Reference to South Africa." In *The*

Future of African Customary Law, edited by Jeanmarie Fenrich, Paolo Galizzi, and Tracy E. Higgins, 31–57. Cambridge: Cambridge University Press.

Holden, Livia. 2003. "Custom and Law Practices in Central India: Some Case Studies." *South Asia Research* 23(2): 115–134.

Holden, Livia. 2008. *Hindu Divorce*. Aldershot: Ashgate.

IANS. 2014. "Shariat Courts Have No Legal Sanctity: Supreme Court." *The Hindu*, July 7, 2014. Available at: www.thehindu.com/news/national/shariat-courts-have-no-legal-sanctity-supreme-court/article6185496.ece.

IBN Lokmat. 2015. "Bedhadak: Jaat panchayat Episode." Maharashtra. https://www.youtube.com/watch?v=4aEj1jbQGFw.

Ingole, Anagha. 2015. "Dispensing Justice Through Kangaroo Courts." *Economic and Political Weekly*, Web Exclusives, L (10). Available at: www.epw.in/reports-states/dispensing-justice-through-kangaroo-courts.html.

Ishwaran, K. 1964. "Customary Law in Village India." *International Journal of Comparative Sociology* 5(2): 228–243.

Iyengar, Rishi. 2015. "Two Indian Sisters Ordered to Be Raped by Village Council Beg Supreme Court for Help." *Time*. August 28, 2015. Available at: http://time.com/4014444/india-khap-panchayat-two-sisters-rape-ordered-uttar-pradesh/.

Iyengar, Sushma. 2007. "A Study of Nari Adalats (Women's Courts) and Caste Panchayats in Gujarat." United Nations Development Programme Bangkok.

Jagran. 2016. "Is Nyay Ki Devi Ka Darbar Supreme Court Ki Manyata Liye Hai," March 2, 2016. Available at: www.jagran.com/spiritual/mukhye-dharmik-sthal-the-goddess-is-the-goddess-of-justice-is-the-goddess-of-the-court-for-recognition-of-the-supreme-court-13663772.html?src=LNewsPriority2.

James, V. 1977. "Marriage Customs of Christian Son Kolis." *Asian Folklore Studies* 36(2): 131–148.

Jauregui, Beatrice. 2011. "Law and Order: Police Encounter Killings and Routinized Political Violence." In *A Companion to the Anthropology of India*, edited by Isabelle Clark-Decès, 371–388. New York: Wiley-Blackwell.

John, Shobha. 2013. "Kangaroo Courts Rise and Thrive in India." *The Times of India*, March 15, 2013. Available at: http://timesofindia.indiatimes.com/india/Kangaroo-courts-rise-and-thrive-in-India/articleshow/18981684.cms.

Kabeer, Naila. 1999. "Resources, Agency, Achievements: Reflections on the Measurement of Women's Empowerment." *Development and Change* 30(3): 435–464.

Kabeer, Naila. 2001. "Conflicts Over Credit: Re-Evaluating the Empowerment Potential of Loans to Women in Rural Bangladesh." *World Development* 29(1): 63–84.

Kaviraj, Sudipta. 1997. "The Modern State in India." In *Dynamics of State Formation: India and Europe Compared*, edited by Sudipta Kaviraj and Martin R. Doornbos, 225–250. New Delhi: SAGE Publications.

Khare, R. S. 1972. "Indigenous Culture and Lawyer's Law in India." *Comparative Studies in Society and History* 14(1): 71–96.

Khilnani, Sunil. 1999. *The Idea of India*. New York: Farrar Straus Giroux.

Kidder, Robert L. 1973. "Courts and Conflict in an Indian City: A Study in Legal Impact." *Journal of Commonwealth Political Studies* 11(2): 121–139.

Kidder, Robert L. 1974a. "Litigation as a Strategy for Personal Mobility: The Case of Urban Caste Association Leaders." *The Journal of Asian Studies* 33(2): 177–191.

Kidder, Robert L. 1974b. "Formal Litigation and Professional Insecurity: Legal Entrepreneurship in South India." *Law & Society Review* 9(1): 11–37.

Kirsch, Thomas G. 2008. *Spirits and Letters: Reading, Writing and Charisma in African Christianity.* New York [u.a.]: Berghahn Books.

Koch, Klaus-Friedrich. 1974. *War and Peace in Jalémó: The Management of Conflict in Highland New Guinea.* Cambridge, MA: Harvard University Press.

Kokal, Kalindi. 2013. "Hope for Justice." *Economic and Political Weekly* 48(45–46): 22–23.

Kokal, Kalindi. 2014. "To Lead or To Follow?" *Economic and Political Weekly* 49(50): 19–21.

Kokal, Kalindi. 2018. "Tamāshā: The Theatrics of Disputing and Non-State Dispute Processing." In *Normative Pluralism and Human Rights: Social Normativities in Conflict*, edited by Kyriaki Topidi, 189–206. Abingdon, Oxon: Routledge.

Korteweg, Anna. 2006. "The Sharia Debate in Ontario." *ISIM Review* 18: 50–51.

Kotiswaran, Prabha. 2008. "Born unto Brothels: Toward a Legal Ethnography of Sex Work in an Indian Red-Light Area." *Law & Social Inquiry* 33(3): 579–629.

Kötter, Matthias, Tilmann Röder, Gunnar Folke Schuppert, and Rüdiger Wolfrum. 2015. *Non-State Justice Institutions and the Law.* London: Palgrave Macmillan.

Krengel, Monika. 1999. "Spirit Possession in the Central Himalayas. Jāgar-Rituals: An Expression of Customs and Rights." In *Possession en Asie du Sud: Parole, Corps, Territoire* edited by Jackie Assayag, Collectif, and Gilles Tarabout. Éditions de L'École des Hautes Études en Sciences Sociales. Paris: Collection Purusartha, 21.

Krishnan, Jayanth K. 2014. "Legitimacy of Courts and the Dilemma of Their Proliferation: The Significance of Judicial Power in India." In *Asian Courts in Contexts: A Comparative Study*, edited by Jiunn-rong Yeh and Wen-Chen Chang. Cambridge: Cambridge University Press.

Krishnan, Jayanth K., Shirish Naresh Kavadi, Azima Girach, Dhanaji Khupkar, Kalindi Kokal, Satyajeet Mazumdar, MsNupur, et al. 2014. "Grappling at the Grassroots: Access to Justice in India's Lower Tier." *Harvard Human Rights Journal* 27(1): 151–189.

Kulkarni, Dhaval. 2015. "Soon, a Law against Social Boycott by Caste Panchayats in Maharashtra." *DNA*, June 14, 2015. Available at: www.dnaindia.com/mumbai/report-coming-soon-a-law-against-social-boycott-by-caste-panchayats-in-maharashtra-2095364.

Kumar, Ajay. 2012. "Khap Panchayats: A Socio-Historical Overview." *Economic and Political Weekly* 47(4): 59–64.

Kumar, Alok Prasanna. 2016. "Social Boycott Act." *Economic and Political Weekly* 51(21): 10–11.

Kumar, Nita. 1992. *Friends, Brothers, and Informants: Fieldwork Memoirs of Banaras.* Berkeley, CA: University of California Press.

Kushawaha, R., and Laxmi Mall Singhvi. 1977. *Working of Nyaya Panchayats in India: A Case Study of Varanasi District.* New Dehli: Young Asia Publications.

Lal, Anshu. 2015. "Madras HC Grants Rapist Bail for 'Mediation': Why the Verdict Makes a Bad Joke out of Justice." *Firstpost.* June 24, 2015. Available at: www.firstpost.com/india/madras-hc-grants-rapist-bail-mediation-verdict-makes-bad-joke-justice-2309902.html.

Larouche, Catherine. 2017. "Bridging a Gap?: Muslim Charitable Organizations, Politics of Development and Violence in Uttar Pradesh." PhD Dissertation (unpublished manuscript), Montreal: Mc Gill University.

Lemons, Katherine. 2010. "At the Margins of Law: Adjudicating Muslim Families in Contemporary Delhi." PhD Dissertation, Berkeley, CA: University of California. Available at: http://escholarship.org/uc/item/6f66n4dn.

Lingat, Robert. 1973. *The Classical Law of India.* Berkeley. CA: University of California Press.

Lipner, Julius. 1998. *Hindus: Their Religious Beliefs and Practices.* London: Routledge.

Lokur Committee. 1965. "Revision of the Lists of Scheduled Castes and Scheduled Tribes." Government of India, Department of Social Security. New Delhi.

Magar, Veronica. 2003. "Empowerment Approaches to Gender-Based Violence: Women's Courts in Delhi Slums." *Women's Studies International Forum* 26(6): 509–523.

Mahapatra, Dhananjay. 2013. "Norms Must to End Khap Violence: SC." *The Times of India*, January 5, 2013. Available at: http://timesofindia.indiatimes.com/india/Norms-must-to-end-khap-violence-SC/articleshow/17894540.cms.

Malik, Aditya. 2016. "The Darbar of Goludev." In *The Law of Possession*, edited by William S. Sax and Helene Basu, 193–225. New York: Oxford University Press.

Mallampalli, Chandra. 2010. "Escaping the Grip of Personal Law in Colonial India: Proving Custom, Negotiating Hindu-Ness." *Law and History Review* 28(4): 1043–1065.

Mander, Harsh, Akram Akhtar Chaudhary, Zafar Eqbal, and Rajanya Bose. 2016. "Wages of Communal Violence in Muzaffarnagar and Shamli." *Economic and Political Weekly* 51 (43): 39–45.

Marcus, George E., and Michael M. J. Fischer. 1999. *Anthropology as Cultural Critique*. 2nd edition. Chicago, IL: University of Chicago Press.

Mathur, Nayanika. 2015. "A 'Remote' Town in the Indian Himalaya." *Modern Asian Studies* 49(02): 365–392.

Menski, Werner, ed. 1998. *South Asians and the Dowry Problem*. Stoke-on-Trent: Trentham Books.

Menski, Werner, ed. 2001. *Modern Indian Family Law*. Richmond: Curzon.

Menski, Werner, ed. 2003. *Hindu Law: Beyond Tradition and Modernity*. Oxford: Oxford University Press.

Menski, Werner, ed. 2006a. "Asking for the moon: Legal uniformity in India from a Kerala perspective." *Kerala Law Times* 2: 52–78.

Menski, Werner, ed. 2006b. *Comparative Law in a Global Context: The Legal Systems of Asia and Africa*. 2nd edition. Cambridge: Cambridge University Press.

Menski, Werner, ed. 2011. "Flying Kites in A Global Sky: New Models of Jurisprudence." *Socio-Legal Review* 7: 1–22.

Menski, Werner, ed. 2016. "Still Asking for the Moon? Opening Windows of Opportunity for Better Justice in India." *Verfassung und Recht in Übersee* 49(2): 125–147.

Merry, Sally Engle. 1988. "Legal Pluralism." *Law & Society Review* 22(5): 869–896.

Merry, Sally Engle. 1992. "Anthropology, Law, and Transnational Processes." *Annual Review of Anthropology* 21(January): 357–379.

Merry, Sally Engle. 2004. "Colonial and Postcolonial Law." In *The Blackwell Companion to Law and Society*, edited by Austin Sarat, 569–588. Malden, MA: Wiley-Blackwell.

Merry, Sally Engle. 2009. "Legal Transplants and Cultural Translation: Making Human Rights in the Vernacular." In *Human Rights: An Anthropological Reader*, edited by Mark Goodale, 265–302. Malden, MA: Wiley-Blackwell..

Merry, Sally Engle. 2012. "Legal Pluralism and Legal Culture: Mapping the Terrain." In *Legal Pluralism and Development: Scholars and Practitioners in Dialogue*, edited by Brian Z. Tamanaha, Caroline Sage, and Michael Woolcock, 66–82. Cambridge: Cambridge University Press.

Merry, Sally Engle. 2015. "International Law and Sociolegal Scholarship: Towards a Spatial Global Legal Pluralism." In *Negotiating State and Non-State Law: The Challenge of Global and Local Legal Pluralism*, edited by Michael A. Helfand, 59–82. ASIL Studies in International Legal Theory. New York: Cambridge University Press.

Meschievitz, Catherine, and Marc Galanter. 1982. "In Search of Nyaya Panchayats: The Politics of a Moribund Institution." In *The Politics of Informal Justice: Vol 2 Comparative Studies*, edited by Richard Abel, 47–77. New York: Academic Press.

Meyers, Diana Tietjens. 2000. "Feminism and Women's Autonomy: The Challenge of Female Genital Cutting." *Metaphilosophy* 31(5): 469–491.

Michaels, Axel. 2004. *Hinduism: Past and Present.* Princeton, NJ: Princeton University Press.

Michaels, Ralf. 2015. "What Is Non-State Law? A Primer." In *Negotiating State and Non-State Law: The Challenge of Global and Local Legal Pluralism*, edited by Michael A. Helfand, 41–58. ASIL Studies in International Legal Theory. New York: Cambridge University Press.

Miller, Richard E., and Austin Sarat. 1980. "Grievances, Claims, and Disputes: Assessing the Adversary Culture." *Law & Society Review* 15(3/4): 525–566.

Mnookin, Robert H., and Lewis Kornhauser. 1979. "Bargaining in the Shadow of the Law: The Case of Divorce." *The Yale Law Journal* 88(5): 950–997.

Moore, Erin. 1985. *Conflict and Compromise: Justice in an Indian Village.* Monograph Series (University of California, Berkeley. Center for South and Southeast Asia Studies); No. 26. Berkeley, CA: Center for South and Southeast Asia Studies, University of California; Lanham, MD: University Press of America.

Moore, Erin. 1990. "Dream Bread: An Exemplum in a Rajasthani Panchayat." *The Journal of American Folklore* 103(409): 301–323.

Moore, Erin. 1993. "Gender, Power, and Legal Pluralism: Rajasthan, India." *American Ethnologist* 20(3): 522–542.

Moore, Sally Falk. 1973. "Law and Social Change: The Semi-Autonomous Social Field as an Appropriate Subject of Study." *Law & Society Review* 7(4): 719–746.

Moore, Sally Falk. 1978. *Law as Process: An Anthropological Approach.* London, Henley and Boston, MA: Routledge & Kegan Paul.

Mukherji, Anahita. 2014. "The Other Durga Shakti." *The Times of India*, June 22, 2014. Available at: http://timesofindia.indiatimes.com/home/stoi/deep-focus/The-other-Durga-shakti/articleshow/36986821.cms.

Nadel, Lynn, and Walter Sinnott-Armstrong, eds. 2012. *Memory and Law.* Oxford Series in Neuroscience, Law, and Philosophy. New York: Oxford University Press.

Nader, Laura. 1978. *The Disputing Process: Law in Ten Societies.* New York: Columbia University Press.

Nader, Laura. 1990. *Harmony Ideology: Justice and Control in a Zapotec Mountain Village.* Stanford, CA: Stanford University Press.

Nader, Laura. 2002. "Moving On: Comprehending Anthropologies of Law." In *Practicing Ethnography in Law: New Dialogues, Enduring Methods*, edited by June Starr and Mark Goodale, 1st edition, 189–200. New York: Palgrave Macmillan.

Nagaraj, Vasudha. 2010a. "Law and Other Things: The Gram Nyayalaya: The New Face of the Judiciary." 2010. Available at: http://lawandotherthings.blogspot.de/2010/11/gram-nyayalaya-new-face-of-judiciary.html.

Nagaraj, Vasudha. 2010b. "Local and Customary Forums Adapting and Innovating Rules of Formal Law." *Indian Journal of Gender Studies* 17(3): 429–450.

Nairita. 2014. "Historical Judgment in India: Fatwas, Sharia Courts Illegal, Says Supreme Court." *News.Oneindia.* July 7, 2014. Available at: www.oneindia.com/india/fatwas-sharia-courts-illegal-says-supreme-court-1478414.html.

Nandy, Ashis. 1989. "The Political Culture of the Indian State." *Daedalus* 118(4): 1–26.

Naples, Nancy A. 2003. *Feminism and Method: Ethnography, Discourse Analysis, and Activist Research.* New York: Routledge.

Narayan, Kirin. 1993. "How Native Is a 'Native' Anthropologist?" *American Anthropologist* 95(3): 671–686.

Negi, B. S., D. S. Chauhan, and N. P. Todaria. 2012. "Administrative and Policy Bottlenecks in Effective Management of Van Panchayats in Uttarakhand, India." *Law Environment and Development Journal* 8(1): 143–159.

Nussbaum, Martha C. 2001. *Women and Human Development: The Capabilities Approach.* Cambridge: Cambridge University Press.

Obeng, Pashington. 2014. *Rural Women's Power in South Asia.* Basingstoke: Palgrave Macmillan.

Paine, Robert. 1967. "What Is Gossip About? An Alternative Hypothesis." *Man* 2(2): 278–285.

Pal, Mahi. 2004. "Caste and Patriarchy in Panchayats." *Economic and Political Weekly* 39 (32): 3581–3583.

Palriwala, Rajni. 1991. "Transitory Residence and Invisible Work: Case Study of a Rajasthan Village." *Economic and Political Weekly* 26(48): 2763–2772.

Pandey, Anshul Kumar. 2014. "Kangaroo Courts Must Go!" *DNA*, January 25, 2014, sec. Blogs. Available at: www.dnaindia.com/blogs/post-kangaroo-courts-must-go-1956917.

Parashar, Archana. 2013. "Religious Personal Laws as Non-State Laws: Implications for Gender Justice." *The Journal of Legal Pluralism and Unofficial Law* 45(1): 5–23.

Pereira, Melvil, and R. P. Athparia. 2018. "The Resilience of Tribal Conflict Resolution Systems in North East India: A Panoramic View." In *Legal Pluralism and Indian Democracy: Tribal Conflict Resolution Systems in Northeast India*, edited by Melvil Pereira, Bitopi Dutta, and Binita Kakati, 1st edition. London: Routledge.

Pereira, Melvil, Bitopi Dutta, and Binita Kakati. 2018. *Legal Pluralism and Indian Democracy: Tribal Conflict Resolution Systems in Northeast India.* 1st edition. London: Routledge.

Pirie, Fernanda. 2013. *The Anthropology of Law.* 1st edition. Clarendon Law Series. Oxford: Oxford University Press.

Plumber, Mustafa. 2015. "Bombay High Court Quashes Rape Charge after Man Promises to Marry Victim." *DNA*, June 22, 2015. Available at: www.dnaindia.com/india/report-bombay-high-court-quashes-rape-charge-after-man-promises-to-marry-victim-2097669.

Polanki, Pallavi. 2014. "No, the Supreme Court, Didn't Say That Fatwas Are 'Illegal'." *Firstpost.* July 9, 2014. Available at: www.firstpost.com/india/no-the-supreme-court-didnt-say-that-fatwas-are-illegal-1610405.html.

Pospisil, Leopold. 1978. "The Structure of a Society and Its Multiple Legal Systems." In *Cross-Examinations: Essays in Memory of Max Gluckman*, edited by Phillip Gulliver, 96–109. Leiden: Brill.

Press Trust of India. 2014. "State Governments Must Put down Kangaroo Courts: Bengal Governor." *The Times of India*, January 25, 2014. Available at: http://timesofindia.indiatimes.com/india/State-governments-must-put-down-kangaroo-courts-Bengal-governor/articleshow/29367506.cms.

Press Trust of India. 2018. "Aadhaar Covers over 89% Population." *The Times of India*, March 7, 2018. Available at: https://timesofindia.indiatimes.com/business/india-business/aadhaar-covers-over-89-population-alphons/articleshow/63202223.cms.

Punekar, Vinaja B. 1959. *The Son Kolis of Bombay.* Mumbai: Popular Book Depot.

Pur, Kripa Ananth, and Anirudh Krishna. 2009. "Formal Perceptions of Informal Justice Village Councils and Access to Justice." In *Strengthening Governance through Access to Justice*, edited by Amita Singh and Nasir Aslam Zahid, 52–64. New Delhi: PHI Learning.

Purkayastha, Bandana, and Mangala Subramaniam, eds. 2004. *The Power of Women's Informal Networks: Lessons in Social Change from South Asia and West Africa.* Lanham, MD: Lexington Books.

Rai, Shirin. 1996. "Women and the State in the Third World – An Overview." In *Women and the State: International Perspectives*, edited by Shirin Rai and Geraldine Lievesley. London; Bristol, PA: Taylor & Francis.

Ram, Kalpana. 1991. *Mukkuvar Women: Gender, Hegemony and Capitalist Transformation in a South Indian Fishing Community*. Women in Asia Publication Series. London: Zed.

Ramsbotham, Oliver, Tom Woodhouse, and Hugh Miall. 2011. *Contemporary Conflict Resolution: The Prevention, Management and Transformation of Deadly Conflicts*. 1st edition. Cambridge: Polity Press.

Ranade, Sanjay V. 2008. "The Kolis of Mumbai at Crossroads: Religion, Business and Urbanisation in Cosmopolitan Bombay Today." In *Proceedings of the 17th Biennial Conference of the Asian Studies Association of Australia (ASAA)*, edited by A. M. Vicziany and R. Cribb, Vol. 1: 1–11. Melbourne: Monash University Publishing.

Razack, Sherene H. 2007. "The 'Sharia Law Debate' in Ontario: The Modernity/Premodernity Distinction in Legal Efforts to Protect Women from Culture." *Feminist Legal Studies* 15(1): 3–32.

Redding, Jeffrey A. 2013. "Secularism, the Rule of Law, and 'Shari'a Courts': An Ethnographic Examination of a Constitutional Controversy." *St. Louis University Law Journal* 57(February): 339–376.

Redding, Jeffrey A. 2014. "The Case of Ayesha, Muslim 'Courts', and the Rule of Law: Some Ethnographic Lessons for Legal Theory." *Modern Asian Studies* 48(4): 940–985.

Rubinoff, Janet Ahner. 1999. "Fishing for Status: Impact of Development on Goa's Fisherwomen." *Women's Studies International Forum* 22(6): 631–644.

Rudolph, Lloyd I., and Susanne Hoeber Rudolph. 1965. "Barristers and Brahmans in India: Legal Cultures and Social Change." *Comparative Studies in Society and History* 8(01): 24–49.

Rudolph, Susanne Hoeber, and Lloyd I. Rudolph. 1987. *In Pursuit of Lakshmi: The Political Economy of the Indian State*. 1st edition. Chicago, IL: University of Chicago Press.

Saberwal, Satish. 1996. *Roots of Crisis: Interpreting Contemporary Indian Society*. New Delhi, Thousand Oaks, CA: SAGE Publications.

Sachs, Carolyn E. 1996. *Gendered Fields: Rural Women, Agriculture, and the Environment*. Boulder, CO: Westview Press.

Samal, P. K., and P. P. Dhyani. 2007. "Gender Considerations of Technological Interventions in Agriculture, Sustainable Management and Development in Indian Central Himalaya." *South Asia Research* 27(2): 153–172.

Sandole, Dennis J. D., ed. 2011. *Handbook of Conflict Analysis and Resolution*. London: Routledge.

Santos, Boaventura de Sousa. 2002. *Toward a New Legal Common Sense: Law, Globalization and Emancipation*. 2nd edition. Law in Context. London: Butterworths LexisNexis.

Sarat, Austin, ed. 1995. *Law in Everyday Life*. 1st paperback edition. Amherst Series in Law, Jurisprudence, and Social Thought. Ann Arbor, MI: University of Michigan Press.

Sbriccoli, Tommaso. 2013. "Legal Pluralism in Discourse: Justice, Politics and Marginality in Rural Rajasthan, India." *The Journal of Legal Pluralism and Unofficial Law* 45(1): 143–164.

Schiff Berman, Paul. 2009. "The New Legal Pluralism." *Annual Review of Law and Social Science* 5(1): 225–242.

Searle-Chatterjee, Mary. 1981. *Reversible Sex Roles: The Special Case of Benares Sweepers*. Women in Development. Oxford, New York: Pergamon Press.

Sen, Amartya. 1990. "Gender and Co-Operative Conflicts." In *Persistent Inequalities: Women and World Development*, edited by Irene Tinker, 123–149. Oxford: Oxford University Press.

Sen, Amartya. 2009. *The Idea of Justice*. London: Allen Lane.

Sezgin, Yüksel. 2013. *Human Rights under State-Enforced Religious Family Laws in Israel, Egypt and India*. Cambridge Studies in Law and Society. Cambridge [u.a.]: Cambridge University Press.

Shachar, Ayelet. 2001. *Multicultural Jurisdictions: Cultural Differences and Women's Rights*. Contemporary Political Theory. Cambridge: Cambridge University Press.

Shariff, Fauzia. 2008. "Power Relations and Legal Pluralism: An Examination of Resistance to Injustices Amongst the Santal Adivasi of India and Bangladesh." *Journal of Legal Pluralism and Unofficial Law* 57: 1–43.

Shariff, Fauzia. 2013. "Harmony Ideology Revisited: Spatial Geographies of Hegemony and Disputing Strategies amongst the Santal." *Journal of Legal Pluralism and Unofficial Law* 45(1): 124–143.

Sharma, Betwa. 2016. "Maharashtra's New Law Against Social Boycott Could Spark a Renaissance, Say Activists." *Huffington Post India*, April 14, 2016. Available at: www.huffingtonpost.in/2016/04/14/maharashtras-new-law-against-social-boycott-could-spark-a-renai.

Sharma, Ritu. 2014. "Verdict in Birbhum Gangrape Case Tells Why Kangaroo Courts Should Be Prudent in Their Judgement." *Oneindia*, September 20, 2014. Available at: www.oneindia.com/feature/verdict-birbhum-gangrape-case-tells-why-kangaroo-courts-should-prudent-in-judgement-1525949.html.

Shedge, Amruta. 2014. "Lawlessness of Maharashtra's 'Gavki' Panchayats." *Headlines today*. Maharashtra. Available at: www.youtube.com/watch?v=QUMBCETXlWU.

Singh, Amita, and Nasir Aslam Zahid. 2009. *Strengthening Governance through Access to Justice*. New Delhi: PHI Learning.

Singh, Mahendra Pal, and Niraj Kumar. 2017. "Examining India's Common Las Identity: An Inquiry into India's Legal Systems and Tradition." New Dehli: Centre for Comparative Law, National Law University Delhi.

Smith, Michael G. 1974. *Corporations and Society*. London: Duckworth.

Solanki, Gopika. 2011. *Adjudication in Religious Family Laws: Cultural Accommodation, Legal Pluralism, and Gender Equality in India*. Cambridge Studies in Law and Society. Cambridge: Cambridge University Press.

Srinivas, M. N. 1955. "The Social System in a Mysore Village." In *Village India*, edited by McKim Marriot, 1–35. Chicago, IL: University of Chicago Press.

Srinivas, M. N. 1976. *The Remembered Village*. Berkeley, CA: University of California Press.

Srinivas, M. N. 1997. *Village, Caste, Gender and Method: Essays in Indian Social Anthropology*. New Delhi: Oxford University Press India.

Srinivas, M. N. 2009a. "A Caste Dispute among Washermen of Mysore." In *The Oxford India Srinivas*, Part I: Village Studies: Rampura, 5: 100–121. New Delhi: Oxford University Press.

Srinivas, M. N. 2009b. "A Joint Family Dispute in a Mysore Village." In *The Oxford India Srinivas*, Part I: Village Studies: Rampura, 6: 122–142. New Delhi: Oxford University Press.

Srinivas, M. N. 2009c. *The Oxford India Srinivas*. New Delhi: Oxford University Press.

Srinivas, M. N. 2009d. "The Study of Disputes in an Indian Village." In *The Oxford India Srinivas*, Part I: Village Studies: Rampura, 4, 93–99. New Delhi: Oxford University Press.

Starr, June, and Mark Goodale, eds. 2002. *Practicing Ethnography in Law: New Dialogues, Enduring Methods.* 1st edition. New York: Palgrave Macmillan.

Strathern, Marilyn. 1985. "Discovering 'Social Control'." *Journal of Law and Society* 12(2): 111–134.

Subramani, A. 2016. "Madras High Court Bans Unauthorised 'Sharia Courts'." *The Times of India*, December 20, 2016. Available at: http://timesofindia.indiatimes.com/city/chennai/madras-hc-bans-sharia-courts/articleshow/56061972.cms.

Subramanian, Narendra. 2014. *Nation and Family: Personal Law, Cultural Pluralism, and Gendered Citizenship in India.* Stanford, CA: Stanford University Press.

Sundar, Nandini, ed. 2009. *Legal Grounds: Natural Resources, Identity, and the Law in Jharkhand.* New Delhi: Oxford University Press.

Suzuki, Masataka. 2008. "Bhuta and Daiva: Changing Cosmology of Rituals and Narratives in Karnataka." *Senri Ethnological Studies (SES)* 71(March): 51–85.

Tamanaha, Brian Z. 2008. "Understanding Legal Pluralism: Past to Present, Local to Global." *Sydney Law Review* 30: 375–411.

The Hindu. 2014. "Stamp out Kangaroo Courts," January 25, 2014. Available at: www.thehindu.com/opinion/editorial/stamp-out-kangaroo-courts/article5614885.ece?homepage=true.

Thompson, Paul. 1985. "Women in the Fishing: The Roots of Power between the Sexes." *Comparative Studies in Society and History* 27(1): 3–32.

Topidi, Kyriaki, ed. *Normative Pluralism and Human Rights: Social Normativities in Conflict.* Abingdon: Routledge, 2018.

Tschalaer, Mengia Hong. 2009. "Women Entering the Legal Landscape: Negotiating Legal Gender Reforms in a 'Tribal' Women's Forum in South Rajasthan, India." SSRN Scholarly Paper ID 1868565. Rochester, NY: Social Science Research Network. Available at: http://papers.ssrn.com/abstract=1868565.

van Binsbergen, W. M. J. 1993. "African Independent Churches and the State in Botswana." In *Power and Prayer: Essays on Religion and Politics*, edited by M. Bax and A. de Koster, 24–56. Amsterdam: VU [Free University] University Press.

van Rossum, Wibo, and Sanne Taekema. 2013. "Introduction to Law as Plural Phenomenon: Confrontations of Legal Pluralisms." *Erasmus Law Review* 6(3/4): 155–157.

Vatuk, Sylvia. 2013. "The 'Women's Court' in India: An Alternative Dispute Resolution Body for Women in Distress." *The Journal of Legal Pluralism and Unofficial Law* 45(1): 76–103.

Virdi, Preet Kaur. 2013. "Barriers to Canadian Justice: Immigrant Sikh Women and Izzat." *South Asian Diaspora* 5(1): 107–122.

Virdi, Preet Kaur. 2016. "Marriage/Breakdown amongst Punjabi-Sikhs in Canada: A Legal Ethnography of Disputants, (Un)Official Forums, and Access to Family Justice in Ontario, Canada." PhD Dissertation (unpublished), London: SOAS University of London. Available at: https://eprints.soas.ac.uk/24907/.

von Benda-Beckmann, Franz. 2006. "The Multiple Edges of Law: Dealing with Legal Pluralism in Development Practice." In *The World Bank Legal Review: Law, Equity, and Development*, edited by Ana Palacio and T. W. Bank, 51–86. Washington, DC: The World Bank [et al].

von Benda-Beckmann, Keebet. 1981. "Forum Shopping and Shopping Forums: Dispute Processing in a Minangkabau Village in West Sumatra." *Journal of Legal Pluralism* 19: 117–159.

Waghmode, Vivek. 2015. "MANS to Raise Voice against Caste Panchayats." *The Times of India*, January 23, 2015. Available at: http://timesofindia.indiatimes.com/city/kolhapur/MANS-to-raise-voice-against-caste-panchayats/articleshow/45989425.cms.

Whitson, Sarah Leah. 1992. "Neither Fish, Nor Flesh, Nor Good Red Herring Lok Adalats: An Experiment in Informal Dispute Resolution in India." *Hastings International and Comparative Law Review* 15: 391–445.

Williams, B. F. 1996. "Skinfolk, Not Kinfolk: Comparative Reflections on the Identity of Participant Observation in Two Field Settings." In *Feminist Dilemmas in Fieldwork*, edited by Diane L. Wolf, 72–95. Boulder, CO: Westview Press.

Woodman, Gordon R. 2001. "Customary Law in Common Law Systems." *IDS Bulletin* 32(1): 28–34.

Zainulbhai, Tameem. 2011. "Justice for All: Improving the Lok Adalat System in India." *Fordham International Law Journal* 35(1): 248–278.

Cases:

Aadhaar Judgment, K. S. Puttaswamy vs. Union of India, 2018, *SCC Online*, SC 1642.

Abdur Rahman vs. The Secretary to Government, Writ Petition No. 33059 of 2016 Madras High Court.

Arumugam Servai vs. State of Tamil Nadu, 2011, 6, *Supreme Court Cases* 405.

Joseph Shine vs. Union of India, 2018, *SCC Online*, SC 1676.

Re: "Indian Woman says gang-raped on orders of Village Court". 2014. *Business & Financial News*. January 23, 2014. 2014 *All India Reporter* (Supreme Court) 2816.

Meenakshi Kumari v State of Uttar Pradesh and Ors. 2015.

Shabnam Hashmi vs. Union of India & Ors. 2014. *Supreme Court Cases*, Vol. 1, pp. 4.

Shakti Vahini vs. Union of India & Ors. 2018. *Supreme Court Cases*, Vol. 7, pp. 192.

Vishwa Lochan Madan vs. Union of India & Ors. 2014. *Supreme Court Cases*, Vol. 7, pp. 707.

Navtej Singh Johar vs. Union of India (2018) 1 *SCC* 791.

Statutes and Government Reports

Protection of Women from Domestic Violence Act, 2005.

The Uttar Pradesh Panchayat Raj Act, 1947, (Uttaranchal Amendment) Act, 2002.

Bombay Village Panchayats Act, 1958.

Government Reports

Government of India. 1967. "District Gazetteer Pithoragarh." Available at: http://pithoragarh.nic.in/files/Gazetteer/People.pdf.

Central List of Other Backward Classes (OBCs). National Commission for Backward Classes [a statutory body under the ministry of social justice & empowerment]. Available at: www.ncbc.nic.in/User_Panel/GazetteResolution.aspx?Value=mPICjsL1aLsN%2bCCWgSsv8%2buAyaBuDqnRoSLrvXbEEJTY%2by0eazrlMjhC5BUvBdUU.

Other Plans [List of Social Welfare Schemes]. 2017. Social Welfare Department, Government of Uttarakhand. Available at: http://socialwelfare.uk.gov.in/pages/display/107-other-schemes.

Index

www.ingramcontent.com/pod-product-compliance
Ingram Content Group UK Ltd.
Pitfield, Milton Keynes, MK11 3LW, UK
UKHW011010180926
475701UK00004B/659
9780367726829